LIBERATING
TRADITION

RenewedMinds

LIBERATING
TRADITION

Women's Identity and Vocation
in Christian Perspective

Kristina LaCelle-Peterson

Baker Academic
a division of Baker Publishing Group
Grand Rapids, Michigan

© 2008 by Kristina LaCelle-Peterson

Published by Baker Academic
a division of Baker Publishing Group
P.O. Box 6287, Grand Rapids, MI 49516-6287
www.bakeracademic.com

Printed in the United States of America

Library of Congress Cataloging-in-Publication Data
LaCelle-Peterson, Kristina, 1960-
    Liberating tradition : women's identity and vocation in Christian perspective / Kristina LaCelle-Peterson.
        p.   cm. — (Renewed minds)
    Includes bibliographical references and index.
    ISBN 978-0-8010-3179-3 (pbk.)
    1. Women in Christianity. 2. Women—Religious aspects—Christianity. I. Title.
BV639.W7L34 2008
270.082—dc22   2007045675

For Mark
and Nathaniel and Linnea

CONTENTS

Acknowledgments   9

Introduction: Peril and Promise: Women's Experience and the
    Christian Faith   11

Part One: Women's Identity, Human Identity

1. Made in God's Image   27
2. Women Characters in Scripture   43
3. Supermodels for Jesus? Christian Women and Body Image   73

Part Two: We're in This Thing Together

4. The Good, the Bad, and the Downright Strange: Marriages
   in the Bible   97
5. Mistaking the Industrial Revolution for the Garden of Eden:
   The Myth of the "Traditional" Marriage   117
6. Two Heads Are Better Than One: Marriage as Partnership   129

**Part Three: Women in the Church and the World or Why
Watching TV Is Not Enough**

7. Seeing the Invisible: Women in the Early Church   151
8. Abbesses, Mystics, and Reformation Women   167
9. Changing the World: Women in Missions, Social Reform,
   and Church Work in American Evangelicalism   181

Part Four: I Said What I Meant, and I Meant What I Said

10. Not Counting Women and Children: Linguistic Invisibility
      in the Church   197
11. The Discarded Images: Reasserting Biblical Language
      for God   205

      Conclusions: Up and Out   229
      Notes   233
      Scripture Index   245
      Subject Index   249

Acknowledgments

A book like this is the product of years of conversations and reading, of taking classes and teaching classes, of living life in this wonderful yet complex world. It would be impossible to name, or even remember, all the people who have contributed to my thinking on what it means to be a female human being, and specifically a Christian one. It is safe to say, though, that all sorts of people—family, friends, colleagues, and students—deserve a great deal of credit. First I want to express gratitude for my parents who passed along the conviction that Christians, even Christian women, can and should think for themselves. Their ongoing love and support have buoyed my spirits through many eras of my life. My seminary friends also informed my thinking in significant ways as we conversed about being women in the church. More recently my students at Houghton College, particularly in courses such as Women in the Bible and Women in Church History, have challenged me to think in new ways through their questions and insightful observations.

More specifically related to the book, I am grateful to Baker Academic and the Coalition of Christian Colleges and Universities (CCCU) for their willingness to take on this project. In particular, I am thankful to Bob Hosack and Jeff Wittung at Baker Academic for all their efforts to bring this book to print in its best possible form. It was a pleasure working with them.

When it comes to acknowledging the contributions of people directly concerned with this book, two former colleagues from Roberts Wesleyan College immediately come to mind: Dave Basinger and Linda Quinlan. Dave's belief that this book was worthwhile and his suggestions in constructing a proposal got the project off the ground. Linda's contributions to this undertaking were immeasurable: she and I spent hours over the course of several years talking through the issues that fill the following pages, both informally as we compared notes on juggling academic responsibilities with those of the domestic side of our lives and also as we dreamed together about the shape of the book. Her empathy and sense of humor helped sustain me, and our conversations helped to mold me and this project more than she will ever know.

I appreciate the input of Houghton College colleagues as well. Linda Mills Woolsey read the manuscript carefully and offered extremely helpful suggestions for improvement. Olga González Nichols, going far beyond the call of duty, read multiple versions of each chapter with a discerning eye and offered comments with grace and élan. More than that, though, she has been a constant champion of the project, reminding me of the need to once more proclaim the message that the gospel is indeed good news for all.

Most of all I am grateful for my spouse and children, whose presence in my life has made all the difference. Nathaniel and Linnea, in their own ways, have taught me more about love than I thought I could know. In the past couple of years they have also exhibited a great deal of patience with their mother, who had to forego some walks in the woods and trips to Minnesota, among other things, to work on her writing. I have certainly been encouraged by their good humor and their pride in my work. Finally, though there is no way to adequately express my gratitude, I would like to thank Mark, who not only read many versions of the following chapters but also has been my constant discussion partner about these and all other life issues over the course of twenty years. My life has been immeasurably enriched by his presence in it.

Introduction

Peril and Promise

Women's Experience and the Christian Faith

This is a book about listening, or learning to listen. Imagine this: two friends run into each other after a couple years apart and the first one begins a long narration about the places he has been and the strange jobs he has had. Without taking a breath, he moves from one topic to another and then glances at his watch. "Oh, I have to meet someone in ten minutes. Sorry. Let's get caught up again sometime." The second person nods, but she feels like yelling out, "Wait, I want to tell you what is going on with me."

In our culture, we have heard all about men and their experiences and exploits, but we have often forgotten to pay attention to the lives and achievements of women. For instance, without putting this book down, name ten women who were authors or artists or composers. Or what about women in mathematics and women who were chemists or physicists or biologists? How many inventors and leading business women can you name? Can you identify ten women in American history who were not part of the entertainment industry or married to a president? If you have church background, can you name ten women leaders in the Bible or ten women in church history, not including Mary? Ask your friends these questions, and if you or they have trouble filling the lists of ten, ask yourselves why.

To remedy the situation, we have to begin to talk about women's participation in human society—about women's contributions to it and also how women have experienced life in various periods of history. As Christians we might speak more intentionally about women in the Bible or find out how women functioned in the history of the church; it's like saying, "Wait, I want to tell you what is going on with me." We need to listen in new ways.

To say that we want to find out what women were doing or thinking in any given moment in history is not to say women are more important, but they are *as* important as men. It is to say, let's listen to the other half of the human race; let's hear about their activities, listen to their perspectives. Let's weep together about the sad and harmful aspects of our tradition, and then move on, resolved to be better; let's rejoice about those things that have brought life to us all.

So this book is about listening to each other.

For women, it is also about listening to how we talk about ourselves. How do we think about our bodies, our friendships, our identity as people involved in webs of social relationships?

Can all of us—women and men—shut out the din of cultural messages a bit and listen again to Scripture's amazing affirmation: that all of us are beings formed in the image of the immensely powerful, yet gentle God?

This is also a book about listening to what we say about God, both what we intend to say and what we say without meaning to say it. What stories do we tell of God? What image of God do we have in our minds as we pray? How do we picture the ways in which God invites us in, and the ways in which God sends us out in service? Do we hear the welcome of God, the love of God, in the darkest parts of ourselves?

At the heart of it all, then, this is a book about love. We listen deeply because we are called to love deeply—love God and all those around us. When we love other people, we want them to have the best life possible. We try to amuse them with our jokes, surprise and delight them with the gifts we give, encourage them to spend time painting if that's their passion, or riding a bike across the country, or writing a poem for someone's wedding. When we love people, we listen to their dreams and hope with all our hearts that we can help them come to pass; we want to contribute to their happiness. In the body of Christ, when we love other people, we work for their fullest spiritual development and find ways to help them use all that they are for God's glory.

This is a book of leaning into all that God created us to be, of living in gratefulness for the unique combination of things that make us who we are. We don't have to be hyperfeminine or hypermasculine or any other stereotypical thing in order to please God: all we have to be is ourselves in all of our crazy diversity. This, then, is a liberating message for us all.

Of course, some of my students tell me that everything is fair now. What is the point, they ask, of scholarship focused on women? As suggested above, it is to listen to the other half of the human experience; it is to hear how human society has been created in part by women and to hear how it has treated women. But more than that, it is to help women believe at a deep level something that our laws and our theology affirm—that women and men are equally valuable—but that our societal and church practices often deny.

Once, on a retreat, I met a young woman who had grown up in the church but somehow had never really believed that women and men are made equally in the image of God; in her heart of hearts she feared that in God's design, women are only second-class citizens. She may have heard the words about women's equal value before God, but she had doubtlessly received the opposite message many, many times in subtle and explicit ways: likely almost all the Sunday school lessons and sermons she had ever heard were about male characters, with illustrations from male experience (football, struggles with pornography, war), spoken with masculine terms such as "sons of God" or "men of God" or "God and man" and always in a man's voice. And to top it off, God, in many pastors' depictions, *is* male. Hearing her talk, I wondered how many other women felt just as she did, and it struck me that to challenge the misperception that men are central and women peripheral to God's project is not just to call for an intellectual restructuring, a correction of thinking. Rather, it is to invite women and men to live out life together in ways that reflect what we say we believe.

Whenever cultural assumptions are challenged, however, there is potential discomfort, and perhaps that is most clearly seen in the study of gender issues since it challenges ways in which we define our very selves, our relationships, and our world. For people raised in conservative Christian circles, this type of study may be particularly difficult since the cultural assumptions about gender are often delivered to us as coming straight from God. That is, gender roles that bear striking resemblance to middle-class American gender mores have been baptized by church tradition and repackaged as "the will of God" and "what the Bible says women should be" or "what men should be." Consequently, to challenge gender assumptions and gender roles feels as if we are rejecting Christianity, or at least parts of the Bible. But that is not what this book will do.

This book will assume that Scripture is normative in the Christian life and Christian community, and will therefore look to the biblical material for direction regarding each of the issues raised. We will take into consideration the broad sweep of Scripture rather than simply look at a few texts that say things about women, and we will use the main themes in Scripture to help us understand notoriously difficult passages. First we will consider the biblical ideal for human beings given in Genesis 1 and 2 and then offer a scriptural foundation for each of the topics under discussion, such as identity, body image, relationships, and vocation. Along the way we will examine the cultural nature of gender roles and the ways in which they have become entangled with churchly expectations. Before we begin, however, it would be helpful to discuss how the terms "feminism," "gender," and "gender roles" will be used in this book, and also to offer a few words about my assumptions about Scripture and biblical interpretation.

Compatible or Combustible: Can Feminism and Christianity Mix?

Imagine growing up in a conservative Christian church (unless you did, and then you can simply remember) in which men were always in control. In the church of my childhood, the pastors and all guest preachers were always men. The board was all men; in fact, when finally one woman was allowed to join, it caused some people to leave the church, though her job was simply to take minutes. The church treasurer was always a man, the trustees were men, the ushers were men, the lay leadership always fell to a man, the camp directors were men, even the missionaries were men (and their spouses were called "missionary wives" even if they worked just as hard to address people's physical or spiritual needs somewhere else in the world). Where were the women? In the kitchen or in the children's wing of the church or running vacation Bible school or being missionaries, which is what they were called if they were single. The modern feminist movement was under way for quite some time before I heard of it through the antifeminist rhetoric in Christian publications and in conversations at a conservative seminary. Feminists, the story went, were a bunch of men-hating, God-hating, family-hating, selfish women who "just wanted rights" as if justice for women was somehow anathema to Christian faith.

Now imagine my complete shock to discover in my thirties that the birthplace of the first feminist movement in this country (in the 1840s) was an evangelical church—a fact that both evangelicals and secular feminists have been embarrassed about. In fact, it was in a chapel of the very denomination in which I was raised! This seemed preposterous at first because I had learned that I could be either a good Christian woman or, heaven forbid, a feminist. Even though I hated it when men put down women, I had internalized the notion that Christianity and feminism were polar opposites—to such an extent that the first time I read about the Women's Rights Convention being held in a Wesleyan Methodist chapel, I thought the author had gotten it wrong. And then came the most surprising but most welcome discovery of all: that the organizers were themselves earnest Christians who promoted the rights of women in all areas of life *because of*, not *in spite of*, their Christian faith. In fact, their first concern had been to end the horror of slavery in the United States, but they discovered that as women they had no right to speak publicly or vote in antislavery conventions. They realized that they had to work on their own standing in society before they would have any way to work on behalf of others. Not only did that first Women's Rights Convention press for women's right to vote as an issue of justice (that taxation-without-representation thing again), but they touched on all areas of life, including child custody rights in the case of a husband's death or divorce, women's right to work for the causes of justice, and the right to participate fully in the promotion of the kingdom of God. They called for an end of men's tyranny over the pulpit, asking things like: Can't God communicate to and through women as well as men? Do women need men to tell them what God wants of them?

More than a decade before the convention, some of the groundwork had been laid. Two sisters, Sarah and Angelina Grimké, originally from a plantation in the South, had moved to Boston to fight against slavery—and were attacked by a mob. Simply for daring to speak in public, they were denounced by a widely circulated letter from Protestant clergy. Their response? A book titled *Letters on the Equality of the Sexes*, published in 1836, in which they argue from Scripture that God created women and men as equals and calls people to use their gifts, particularly for addressing the injustices they observe around them.

So began my realization that the feminist movement and orthodox Christian thought have historically been intertwined; in fact, it would be accurate to say that the concern for women's equality—what was later called feminism—grew, in part, directly from the Christian commitments of these nineteenth-century evangelical women. Can a conservative Christian person take seriously the issues raised by the feminist movement without abandoning orthodox Christian thought? Yes; in fact, these examples show that people have been negotiating the intersection of Christian faith and justice for women for at least 170 years. This book, then, is part of a tradition that goes back to the early nineteenth century in this country and taps movements in the church that go back much further than that.

Before getting into the topic at hand, I need to introduce some of the assumptions that will inform the discussions in the various chapters. First, a few things need to be said about the difference between sex and gender and then about gender difference and how our culture talks about these things. Finally this introduction will give a brief look at my approach to Scripture.

Difference between Sex and Gender

Though often used interchangeably, the words "sex" and "gender" refer to different things. Sex is what is biologically given and has to do with differing reproductive function, whereas gender encompasses the social expectations placed on people of each sex. In the words of a couple of linguists, "gender is the social elaboration of biological sex."[1] For instance, it is biological fact that in general men's musculature is more robust than women's; that is a sex difference. But to go on from there to claim that only men should be astronauts is a social distinction that we have linked to sex difference. That is gender.

The problem is that often we assume that the social distinctions we live with flow naturally from biological difference. But they simply don't. There is no reason, for instance, that a woman should push a vacuum cleaner whereas a man should rake leaves. There is no biological reason for it to be more acceptable for women to have long hair, or for boys to wear blue.

That gender is based in social conventions is easily demonstrated: look at how gender assumptions vary from culture to culture, or even in different classes within a society, and how they change over time. For instance, it used to be assumed that it was masculine to take showers and therefore not something a woman would do; women would take baths. Advertisers of bathing products still pander to women, but probably not too many people would think a woman masculine for taking showers. Driving is a somewhat more serious example: when cars were first invented it was assumed that they would be too much for a woman to handle. Any woman who did drive was said to be manly, or trying to act like a man. Now, as it turns out, it is statistically proven (and capitalized on by insurance companies) that far more men have a hard time controlling motor vehicles than women do. So much for all the "women-driver" jokes! What seemed "natural" at the time—that it was masculine to handle a big machine—was merely a social assumption.

If social constructions of gender originate in human culture, then when we examine them and critique them we are not calling the Bible into question or challenging the laws of God. We are simply observing that human beings construct their own ways of making their societies work, but that societies often undergo changes (for a variety of reasons). We happen to live in an era and in a cultural milieu in which ideas of gender—ideas of both femininity and masculinity—are changing. The givens look a little less given. What our grandparents thought were options for a woman's life or a man's life may look quite different from our own. Since ideas about gender are fluid and ever-changing, we have to exercise caution in ascribing them to God unless we think that God changes course whenever cultural ideals change. Of course Christians have often pinned their gender assumptions on divine law, but then their spiritual descendants end up looking back with either amusement or shame at how their forebears confused social mores with the will of God. My students, for instance, are bemused to think that there were churches where women would have been turned away at the door if they were not wearing bonnets. They are often disgusted when they hear that Puritan men gave their testimonies in church before they could become members, whereas the women had to give written copies to the pastor, who would read them to the congregation.

What about Gender Differences?

This book is not the place to settle the question of origin of differences between men and women—that is, what is legitimately linked to sex and what is simply the product of socialization into gender expectations—but we can observe with certainty that our culture is obsessed with the elaboration of difference.[2] Similarities between the sexes are downplayed and differences become the stuff of late-night talk show monologues and popular-level theorizing about how to get along with, or worse, how to triumph over, the other. The epitome of this is the book *Men Are from Mars, Women Are from Venus*, in which the author, John Gray, assumes that women and men are practically aliens to each other. In response, a spate of books and articles have come out rejecting the idea of fundamental differences between the sexes: for instance, two books titled *Men Are from Earth, Women Are from Earth, Deal with It!*—one a cartoon spoof of Gray's book and the other a more serious treatment—as well as an inspirational book, *Men Are from Israel, Women Are from Moab: Insights about the Sexes from the Book of Ruth*, in which, contrary to the expectation that the title sets up, the authors affirm that people of both sexes can exhibit all sorts of behavior, and they advocate egalitarian relationships based on personalities rather than gender roles. The authors of the academic book *Same Difference: How Gender Myths Are Hurting Our Relationships, Our Children, and Our Jobs*[3] argue that focusing on sex difference obscures the overwhelming extent to which women and men are alike and stalls the process of making the society just for women.

The debate is complicated by the way studies about difference are reported and interpreted. Suppose, for instance, that someone did a study that showed that 56 percent of the time men could find things on maps more quickly than women. The title of the article would probably be something like "Men Are Better Guides" or "It's Good Women Don't Mind Stopping to Ask for Directions." This would make it seem as if all men are good map-readers and women are hopeless at it, despite the fact that in 44 percent of the cases women were faster than men at reading the map. Would a study such as this have any bearing on whether or not a woman can be a good cartographer or a pilot? No, because any individual woman could be better at map-reading than most men, and in addition, even if she had scored lower than some of the men in the study, the question remains whether she *could* learn to read maps well. The initial score might not actually predict the level to which a person can rise and certainly would not address the causes of disparities between the sexes. For instance, could women's slightly lower scores reflect the fact that they read maps less, since in many couples the husband plans the routes?

The reporting and interpretation of medical studies can be equally problematic. In other words, what parades as scientific fact is often simply a reflection of social assumptions about different classes of human beings. For instance, in the late nineteenth century when most colleges and universities did not allow women to enroll, medical experts warned that if women did go to college, their brains would develop at the expense of their ovaries; the mental energy required to engage in collegiate study would siphon off to the brain the life that the ovaries needed, rendering women infertile. In other words, the medical experts and psychologists used science to provide justification for keeping women out of higher education; their supposedly value-free, scientific advice to women actually reflected the then-current assumptions about women's frailty, irrationality, and unfitness for anything but domestic roles.[4]

In any case, what should we as Christians make of all this focus on gender difference? Certainly we are embodied as sexually male and female—a truly delightful aspect of our human selves—but, as author Lisa Graham McMinn observes, we are also embedded in a culture that offers explanations of what our maleness and femaleness should mean, how gender should be lived out.[5] These latter explanations often involve the elaboration of sexual difference into gender ideals that on closer examination do not allow either sex the full expression of humanity. Longtime Southern Baptist pastor Paul Smith comments that "Dividing up good and beautiful characteristics of humankind and assigning them to one sex or the other does injustice to us all."[6] As Christians, perhaps we are required to work for the full human flourishing of ourselves and those around us as a way of expressing gratitude to the God who made us.

Approach to Scripture

If we are Christians, we take seriously the role of Scripture in forming us for the enterprise of living out our lives in this world and in the presence of God. However, we are all aware that the Bible has often been wielded by the powerful at the expense of the vulnerable; in fact there are egregious (and sadly enough, ongoing) examples of abuse done in the name of God, using Scripture as justification. For instance, domestic violence in Christian homes is virtually an epidemic and, according to some studies, may even have a higher rate of incidence than in the culture at large. Some Christian men think this violence is justified by the Bible.[7] We could also mention the genocide of Muslims and Jews during the Crusades, the burning of hundreds of women as witches in early modern Europe, the enslavement of millions of Africans after the colonizing of the New World, and so forth. The Bible has certainly been used to oppress "the other." I am sympathetic, then, to the concerns that have led people to consider Christianity and even Christian Scripture as sexist or otherwise oppressive.

However, I do not believe the Bible *must* lead to oppression, and in fact, Christian history cannot be said, with any degree of fairness, to be simply a litany of abuse. It is also replete with positive expressions of concern for the vulnerable and most outcast in society, as evidenced by those Christians who seek to alleviate the plight of the poor, such as Jane Addams or Mother Teresa, or by those who champion the cause of the oppressed, such as the Christians who participated in abolitionism, and those Christian organizations that work against sex slavery today or endeavor to curb the devastation of the AIDS pandemic or work against illiteracy. For centuries, Christians have been at work in educational and health-care endeavors.

I believe that Scripture was not intended to justify male domination or the abuse of women (or anyone else for that matter), but was meant to call us all to interact with each other on the basis of justice and love. Some of the harshest words in the Hebrew Scriptures are for those who oppress the poor and refuse to care for the widow; the most fundamental instruction regarding the treatment of the other is to love others as much as one loves oneself.

How does my approach to Scripture compare with that of other feminists? Obviously there are many ways that people have assessed Scripture, but most feminist writing falls roughly within one of the three main approaches described below.

The Bible as Oppressive to Women

First, some secular feminists (and biblical traditionalists, an ironic pairing to be sure) assume that the Bible reifies male power and privilege;

that is, they view Scripture as justifying male domination over women. For secular feminists this assumption leads to a rejection of Scripture as a hopelessly patriarchal set of texts that oppress women. Mary Daly, for instance, would be in this camp, because, to her sensibilities, the Bible is thoroughly sexist and therefore should be discarded by women and men who would claim their full humanity. She is not a Christian feminist, by any means, since even by 1978 with the publication of *Gyn/Ecology: The Metaethics of Radical Feminism* Daly had repudiated all the central doctrines of traditional Christianity and identified herself as post-Christian. This fact has not somehow dissuaded critics from using her as an example of radical Christian feminism in order to vilify the entire cadre of scholars who take the label "Christian feminist."

For biblical traditionalists, the perceived lower status of women in the Bible translates into the common church practice of keeping women in the kitchen and nursery and off the board and away from the pulpit. It is comfortable for many men and women in conservative churches because it is the status quo; it is what they are used to.

The Bible as a Mixed Bag

Then there are those who think the Bible contains some texts that are degrading or insulting to women, but also other texts that are liberating. These writers choose to focus on the positive texts, and consider the others to have no binding authority, since they are simply wrong. They use liberating texts in the Bible to critique patriarchy, both in other parts of Scripture as well as in the church and society. This method has been called a canon-within-the-canon approach, as some texts are elevated to a normative level and others are rejected as not being inspired. The stories of Jesus' positive interaction with women, for instance, would, in this view, trump Paul's negative statements about women, which are taken to be expressions of his sexism. The measuring stick for determining what is "in" and what should be thrown out is the experience of women, particularly their experience of exclusion and oppression in male-dominated societies. So, for instance, Elisabeth Schüssler Fiorenza, a feminist liberation theologian, considers women's experience in the *ekklesia gynaikon* (congregation of women, literally translated) to be the arbiter on questions of validity of texts, much in the same way that liberation theologians give priority to the experiences of poor people in base communities. Pioneer feminist theologian Rosemary Radford Ruether also employs this approach, though she is "focusing on how women's biological experiences, such as menstruation, are understood in a male-dominated society in ways that alienate women from our bodies and minds and place us in lesser, more derivative, and more dependent positions than males hold in society."[8]

Ruether refers to women's experiences socially and historically and not simply in Christian community. Womanist theologians Katie Cannon and Delores Williams employ a similar methodology, though their project is to highlight the experience of black women, since womanism is the term coined by feminist women of color.[9]

Traditionally Christians have affirmed that Scripture is the revelation of God (in the texts themselves) and is revelatory as people and communities of faith engage with it. In other words, they have argued that it is not simply a set of propositions, but the living and active word of God that stimulates a new understanding of God and new communion with God and others in Christian community. The difference in many modern approaches to Scripture, including the canon within the canon here under discussion, is that the weight of that balance has moved from the text as authoritative to experience as authoritative.

The Bible as a Liberating Text for Women

The oldest feminist approach to Scripture, and the one taken here, claims that Scripture, rightly understood, is affirming of women's full humanity and full participation in the people of God. This was the approach of the Grimké sisters, mentioned earlier. In this tradition no texts are rejected; instead, scholars seek to appreciate them in their context and for the purposes (as much as we can discern them) for which they were written. That is, evangelical feminists, such as Catherine Clark Kroeger or Craig Keener, assert that the Bible, interpreted fairly, affirms women, and that the church's teaching of women's inferiority is a problem of sexist interpretation rather than a directive in the texts themselves. Thus the sexism evident in the treatment of women through the ages of church history does not necessitate giving up on Christianity, or on Scripture, or even on parts of Scripture; rather it calls all of us back to Scripture and the high standards found there regarding love and the just treatment of all human beings. (See, for instance, the "Men, Women, and Biblical Equality" statement signed by over 200 prominent evangelicals that appeared in *Christianity Today* and *Leadership* in 1990.)

A Word about Biblical Interpretation

Often when women have challenged "traditional" interpretations of Scripture, their critics have accused them of being biased and of using the Bible for a political agenda, that is, the promotion of women's issues. Is this a fair criticism? Maybe we could just as easily ask the question the other way around: is a person who advocates "traditional" marriage—man off to work, woman at home—and church mores biased in favor of keeping things the way they are? In other words, is seeking to introduce change any more political than seeking to ensure that change does not happen?

Let's suppose a country-club owner and street person read the interchange between Jesus and the rich young ruler in Luke 18. In the passage, a pious young man asked Jesus what he still lacked to please God, and Jesus told him to give his money away to the poor and follow him. The street person reading this might interpret Jesus' words literally and think they apply universally: rich people should give their money to the poor. The country-club owner might interpret it differently, something like this: Jesus was only telling the man he should be *willing* to give up his money for the sake of following Christ—as we should be as well—but Jesus never meant that all rich people have to give away their money. The street person sees the passage in a way that benefits her and the country-club owner interprets the passage in a way that benefits him. Which one is political, or more political than the other? Which one is biased? They each have something at stake in their interpretation.

Perhaps it is safe to say that there is no objective place to stand and that we all come to Scripture from our particular social locations and from our individual sets of experiences. Whether we are rich or poor, urban or suburban or rural, from one region of the country or another, female or male, a person of European descent or of African or Asian descent—all these things influence how we see what we see in the Bible. Not only that, but if we have grown up in the church, we bring a certain Christian tradition to our reading of the text, and this tradition is often equated with "what Scripture says," making it hard to challenge. No one has an objective approach to the Bible, and those who protect their own power or protect the status quo are not more objective and are not apolitical, though it may feel that way because for so long it was a one-party system (only educated white males need apply). Now, when various voices challenge traditional assumptions about women in the church, for instance, they are not necessarily more biased, but simply coming from a different location. The question for us is: can we learn to listen to Scripture in a new way?

This is not to say that all interpretations are equally valid, but it is a plea to listen to others who take the Bible very seriously but do not agree with our approach.

The Flow of the Book

The first section of the book will deal with identity issues, beginning with these questions: what does it mean to be made in the image of

God, and what does the range of women's roles in Scripture have to say to contemporary women's concepts of themselves? Related to this, of course, are ideas of self-concept and body image. How well do we agree with God's assessment in Genesis 1 that the human beings—body, mind, spirit, everything—were created "very good"? How does that fit with the way we often evaluate our worth according to societal standards about appearance and beauty?

The second section of the book will consider Christian marriage. First we will survey what the Bible has to say about it and discuss what it does not say. Then we will consider a mutual-regard model for marriage in which each person's labor inside and outside the domestic sphere is equally valued. We will ask: Is it scriptural? Is it possible to achieve? Is it beneficial, and for whom?

In the third section, we will look at some ways women have participated in the history of the Western church. We will listen to their stories as a way to stretch our understanding of how women and men can function in the church together, to broaden our notions of Christian-life options for women and to remind us that, whatever we undertake, we stand on the shoulders of those who came before. Due to space constraints, only women's labors in the church are addressed, but I certainly celebrate the history of women's work, both domestic and professional, both explicitly Christian or not, as a sure sign of the creative invitation of God in people's lives.

The book will close with a discussion of language: how gendered language affects and defines us, as well as how it displays and forms our image of God. We will come full circle as we recognize that the God who created us male and female in the very image of the divine is, in fact, above the limitations of sex and gender. The God of Scripture is the powerful, personal, infinitely creative, and loving being who invites us all into dynamic human life.

Our concepts of God, ourselves, our relationships, and our potential usefulness in the world contribute to the size of our dreams. It is my hope that these reflections might help women, as well as men, have the freedom to dream big dreams!

Part One

WOMEN'S IDENTITY, HUMAN IDENTITY

1

MADE IN GOD'S IMAGE

What does Scripture actually say about women, about gender, and about how we conduct our lives together? And how do we go about discovering, or uncovering or recovering, what Scripture says? If we rely on Sunday school and sermons, we probably hear about five or six women in the biblical texts—Eve, Sarah, Ruth, Esther, Mary the mother of Jesus, and Mary Magdalene—and we hear about how women are supposed to submit to their husbands and be quiet in church. That is about all many churches have to say to and about women. We can expand that picture by considering the creation stories (there are two in the first couple chapters in Genesis) to see what is being taught about the woman and the man, and then by surveying the ways in which women figure into the drama of salvation in both the Old and New Testaments. Surely the stories of women in the Bible should have something to say about women's value in the community of God's people.

Equally in the Image of God

Secular feminists and feminist Christians, as well as people who would not choose the label "feminist" at all, often agree on this one point: the equal worth of men and women. Obviously the source of that belief might be very different: secular writers might argue from Enlightenment notions of the value of all human beings, whereas Christians might root their discussion in Scripture, starting with the creation narrative in Genesis 1. Since Jesus himself appealed to this passage to highlight God's intentions for humanity in marriage (Mark 10), it seems fair to look to the pre-fall Genesis account to learn about God's design for the race.

First, Genesis tells us, God states intentions regarding the human race in 1:26 (to make the race in God's image and to have dominion over the rest of creation) and then proceeds to create according to that intention. The result? In verse 27 we find this:

> So God created humankind in his image,
> in the image of God he created them;
> male and female he created them.

Amazingly enough, the man and woman bear God's image or reflect God's image, though what the phrase "image of God" refers to has been the subject of considerable debate. Some have suggested that the *imago Dei* refers to some sort of likeness to God, such as human rationality, or moral nature, or the ability to love deeply, or even the capacity for creativity. Others have suggested that the *imago Dei* has to do with humans being created for relationship with God, and still others link it to the rulership the humans were to have or the care they were supposed to exercise over creation on God's behalf. Finally, some have suggested that the *imago Dei* is a royal image signifying that human beings represent God much as monarchs in ancient societies were thought to represent the divine, or even in the way statuary was said to represent a deity, by being the location of a deity's presence. In this sense, human beings would be the bearers of God's presence in the world.[1] Whatever interpretation of the *imago Dei* we embrace, though, the point is that the man and the woman both bear a likeness to God and/or reflect God to this world. The text does not suggest that men bear a greater resemblance to God, or bear God's image more fully. Simply, human beings were created in the image of God.

Some of the confusion has come, one may surmise, from the word translated *humankind* here, traditionally translated *man*. The word in Hebrew is *adam*, "Let us make humankind (*adam*) in our image." The word *adam* is used in a few different ways in the Hebrew text of the Old Testament. It can distinguish the living (*adam*) from the dust of the ground (*adamah*). It can be used to distinguish human life from other forms of life. And it can be used, and is used later in the account, to distinguish the male human, *Adam*, from the female human, *Eve*, the mother of all living. In Genesis 1:27, the text is not designating the male human being; this is clearly demonstrated by the latter part of the verse: "male and female [God] created them." It is not the male human being who is made in God's image but both the male and the female humans who are to bear God's image in the creation. Further, because both of them bear God's image, neither one can be considered to be more in the image of God.

However, the church has not done an effective job in communicating this message. For one thing, if we focus on the masculine images of God in Scripture and overlook the feminine ones, we may gradually begin to think that God *is* male; this will make it more or less impossible to consider women as being equally made in God's image. If God *is* male, then men are by nature more closely formed in the image of God, and therefore represent God more fully in this world. If this is true, then men have divine justification for ruling over women, who are naturally inferior, an argument used for centuries to justify unjust relations between men and women. However, the Genesis text calls this into question through its assertion that both male and female are made in God's image, suggesting that God is large enough to encompass both.

Further, there is a complete dearth of sexualized language for Yahweh in the Old Testament (now often referred to as the Hebrew Scriptures), especially compared with the sexual deities of the ancient Near East during the time frame of the Old Testament events and writing. It was not the maleness of God that was significant, but what this God did: rescuing them from Egypt, giving them the Law, guiding them in the wilderness, and planting them in the land promised to them. Finally, we have to remember the female images of God given in Scripture and allow them to call into question taking too literally any male image of God.

The high and almighty God of Scripture cannot be limited to either gender or even simply a composite of "feminine" and "masculine" characteristics. One popular misunderstanding of the *imago Dei* assigns women the "feminine" characteristics of God's image, and men the "masculine" ones, but this is neither suggested by the text nor sustained by the text.[2] Rather, Genesis 1 affirms that human beings bear God's image in the world in a manner distinct from all other created beings. Nowhere in Scripture are we given the warrant to divide God into female and male "sides"; in fact, this view of God resembles the yin/yang, male/female balance found in Eastern religions such as Daoism, and not the God of the Bible. Further, the practice of dividing up the human traits into categories of "feminine" and "masculine" does not derive from Scripture, since these words are not even mentioned by biblical writers. They seem unconcerned about teaching femininity and masculinity—indeed, many of the stories of women don't fit our ideals of a "good woman" at all—and they certainly do not assign different characteristics of God to each sex on that basis.

Though the equality of male and female in their bearing of the *imago Dei* has been the explicit theology of most churches in orthodox Christian circles, still many exegetes have allowed their assumption of female inferiority to influence their interpretation of the text. For instance, some have been unable to affirm the plain sense of the verse—that all humanity is made equally in the image of God—because they consider the maleness of Jesus' incarnation to be theologically significant. In other words, they assume that Jesus' being a male was indicative of something inherently male in the nature of God. This, in turn, would mean that men approximated the divine more closely, that they were, in fact, made more in the image of God somehow. Though this issue will be taken up in chapter 11, it is worth noting here that the maleness of Jesus is not what is significant about the incarnation; rather, it is the fact that God became human, became one of us. It is the humanity of Jesus, along with his divinity, that extends salvation to humanity. Therefore, the maleness of Jesus does not imply anything about men's superior bearing of God's image.

Another problematic assumption that has plagued the church ever since Augustine (354–430 CE) is that the image of God in humanity primarily refers to our rationality, including things such as the memory, intellect, and will. We are like God, says Augustine, in our ability to reason and reflect on our existence. Augustine, and of course many others, also assumed that men are more rational than women, which leads to the conclusion that men are inherently more in the image of God than women are. Of course the text does not specify that rationality is the essence of that image, nor that men are more rational, but these felt like givens in his cultural milieu.

In fact, scholars recently have critiqued this assignment of rationality to men and emotionality to women as part of a larger set of Greek dualisms that crept into our interpretation of Scripture via people such as Augustine. Whereas Adam and Eve are named co-reflectors of God's image in Genesis 1, exhibiting mutuality and variety, the concepts of male and female came to be seen as opposites, even as oppositional constructs: men/reason/spirit versus women/emotion/body. This type of thinking, that femaleness is linked to emotions or physicality, is not taught in the Bible but is a constant lens through which people have read the Scriptures. And because of that supposed link, women were considered unable to represent God, which calls into question their bearing of the image of God in creation. Taking it one step further, theologian Elizabeth Johnson observes that "this dichotomization of humanity proceeded to the point where women were even projected to be the symbol of evil, the anti-image of God, the representative of evil tendencies in the sin-prone part of the male self."[3] At this point, women were considered not just less like

God in their essence, but also evil and dangerous to men on account of Eve's fall. Yet, as we shall see, Genesis 3 describes Adam and Eve eating together, which makes them both culpable. And in the New Testament, Paul mentions Eve's sin just one time; generally his shorthand for the fall of humanity is the sin of Adam (e.g., see Rom. 5).

Of course, to admit that the text may actually affirm the equal essence of men and women, or their equal capacity to bear God's image in this world, would have far-reaching ramifications for how we treat one another. If we really believe that someone else is made in the image of God, we might have to engage with that person as our equal, treating him or her with the same high regard we have for ourselves. We would have to respect or even love that person. And we might even have to give up playing gender wars.

Equally Commissioned by God

Significantly, the two human beings in Genesis not only bear the image of God equally, but they are commissioned by God to carry out God's work in the world together. In other words, women and men share the same essence and have, in a general sense, the same function. Again we see that this is God's stated intention (1:26), and then it is realized as God creates them.

Genesis 1:28 reads: "God blessed them, and God said to them, 'Be fruitful and multiply, and fill the earth and subdue it; and have dominion over the fish of the sea and over the birds of the air and over every living thing that moves upon the earth.'" Clearly this is not simply a directive to Adam, the male human being, since he obviously could not be fruitful and multiply without the woman. We know that at least the first part of the command is given to both of them, and in the verses that follow, there is nothing to indicate that the rest of the commission isn't also given to both Adam and Eve. In other words, God commissions Adam and Eve to be fruitful and then goes on to give them dominion over the rest of creation. The text does not suggest that Adam is the big boss over creation in general or over Eve in particular; rather, the woman, along with the man, is commissioned jointly with him to carry out God's work in this world. Here we see God's original intention for the human race: a collaborative model of mutual dominion, or care-taking. Before sin enters the picture we have a model of joint responsibility. In God's original economy, human beings would work together to produce progeny and to care for creation.

This means, of course, that the cultural messages about women's secondary importance in the human project are simply not true from the perspective of Genesis 1. The humans equally display or bear God's image, and they are equally commissioned to care for and tend this earth. There is no hierarchy designed by God according to Genesis 1, and the text does not imply any. Whatever priority has been given to men in Christian and secular circles does not reflect God's stated design, and therefore does not represent the way things have to be. It is not the "natural" way of doing things. In fact, one could argue just the opposite: the "natural" way, that is, according to the nature given them by God, is that men and women collaborate in doing God's work. The gender wars, seen in this light, are nothing more than a profound expression of the brokenness of humanity since the fall. Similarly, the male chauvinism that has characterized the church is not a standing against culture, but an expression of the sinfulness of cultural practices. In their book *Why Not Women? A Fresh Look at Scripture on Women in Missions, Ministry, and Leadership*, the leaders of Youth with a Mission assert that to treat women as second-class beings is an affront to God's character (since God is just) and a rejection of the image of God in them. In fact, they contend that the restriction of women in the church is nothing but the negative treatment of women the world over brought into Christian circles.[4]

This is also the thesis of the book *Veiled and Silenced*, in which the author, Alvin Schmidt, shows how sexist societal practices have hamstrung the church throughout its history. The old jab made by traditionalists at feminist Christians—that they are simply capitulating to culture—is turned here against the traditionalists: sexist church practices show that traditional churches are bound by social assumptions about women. It's not the feminists who are bringing (the worst of) culture into the church, Schmidt argues, but the traditionalists who have imbibed male chauvinism so deeply that they think it is synonymous with Christian values.[5]

Because we live in a culture that thrives on the so-called Mars/Venus divide, it can be difficult to hear the generic tone of Genesis 1. The fact that we're all made in the image of God doesn't fit the current societal practice of emphasizing (and even fabricating) differences between men and women, and further, the fact that we're supposed to work together in the project of human life flies in the face of the "gender war" mentality and the competition between the sexes that it fosters. Perhaps many Americans, even Christian Americans, accept the idea of a war between the sexes because by doing so they can avoid the sometimes hard work of listening to each other and cooperating in the large and small things of life. Perhaps we should take to heart Dorothy Sayers's observation from the early twentieth century that "male" and "female" are adjectives that modify the noun "human being." What we have in common far outweighs the differences.[6]

Besides, the overriding concern of the Genesis text is not sexuality, but being created in the image of God and being commissioned to do God's work in the world. The male and female aspect of Genesis 1:27 more likely has to do with fertility, since the commissioning follows directly upon it and begins with the command to be fruitful, multiply, and fill the earth. In other words, this distinguishing feature of personhood—to bear God's image and do God's work—is found equally in the male and female version of the human race, and this separates us, not from each other but from the rest of creation. This approach rejects the idea that the mention of sex here implies that sex is fundamental to being human, or intrinsic to God's nature. Rather, the driving point of the passage is that human beings are the pinnacle of creation, God delights in them, and they represent God in the world.

Genesis 2 Creation Story: Equal in Substance

Some interpreters find their justification for woman's dependent role in Genesis 2. In fact, in rabbinic Judaism (from approximately 200 to 600 CE) the exegetes found their most basic rationale for women's inferiority in this text. For instance, Rabbi Joshua is asked why a woman needs to wear perfume while a man does not. Referring to Eve's being created from Adam's rib, he answers, "Man was created from earth and earth never putrefies, but Eve was created from a bone. For example: if you leave meat three days unsalted, it immediately goes putrid."[7] For Rabbi Joshua, Eve's very essence is corruptible and Adam's is not. Later, he reflects on the Almighty's thinking about "from what part to create her. 'I will not create her from [Adam's] head lest she be swell-headed; nor from the eye, lest she be a coquette; nor from the ear, lest she be an eavesdropper; nor from the mouth, lest she be a gossip; nor from the heart, lest she be prone to jealousy; nor from the hand, lest she be light-fingered; nor from the foot, lest she be a gadabout.'"[8] Here we have, negatively stated, a depiction of ideal womanhood according to rabbinic tradition as well as an argument for women's inferiority, since the rabbi goes on to line up texts from Hebrew Scripture to show how women have fallen prey to all these vices. By citing the negative uses of all of women's "parts," the writer argues implicitly for limiting women's roles in rabbinic society.[9]

Now if this strikes us as a bit unfair, stretching the text to grind a particular axe, we should bear in mind that many Christian exegetes have carried on the same tradition.[10] Christian writers too have sought to find difference and inferiority of the female from the moment of creation and in the portrayals of women in subsequent Scriptural texts.

They too have linked this supposed inherent inferiority to a limitation of women's participation in public worship or leadership.

However, again we should ask what the text actually demands. Does it demand that we read it to mean that Eve is an afterthought of God, a little assistant to God's main man, Adam? Is this why this story was preserved? Many creation stories in other ancient Near Eastern cultures tell of the creation of humanity from mud, but none of Israel's neighbors had a separate story for the creation of the female human. Theologian Victor Hamilton concludes from this that "In biblical thought the woman is not subsumed under her male counterpart."[11] Women's particular existence is highlighted, but the question is, did the writer go out of his way to inscribe women in an inferior position, or to underscore women's elevated place in the design of God? In the next section we will consider both the term "helpmate" used for Eve and the drama of the story to show that Eve was not simply an auxiliary to Adam.

"Helper Suitable for Him" in Genesis 2

The compound word in Genesis 2:18, translated in the King James Version as "helpmeet" and more recently "helpmate," is not used again in Scripture. Nor is it a common word in our everyday conversations, as in, I have to find out if my helpmate picked up milk today. Yet the meaning assigned to the word has had incredible impact on Christian conceptions of women's nature and women's place in marriage. Modern English translations display a range of options:

- NIV: "helper suitable for him"
- NASB: "helper suitable," though a footnote says "corresponding to"
- NRSV: "a helper as his partner"
- NKJV: "helper comparable to"
- NAB, a Catholic version: "suitable partner"
- ESV, the new conservative Protestant version: "a helper fit for him"
- NLT: "a helper who is just right for him."

The first half of the word, *ezer*, translated "help," is most often used in the Old Testament to refer to God's help. Of the nineteen times the word is used in the Old Testament, fifteen times it refers to God helping the nation of Israel or a person.[12] At other times it refers to military assistance. Clearly this is not the helper as subordinate or the unequal partner that many have associated with the term (à la daddy's little helper, or Santa's elves). The scholars who translated the Hebrew text into Greek (the Septuagint), a couple of centuries before Christ, understood this as a term that refers to help "from a stronger one, in no way needing help."[13] Theologian John Stackhouse makes a similar observation, particularly since the word is used most often of God: "Thus, the fundamental concept is of partnership and useful companionship for the man, not of a subordinate to the man."[14] This mutuality is an essential part of being human.

The second half of the word, *kenegdo,* carries the idea of Eve being appropriate for Adam, or on his level. It is translated variously in English versions of Genesis 2:18, usually with terms such as "comparable" or "partner" or "suitable." The point is, this part of the term also does not imply Eve's inferiority, but declares her an appropriate match for Adam. It connotes the fittingness of Eve, the way in which she is on his level. This is the type of help that the other is not capable of living without; Eve, then, offers life-sustaining interaction with Adam. She is capable of befriending him on his level and helping him as a true partner. As theologian Stan Grenz suggests, Eve acts as the rescuer: "This casts the woman in a role exactly opposite of the subservient position one might expect, for she is elevated to the status of being an agent in God's saving design."[15]

Even leaving the discussion of Hebrew words aside, the drama of the story revolves around Adam's aloneness because he is surrounded by inferior beings: no "helper comparable" has been found—a phrase repeated a number of times in the story. God parades the animals before him and nothing is found to be suitable, on his level. In other words, all the other animals are inferior and rejected on that basis. When he wakes up to find Eve there, he is ecstatic because, unlike the animals, she is not inferior to him but "bone of my bones, flesh of my flesh." Eve's creation is a relief precisely because she is not another inferior creature, but someone who is of the same substance and someone who can offer real companionship to Adam. He rhapsodizes that finally there is someone like him, who can engage him fully in all the ways an inferior being couldn't. (In fact, there are scholars who understand this story to be describing the splitting of a sexually undifferentiated human into the two sexes. Then Eve isn't made from a man, but they are both formed from the original human being.)[16] Adam finally has not only someone made of identical substance but someone who is on his level, someone comparable to him. Significantly, he does not awaken with the relief that he finally has his own personal servant: "Finally, someone to cook my dinner and do my laundry." Eve is not God's afterthought, then, but God's fully adequate answer to Adam's situation, and he recognizes it.

In any case, the fact that Eve was created from Adam's rib emphasizes the equality of the two people, rather than from his foot to be walked on or from his head to rule over him. It is a story of mutuality, and not opposition. Adam does not wake and exclaim that she is someone who is his mirror image, or someone from the "female race," or someone who is his opposite. Rather, here is someone comparable to him, someone to enjoy partnership with him. Before sin entered the picture, the man was delighted to have a partner comparable to him, an equal, with whom he could share life and share the responsibility of tending God's garden. It is only later, after the fall, that wives begin to be counted right along with the cattle and other possessions; that is not a reflection of God's design as much as an indication that humanity has not lived up to the ideal depicted in the first two chapters of Genesis.

Before the fall Adam does not have the power to name her either. He recognizes their similarity, that they are *ish* and *ishah,* the Hebrew words for man and woman, but this is not a naming. In fact, many have noted that this is a set of words that emphasizes their connection, demonstrated by the linguistic similarity of the words in Hebrew. Adam's actual naming of her as "Eve" takes place after the fall.

Genesis 2 in Christian Tradition

This reading of the creation narrative has found resonance recently, but it is not a new approach. For instance, Margaret Fell, a founding member of the Society of Friends, argued in 1666 for Eve's equality in creation, and the same sentiment can be found in the nineteenth century, particularly among Methodist writers who affirmed the ministry of women: Phoebe Palmer, herself an evangelist; Adam Clarke, a Methodist bishop; and Frances Willard, who headed the Women's Christian Temperance Union (WCTU), which engaged in many kinds of reforms that would benefit women.[17] In his book *Ordaining Women* published in 1891, B. T. Roberts, the founder of the Free Methodist denomination, argued that "Woman was created, not as the *servant* of man, but as his *companion*, his *equal*."[18] He also observed that they were jointly commissioned to care for the earth.

Of course there are those who soften the mutuality implied in the *imago Dei* by reading this story of Eve's creation in a way that suggests her inferiority. Some Christian writers, both academic and popular, have attempted to affirm the equality of the man and woman, but simultaneously espouse a hierarchy of function that they claim was instituted by God in creation. Karl Barth, for instance, one of the most prominent Protestant theologians of the early twentieth century, could state categorically that men and women "are fully equal before God," and yet claim that the man has to take "the lead as the inspirer, leader and initiator in the common being and action" while "the business of woman, her task and function, is to actualize the fellowship in which man can only precede her, stimulating, leading and inspiring."[19] Barth assumed that the woman was to take the backseat to the man; in fact, she was to create the conditions in which the man could exercise his leadership, and in this structure they would realize their identity as man and woman. In this, Barth takes the gender assumptions of his time and place and reads them back onto the text.

This position, which many have echoed since Barth, is very troubling.[20] For one thing, nowhere in Genesis 1 or 2 is the man said to lead, inspire, or dominate, and these imported notions obscure the mutuality of the Genesis texts. But more than that, this position is troubling for what it says about God. In this scenario, God cares more about stability than about love or justice, and apparently thinks stability can only be achieved through hierarchy. Both of these views are problematic. In other words, if we assert that women are intrinsically inferior and therefore confined by God to the passive role, deferring to men as superior beings, there would at least be some logic to that claim. But if we insist that there is no inner inequality between men and women, then God simply assigned the woman a subordinate place in the hierarchy to keep order. Thus we have a picture of God subordinating a class of people to another class based solely on a desire for order, which makes God more concerned with stability than with the flourishing of women as full human beings or with justice in their regard. This doesn't fit the biblical picture of God, who loves lavishly (Eph. 1) and who exalts the humble and lifts up the downtrodden while the powerful are brought down (1 Sam. 2 and Luke 2).

Furthermore, though many Christians fear that without hierarchy in male/female relations chaos would ensue, we have to ask whether this is necessarily so. If God is three in one, a community of three "persons," existing in mutually loving and interdependent relationship, why would we think that God had to establish hierarchy as the only way to have order? In other words, there seems to be a fairly obvious alternative to hierarchy modeled in the Godhead. And so, to say that God had to set up a hierarchy in human relations either calls the historically orthodox concept of Trinity into question or calls the love of God into question, since God would be setting up an unjust system capriciously.

Even in our human experience mutuality is deemed acceptable and even desirable in certain relationships. Though our lives may contain a variety of relationships, including those in which we receive more than we give (if we are being mentored, for instance) and those in which we give more to the other person (as in caring for the very young or ill, or befriending someone who is disadvantaged in some way), our most significant friendships are often those in which we share more equally in the relationship.

Think of your own friendships. Think of those in which the other people understand your sense of humor, and share some of your central interests, too, whether that means extreme sports or working to stop extreme poverty. With your closest friends sometimes you may be the "strong" one helping another through a sad or difficult time and sometimes the roles are reversed: you may be needy and enjoy the support of the other person. By way of analogy, then, maybe we can understand the delight of Adam: he finally has someone to share laughs with, someone to share his interest in caring for this beautiful world, someone whose love and presence in his life helps sustain him. Perhaps it is fair to assume that if we can build deep friendships based on mutual interests and outlook on life, God is wise enough to place the unfallen man and woman in the garden in a relationship of intimacy and mutuality that enriched their life together.

Equally Fallen

In Genesis 3 Eve and Adam eat the forbidden fruit. Sometimes we read a text many, many times and miss something that later seems incredibly obvious. We saw this in Genesis 1, where interpreters have so often assumed that Adam is given dominion over the earth, but when we search the text we find that Adam and Eve together are commissioned to exercise authority over the created order. Genesis 3:6 contains another of those "overlooked" truths. For years people have said things like: the devil had to tempt the woman because if he had addressed the man, the human race never would have fallen (Luther), or the woman is the devil's gateway (Tertullian). However, the text itself contains a clue that those readings are not really warranted.

The key phrase is in verse 6: "and she also gave some to her husband, *who was there with her*" (emphasis mine). The most straightforward reading of the text suggests that Adam was listening in and that they ate together. Male interpreters through the centuries have enjoyed using Eve as the scapegoat—just as Adam did, which didn't seem to impress God very much—and have blamed Eve for the fall. By extension, they have gone on to blame all women, or to assume that all women are somehow more sinful and prone to sin than men. Jerome (ca. 340–420) called on women to weep every day and ask forgiveness for being women, and Luther quipped that the Tempter had to go to Eve because otherwise the race wouldn't have fallen. In the present era, a New Testament professor in an evangelical college taught that women were more easily deceived and therefore could not be trusted with leadership. Surely this can't be the case if the woman and man together shared the fruit.

Other people have offered downright fanciful interpretations of this event: for instance, some have claimed that Adam was doing his duty to stand by his wife in her fall from grace, that he sacrificed his purity so that they could be on the same level; conversely, others have blamed Eve for seducing him (because in her sin she had become sensuous?), a perennial favorite of the Catholic Church for many centuries. These say much more about the authors' view of women than what the text has to say.

According to the story, we know simply that they were together. We also learn a bit about her motives, while there is no remark on his. Therefore, we cannot say anything definitive about Adam's motives—neither that he was weaker than Eve, succumbing to her when she was tempted by evil itself, nor that he was more moral and partook only out of a sense of pity for her. All we know is that they were there together in the face of temptation and then they ate together.

As a result, they lose Eden together. In three realms of their lives, alienation comes to typify their relationships: between themselves and God, between each other (the first stress between the woman and the man), and between the human race and the rest of the created order. Human life will now become difficult and laced with pain and loss, and the people's sinfulness will taint their relationships from here on out. The rest of the Old Testament bears witness to this new reality. We have stories of slavery, deceit, horrible treatment of women (check out Judg. 19), murder—all of this against the backdrop of the ongoing human struggle to remain aware of and obedient to God.

In the third chapter of Genesis we have what has often been termed "the curse" placed on the serpent, then on Eve, and finally on Adam, a spelling out of the struggles that each will face. Some have understood this as the punishment of God because of their disobedience; in this sense it is prescriptive—God prescribing punishment. Others have seen it to be descriptive—here is what is going to happen to you as a consequence of the sin that has now entered the cosmos.

In any case, after the serpent is destined to crawl about in the dust and live in enmity with the offspring of these human beings, Eve is addressed specifically in 3:16:

> I will greatly increase your pangs in childbearing;
> in pain you shall bring forth children,
> yet your desire shall be for your husband,
> and he shall rule over you.

How do we know that alienation between the man and the woman came at this juncture? It is here that we have the first mention of hierarchy, of one person ruling over the other. The mutuality that is intended by a joint commission is now marred by the altered relationship described in the statement: your desire shall be for your husband, and he shall rule over you. Here, in the aftermath of the fall, in the "curse," is the first mention of male domination and female subjugation. This is certainly *not* the eternal design of God for humanity, but a supreme expression of the brokenness that pervades human existence since sin entered the picture. What could be more insidious than a rupture in the closest of human relationships, that of woman and man in marriage? Though the words are directed to the woman, the tragic implications apply to both people. Obviously if a relationship of mutual delight and respect has degenerated into a situation of subjugation and domination, both people lose.

The consequence for sinning outlined for the man has to do with the human relationship to the created order. No longer will tending the garden be a delight, as apparently it was when things were at their ideal; now it will be backbreaking work, full of impediments. Does this imply that it is only the man who is to work growing the food or that thorns won't grow up in the way of women if women take up food production? Of course not: this, too, is a sad new state for the humans, not just for the man. Interestingly, anthropologist Peggy Reeves Sanday has observed that in societies in which people struggle against harsh environmental conditions, there tends to be, in fact, male domination, whereas in situations of environmental "beneficence" there is more likely to be gender equality.[21] This suggests that the warning to Adam about the difficulties they will face with regard to the environment may be related to the difficulties they will encounter in the relationship between them.

Finally, we might ask: Are the items in Genesis 3 describing the state in which God wishes people to live? For example, since God said that farming would be difficult, does that mean using tractors is contradicting God? Virtually no Christians have read the text that way; rather, throughout the centuries they have affirmed the use of farm implements—even the Amish use metal plows and horses to ease the work, disapproving only of motorized machines. Another example is that of a woman in childbirth: Is it wrong for a woman to have epidural anesthesia in childbirth, since God said that women will have increased pain as they bear children? Even before the advent of modern medicine, midwives and then doctors in Jewish and Christian circles attempted to ease the pain of childbirth through whatever means were at hand. As in the tractor example, we simply have more refined ways to mitigate the toil and pain of the process.

The point is, in general, that people of faith have not interpreted this text as depicting God's eternal will but as the sorry state of things after humans messed things up. If people try to minimize the effects of the fall with tractors, combines, and painkillers, no one seems to bat an eye. Inconsistently enough, however, there is one line in this litany of woes that is taken to be inviolable: the husband's rule over the wife. Why would this be eternally binding and not the others? Why would this depict God's design for things when it, too, is in the section describing the brokenness of post-fall life? Why would God affirm the easing of physical pain and make permanent the heartache brought on by domination and subjugation? The inconsistency with which this text is handled demonstrates the precommitments of the scholars and preachers—most of whom have been male—who have commented on it. They have taken this verse to be normative (that is, the way things should be) and used it to justify the subordination of women in the home, in the church, and even in society.[22]

If we take God's statements in Genesis 3 as the consequences of sin, we will likely see them not as hardships to be endured, but as challenges to be overcome. In the same way, one could argue, we ought to seek to overcome the ongoing practice of ignoring the equality of women and men in God's image. The temptation for men to rule over women and the temptation for women to consent to this rule is just that: temptation to live in ways not designed by God. As speaker and writer Rebecca Merrill Groothuis puts it: "The man's and woman's sinful proclivities (abusive control and irresponsible passivity, respectively) reinforce each other to create a chronic, 'natural' condition of male rule and female subordination."[23] Rather than being God's design, this setup is a gross distortion of human relationships brought about by sin, and reinforced by sinful patterns woven into the fabric of human societies. Theologian Elizabeth Johnson observes in this regard: "Analysis of women's experience is replete with the realization that within patriarchal systems women's primordial temptation is not to pride and self-assertion but rather to the lack of it, to diffuseness of personal center, overdependence on others for self-identity, drifting, and fear of recognizing one's own competence."[24] She goes on to suggest that Sleeping Beauty does not need a message about laying the self down! "In this situation grace comes to the sleeper not as the call to loss of self but as empowerment toward discovery of self and affirmation of one's strength, giftedness, and responsibility."[25] Domination and passivity are things to be resisted, as together men and women seek to live out their joint commission to be fecund and care for the world. We cannot accept the brokenness and sinfulness of post-fall humanity as "just the way things are" if we are people seeking to live out God's design for us.

Whether the "curse" in Genesis 3 was God's punishment on the couple crouching there or simply the natural consequences of sin, the coming of Jesus was to address the effects of the fall and restore the relationships broken there. The next chapter will examine some of the Old Testament record with regard to women because, despite the male-dominated culture of the ancient Near East, women figure prominently in some of the stories and play surprising, though minor, roles in others. What significance, we may ask, is there in the variety of ways in which women participated in the covenant community, and what might this mean for a discussion of female Christian identity? We will close the chapter by looking at the ways in which Jesus interacted with women, since presumably someone who displays the fullness of the Godhead (Col. 1) will give clues about God's estimation of women. This too should form part of the foundation of a Christian woman's identity.

2

WOMEN CHARACTERS IN SCRIPTURE

Old Testament Women after the Fall

In the Hebrew Scriptures, women figure in the narration more than might be anticipated, given the male-dominated societies in which the events took place and were written down. Women function not only as spouses and mothers, roles to be expected, but also as prophets, as redeemer figures, as people who receive direct words from God, and even as the leader of an army.

The first "category" of women we might mention is those whose conversation with God is at least partly recorded in the text. Eve, before she is ever a mother, interacts with God (the serpent made me do it), and God, in the words directed to the serpent, embeds a promise that Eve's offspring shall crush its head. Later, Sarah, the postmenopausal woman who chuckled a bit about bearing a baby, is accused by the Lord of laughing. She denies it, unaware that Abraham had also laughed at the renewed promise that he and she would conceive a child in their old age. (Yes, you may well ask why we hear so much about Sarah's laughter in Genesis 18 when in the previous chapter Abraham also laughed at the idea.) Hagar, Sarah's servant, winds up in the desert twice—once because she ran away, and once because Sarah drove her away—and she cries out to God. When God responds to her, she names him and receives a prophetic word about the nature of her son. Rebekah, too, receives a glimpse of how the lives of her twin sons will unfold. Miriam, the sister of Moses, has an encounter with God when she and Aaron challenge Moses' leadership (Num. 12). She complains, "Hasn't God spoken to us as well?" and God's answer implies she has received communication from God, though not as directly as Moses had. (As punishment, Miriam suffers with a skin ailment for seven days and then is healed and restored to the camp. That Aaron escapes punishment seems to suggest that she was the more guilty party, the instigator of this rebellion.) Samson's mother interacts with an angel about the as-yet-to-be-conceived son she will bear, a fact her husband has trouble believing. After the angel returns and the husband is consulted, he is afraid they are going to die because they have seen the Lord. The wife has to remind him that they won't die since they have just been told they will be having a baby. (So much for men being the conduits of God's will for the family.) In each of these narratives a conversation between God and a woman is recorded, though, as we shall see below, there are other instances in which God's direct interaction with women is assumed if not described.

Women Who Conversed with God

Often the first picture of women in the Old Testament that comes to mind, however, is not women conversing with God, but women bearing children. (Or is it the only picture that comes to mind?) There are a number of stories in which women, particularly barren women, conceive and bear sons who take center stage in the unfolding drama of God's interaction with the covenant people: Sarah, for instance, then Rebekah, Rachel, and Hannah. None of these women passively wait for life to be delivered to them, however.

Sarah, the first in the line of barren women, is cosharer in the promise regarding a great nation and a promised land, though she and Abraham apparently did not initially understand this. She employs a culturally accepted practice of surrogate childbearing in order to become a mother, though her plan goes drastically wrong. The servant, Hagar, bears a son who does not fulfill the promise of God to Abraham, but Hagar receives her own promise from God, parallel to Abraham's, that she will be the mother of a great nation. Sarah finally does conceive and delivers Isaac into the world. Isaac answers the longings of Sarah's heart, but more significantly he is the one through whom God will make a covenant people. Why Sarah's child in particular? In the end Abraham has many sons, Ishmael through Hagar and Isaac through Sarah but also six children through Keturah, Abraham's second wife after the death of Sarah. Furthermore, Genesis 25:5, after listing the six children of

Keturah and Abraham by name, mentions that Abraham also had sons through concubines. Only Isaac is the child of promise, however. Why? God apparently chose not only Abraham to be father of a great nation, but Sarah to be the mother. When the Jews of Jesus' day claimed to be children of Abraham, they really meant children of Abraham and Sarah, since Hagar's son does not figure into the covenant, and neither do any of the other children Abraham fathered. So much for men being the only important ones in the plan of redemption!

Rebekah's main activity as she pursues motherhood is to pray, and get her husband to pray, that they will have children. But after the sons are grown she connives with the younger one, Jacob, to steal the paternal blessing from the older son, Esau. She clearly favored Jacob over Esau and acted to deceive her husband, though some have suggested that she was simply trying to fulfill the words spoken to her by the Lord, that the older would serve the younger. In this reading Rebekah, like Sarah, acts to achieve God's plan in the only way she sees as feasible.

The sisters Rachel and Leah also actively participate in a race to outdo each other in motherhood. Like Sarah, they employ their servants to bear them children in addition to the ones they bear themselves, and it appears that they decide which of them their shared husband, Jacob, will sleep with. Leah, who had many sons, gives the barren Rachel some mandrakes, believing them to possess properties that would promote fertility. In exchange Rachel gives Jacob to Leah for some of the nights that "belong" to her. This results in another son for Leah and a first son for Rachel.

Later, in 1 Samuel 1, we find that Hannah, too, takes an active part in the conception of her child. While her family feasts and celebrates at Shiloh, she makes her way alone to the place of worship in order to make a deal with God. She vows to give to God the very thing that she is asking for: a son. After Samuel is born and weaned, she fulfills her promise of allowing him to serve the Lord in Shiloh, where he becomes a great prophet to God's people.

As we consider motherhood in the texts, we should remember two things. First, in many of these stories the men are also valued only for their fatherhood. Isaac, for instance, has virtually no role except for fathering Jacob and Esau and giving the paternal blessing, and Elkanah functions only as Hannah's husband and eventual father of Samuel. And second, not all the women whose motherhood is described in the Old Testament would make it into the "Mothers to Imitate Hall of Fame." For instance, there are the women who go to great lengths to bear children, and who could be applauded for their courage and wit and ability to survive in a culture such as theirs, yet the means they employ to achieve conception seem downright repulsive to modern readers. Lot's daughters, for instance, rape their father—the very man who had tried to offer them to the rapacious crowd earlier in the story—in order to conceive. The widow Tamar dresses as a prostitute to seduce her father-in-law, Judah, because he refused to give another of his sons to her in marriage so she could raise up a child in her first husband's line as levirate marriage laws required (see Gen. 36).

These last two examples point to the reality that the record of women's experience in the Old Testament is not all positive and, in fact, is at points very troubling. To get a sense of "what the Bible says about women," and by implication how God assesses women, we have to consider these difficult passages as well. Again we have to ask: What is intended by these texts? When we see violence against women depicted, are we supposed to think that God endorses the ill treatment of women? (As one of my students commented after reading Judges: "God must really hate women!") Some outsiders to the faith, and particularly those who are sensitive to the experiences of women, read these texts and assume that God does, in fact, hate women, or at least not care very much about them. But seen within the larger biblical framework, these incidents of violence can be understood, not as God's ideal or even something acceptable to God, but as depictions of human beings who are damaged by the fall and therefore are damaging to each other, even in their most intimate relationships. In the texts, for instance, some husbands and fathers willingly sacrifice the safety of their wives and daughters to protect themselves or other men. They seem to assume that women's well-being and safety are not as important as those of men.

Women Sacrificed to Protect Men

Sarah, the half-sister of Abraham, was so strikingly beautiful that Abraham thought foreign rulers would kill him to take her. So he passed her off on two occasions to be used sexually by complete strangers to save his own hide. Perhaps his rationale was that she would be brought into the harem anyway if he were killed, so at least this meant the possibility of their reunion. In any case, his focus is on his safety, not hers. A generation later, when famine drives them to Philistia, Isaac offers the same lie about Rebekah in order to protect himself from King Abimelech of the Philistines. In the story of the flight from Sodom, Lot's daughters are offered by their own father to a crowd intent on rape, in lieu of the male guests that Lot is hosting. His concern and responsibility for his own daughters apparently took a backseat to his reputation as a host, though in the end the safety of the young women as well as the rest of the family was ensured by the visitors, who turn out to be angels. Tragically, a very similar situation arises again in Judges 19 without the intervention of an angel. A Levite, retrieving his concubine from her father's house where she had fled, stops over in Gibeah (just north of what is now Jerusalem), and the townsmen want to assault him sexually. Rather than that, the host offers his virginal daughter and the Levite's concubine, with the words, "Ravish them and do whatever you want to them" (Judg. 19:24). Finally the Levite's concubine is thrown out to the crowd, and they rape and abuse her all night. In the morning the Levite finds her fallen on the doorstep, so he puts her on his donkey (it is unclear whether she is dead at this point), takes her home, and rather self-righteously cuts her up into twelve pieces and sends her body parts to each of the tribes to show how low the men of the tribe of Benjamin are. (One can only wonder whether he feels even a tinge of guilt, given his part in her demise!) In any case, we see God's judgment on all those responsible for the horrible treatment of this woman through the narration of all the additional violence that it spawns. Nor is the violence against women in other stories endorsed or even treated neutrally; instead, it is explicitly or implicitly condemned.

Other Women Who Were Victimized

Hagar was victimized by a woman's actions and by a man's passivity; apparently she had no choice about her own body, but was offered by Sarah to Abraham to bear a child to him. Hagar conceives and becomes proud, which angers Sarah, who abuses her so severely that Hagar thinks dying in the desert would be preferable to withstanding Sarah's treatment of her. Abraham is passive in all this, allowing the maltreatment of Hagar. Later, after Sarah's son Isaac is born, Sarah sends Hagar and Ishmael out into the desert to die. Sarah herself has been victimized, but she turns around and victimizes Hagar; as biblical scholar Alice Bellis puts it: "Sarah's story is replayed wherever the oppressed oppress those who have even less power."[1] Sarah's good impulses to protect her son, the son of promise, are expressed in harsh and sinful ways; her imperfections are there for us to see, which makes her a real person rather than an idealized perfectly good, or wholly bad, woman. A few generations later, Jacob and Leah have a daughter, Dinah, who is apparently raped by Shechem, the son of a local prince (see Gen. 34). Shechem wants to marry her—in fact, she is living at his house—but Dinah's brothers engage in honor killings and retrieve her. Some interpreters place Dinah's victimization at the time of her first contact with Shechem, and others think she was victimized by her brothers' zeal to clear their name. What if, they claim, she continued in the relationship with this foreign prince willingly? In neither

Hagar's nor Dinah's story, however, is there a sense that this violence is approved by God.

Perhaps most appalling is the story of Jephthah, a military hero introduced in Judges 11, who has promised to kill whoever passes over the threshold of his house first if he comes back from battle victorious. When he comes home having won the battle against the Ammonites, his (virginal) daughter comes out to greet him and receives a death sentence. She is given a three-month reprieve in which to grieve the premature end to her life, after which she is put to death. Sometimes interpreters and preachers commend Jephthah because he did at least fulfill his vow, but this raises the question about the nature of God who heard the vow. Was keeping a rash vow really more important than keeping one of the Ten Commandments? Can a vow to break God's commands be holy in the first place? Was God more concerned that he keep his vow or that he care for the daughter given to him by God? In the New Testament this question is raised again and answered by Jesus in Mark 7:9–13. Jesus criticizes those who pledge their money to God—a practice called *corban*—while their own parents were not being cared for. In this case they have made a vow that seems pious but one that causes them to break the commandment to honor one's parents. Jesus teaches that people's vows are meaningless and even sinful when they fly in the face of the express requirements of God's commands. Jephthah, then, never should have made such a vow, and certainly God did not demand that he keep it, when it meant the death of his own daughter.

Then there are the women around David. Michal, his first wife, who loved him and who rescued him from the murderous intentions of her father, does not even receive a visit from David when he sneaks back; we have only a story of his reunion with Jonathan. Years later, when David returns as king, with a dozen or so wives in tow, he rips Michal out of her second marriage, apparently for his own political security. (Her father Saul had married her off to someone else, because she had been abandoned.) Her husband, Palti, accompanies her, weeping, as she leaves. It should come as no surprise that later, Michal is not impressed with David's dancing, as she watches him bring the ark to Jerusalem. In a subsequent story, David abuses his kingly power to make Bathsheba into a sexual partner, and when he discovers she is pregnant tries to cover it up by bringing her husband home from the battlefront. Unwilling to break ranks with his fellow soldiers, Uriah refuses to sleep with his wife, and so David connives to have him killed in battle. Does God approve? The text is clear that God judges David's actions harshly: the baby dies and Nathan the prophet warns David that the sword would never leave his house. The beginning of that prophecy's fulfillment comes with the rape of Tamar, one of David's daughters, by her half-brother Amnon.

David does nothing about it, likely because Amnon was his firstborn son and because it may have been too difficult to punish his son for something very much like his own sin. Thus begins the bloody story of Absalom, Tamar's full brother, who murders Amnon, is banished from the country, and eventually leads a revolt against David. But none of these stories about the victimization of women is endorsed by the narrator, and in fact they end so tragically that the reader is to assume that these instances of violence were not endorsed by God.

Negative Examples of Powerful Women

Another class of narratives depicts women acting with evil intent. Obviously women as well as men can work against the redemptive activity of God in the world, though the Hebrew Scriptures describe surprisingly few cases involving women, which we will survey here. We have already considered Eve's disobedience, Sarah's abuse of her servant, and the conniving of Rebekah, but these are flaws of sympathetic characters in the text. Other women are characterized primarily for their failings. For instance, Job's wife tells him to curse God and die, when his suffering becomes nearly unbearable. (Her advice represents one unacceptable response to suffering, and the advice of Job's "friends" represents another, since they simplistically equate suffering with punishment for sin.) Delilah perhaps could be considered brave, since she lays traps for someone who is not only fabulously strong but reckless and violent; however, she is not commended in the text since she carries out the plans of Samson's enemies—God's enemies—at Samson's expense, and Samson is someone she purports to love. When King Saul wants a word from Samuel the prophet even though Samuel has died, he consults a medium, though her profession, necromancy, was forbidden. Jezebel, the Canaanite queen of Israel, joins with King Ahab to rid the land of prophets of God, including the particularly audacious ones such as Elijah and Elisha. At one point Ahab desires land that the owner won't sell, so Jezebel plots against and kills this neighbor in order to get his land for her coveting husband. Though she is ruthless and evil, one might ask if this is any worse than a king (such as David) who kills someone because he has coveted that man's wife? Athaliah, the daughter of Ahab, becomes the ruler over Judah for six years and follows her parents' evil program. And then there is the unfaithful wife of the prophet Hosea, Gomer, who engaged in sexual relationships with a variety of men. God instructs Hosea to marry her and to buy her back from her prostitution in order to point to the forgiveness and willingness to redeem that God offers the people of Israel. The practice of having multiple sexual partners was approved for men in ancient Israel, but not for women, which is why the sexual promiscuity of a woman would function as a powerful metaphor for Israel's unfaithfulness to God. (Abraham, David, and Solomon, most notably, had many socially approved sexual partners in the context of polygamous marriages as well as in the concubine system. This double standard is explicitly rejected by Jesus in his discussion of divorce and remarriage in Mark 10 and by Paul in 1 Cor. 7.)

Redeemer Figures

Several women in the Old Testament save or rescue others, a role our fairy tales and children's films still largely deny women. For instance, in the first couple of chapters of Exodus, women collude against Pharaoh, the ruler of the most powerful nation in that region of the world. The midwives refuse to kill the boy babies even though expressly commanded by Pharaoh to do it; Jochobed, Moses' mother, puts her boy baby in the river, but not without a basket-boat to keep him from drowning; Miriam, the older sister, watches the little craft to make sure Moses is safe and pretends to find a nurse for the baby (was this a prearranged ruse to get Moses back into Jochobed's arms, or did Miriam simply think on her feet?); and the daughter of Pharaoh adopts this Israelite boy who has been condemned to die by her own father. At four levels, women act to subvert the dominating man's command and save Moses. Another woman saves Moses' life when he is an adult: his wife, Zipporah. In Exodus 4, as they are traveling from Midian back to Egypt, where he will carry out his role in the salvation of the nation, Zipporah functions in a priest's role, circumcising their son and/or Moses, which averts God's anger.

Women act to save other lives as well. Later, the Canaanite woman Rahab takes her life into her hands to protect a couple of Israelite spies. In Joshua 2, as Joshua plans his attack on Jericho, he sends spies into the city to scope it out. They stay with Rahab, a prostitute, as they gather information, but somehow their whereabouts are made known to the king. He demands that she turn over these dangerous men, but Rahab hides the spies and puts their pursuers off the trail. In so doing she saves the lives of not only the spies but also of everyone in her family, since the Israelites reward her by sparing them when they attack. In the end she and her family are welcomed into the community of the people of God.

Later, another non-Israelite woman functions as a redeemer figure to her family and is highlighted in the historical narrative of ancient Israel: Ruth. Turning her back on her own people, her own country, all that she might have held dear, Ruth travels to Bethlehem with a pledge to care for her destitute mother-in-law for the rest of her life! When they get there, Ruth averts their starvation by engaging in the risky business of gleaning in a stranger's field without the company of other women to serve as protection. In fact, Naomi and her relative Boaz each comment on the dangers inherent in Ruth's practice. At Naomi's request, Ruth offers herself in marriage to Boaz, who is apparently much older than Ruth and who comments about how she, as a young woman, had other options. He is flattered, but also admires her for her self-sacrifice, her noble act of securing Naomi's future through this liaison. She could have gone after younger men if her own happiness was the focus, but instead she initiates a relationship with Boaz, partially if not totally out of a desire to provide a long-term solution to Naomi's plight. Unfortunately the text does not give insight into the inner workings of Ruth's heart, so we don't know what she thought of Boaz. But the women of the town interpret her actions as done on Naomi's behalf: her love is *hesed*, the type of loving-kindness that God is said to show toward people, and she is said to be more precious to Naomi than seven sons. Through her actions the fortune of Naomi is reversed, and Naomi, who is bitter and empty at the beginning of the book, becomes contented and satisfied with the blessings of the Lord.

A few generations later, Michal, who was married to David, protects and saves him much as Rahab saved the spies. When Michal's father, King Saul, wants to kill David, she alerts David to the plot, helps him escape in the night, and then, when the king's messengers come, pretends David is sick in bed by using an idol dressed in clothes. She places the idol in the bed, apparently hoping to delay David's pursuers so he had more time to escape. Interestingly, in the same chapter Jonathan, her brother, and Samuel the prophet also rescue David, though her situation was the most directly dangerous (see 1 Sam. 19).

Another woman who functions as a redeemer figure for her family is Abigail. She saves her household from the revenge of the powerful warlord David and his guerrilla troops, after they were insulted by her husband, Nabal. Through her wise actions and flattering or perhaps even prophetic words—she avers that David will be the next king of Israel—she assuages his anger and saves him, he says, from a retribution he would have later regretted. David tells her: "Blessed be the LORD, the God of Israel, who sent you to meet me today! Blessed be your good sense, and blessed be you, who have kept me today from blood-guilt and from avenging myself by my own hand!" (1 Sam. 25:32–33). For her troubles she is added to David's passel of wives, which to modern ears might not sound glorious, but which might have improved her lot tremendously, compared with marriage to a man whose name means "fool" and who apparently lived up to it.

But women don't act as redeemers only for their families; we know of at least three women—Miriam, Deborah, and Esther—who participated in the salvation of God's people as a whole. First, there was Miriam, who is depicted as a leader of women's worship in Exodus 15 and as a prophet in Numbers. The prophet Micah affirms that Miriam was sent by God, along with her brothers Moses and Aaron, to bring the people out of Egypt (Mic. 6:4). This means that at the foundational moment of the nation of Israel, when the covenant was given and the people of God was being formed, God tapped a woman to lead. It is worth noting that if a woman was welcomed as a leader at such a crucial juncture in Israel's history, God must not be fundamentally opposed to women's leadership.

Deborah, in very explicit ways, also leads the people. She functions as a judge in Israel, before the days of the kings, and also as a prophet (see Judg. 4 and 5). In her role as prophet, she heard from the Lord that a certain man, Barak, should position the army in such a way as to draw Israel's enemy into battle. The Lord promised victory, but Barak was fearful and unwilling to go unless Deborah went with him, so together they led ten thousand soldiers into battle. In the end, though they won, Barak was not honored, since he failed to trust Deborah's prophecy; rather, another woman, Jael, received praise for killing the enemy general, for inviting him into her tent despite his rapacious reputation. "Most blessed of women be Jael," Judges 5:24 says. After this victory the land had forty years of peace, which implies that Deborah continued to be a leader of the people for that amount of time, since in the case of other deliverer figures in the book of Judges, the peace lasts for the duration of the redeemer figure's life.

The most prominent female redeemer figure in the Hebrew Scriptures is, of course, Esther. Taken from her adoptive father, Mordecai, as a candidate for the king's harem, she eventually rises to the position of queen. Even as queen, her life in the harem is so isolated that she is unaware of the decree signed by her husband, the king, which set a day for Jewish people to be slaughtered. Mordecai sends news of this to her with a plea that she try to do something to rescue her people. Though at first reluctant, since her unbidden approach to the king could result in her being put to death, she finally agrees. She develops a plan, outlines it for Mordecai, and gives him directions about his part and the people's part in it: "'Go, gather all the Jews to be found in Susa, and hold a fast on my behalf, and neither eat nor drink for three days.' . . . Mordecai then went away and did everything as Esther had ordered him" (Esther 4:16–17). The tables have turned; Esther has developed in the story from a passive young woman—she likely had no choice about participating in the king's beauty contest—to a decisive leader who works through a corrupt system to effect salvation for her people.

The Hebrew Scriptures, then, offer glimpses of women who functioned as redeemer figures. Some were instrumental in saving another person, some protected their families, and some helped rescue the nation. In this last category it is perhaps significant that women were leaders in different eras of biblical history: Miriam during the exodus, Deborah during the time of the judges, just before the monarchy, and Esther during the exile.

Prophets

In addition to playing the role of savior, some women functioned as prophets in the Old Testament texts. As mentioned above, Miriam was a prophet; she heard from God and delivered the word to people, which is the function of a prophet. There is growing scholarship supporting the notion that the song of victory in Exodus 15 was originally something created by Miriam, since she leads the chorus and since Moses has already complained about how inept he is with articulating things.[2] In any case, as noted earlier, we find in Numbers 12 that Miriam, along with Aaron and Moses, is explicitly affirmed as a prophet, though reprimanded for arrogating for herself a position on par with Moses' position. In other words, when they challenge Moses, Miriam and Aaron are not rebuked by God for claiming to be prophets—this is a given—but because they failed to see that Moses had a closer interaction with God than normal prophets did.

Later we have Deborah, a married woman, who not only led the Israelites into battle, but whose day job was giving out judgments and prophecies of the Lord. Judges 4 informs us that she had a regular "office," a place where people came to her to hear what God had to say, because they recognized her as a prophet. It was called the "palm of Deborah," and the writer tells us just where this was. What's intriguing about the introduction of Deborah in the text is that there are no reasons given or excuses made for why a woman has the role of prophet and of judge. The text does not say, nor even hint, that Deborah has this job because no man could be found to do it. It is simply a fact, unremarked on by the writer. Is this because it was more common at that time than we think now, more unremarkable?

Then there is the prophet Hulda, also a married woman, whose story, related in 2 Kings 22 and 2 Chronicles 34, comes in a very dark time. Near the end of the monarchy in Judah, when idolatry flourished and enemies threatened on every side, Josiah became king in Judah. In contrast to many on the throne before him, he was a God-oriented ruler, and when the "Book of the Law" was found (probably Deuteronomy, though some scholars think it was the entire Pentateuch) and read to him, Josiah was utterly distraught. He tore his robes and instructed the high priest, Hilkiah, and some other officials: "Go, inquire of the Lord for me, for the people, and for all of Judah, concerning the words of this book that has been found; for great is the wrath of the LORD that is kindled against us . . ." (2 Kings 22:12). The high priest Hilkiah went to the prophet Hulda, who gave a fairly dire message about the punishment that was in store for the nation after Josiah's life was over. She declared: "Thus says the LORD, the God of Israel: Tell the man who sent you to me, Thus says the LORD, I will indeed bring disaster on this place . . . you shall be gathered to your grave in peace; your eyes shall not see all the disaster that I will bring on this place." And those who heard her "took the message back to the king" (2 Kings 22:15, 20). No mention is made in the text about why Hilkiah went to Hulda rather than to Jeremiah, who was a well-known prophet at this time, or to Zechariah, or to any of the other prophets in Jerusalem. In a dire situation, hoping to avert the punishment of God for their failure to live up to the law, the high priest and other faithful people of God consult a woman to give them the words of divine instruction.

Finally, we have a couple additional passing references to women prophets, and, as in the other cases listed above, there are no explanatory notes to justify women in that role. It is simply an accepted fact—a fact apparently more acceptable in the ancient Near East than in many churches in our progressive era! The first is in Nehemiah, when the writer mentions the prophet Noadiah by name, who along with the "rest of the prophets" had been prophesying against his work (Neh. 6:14). This at least points to an acceptance of women's prophetic authority alongside that of men, even though in this case the women, along with the men, were wrong. The second passage is in the beginning of Isaiah 8, where God warns the people about the swiftness of judgment coming. To illustrate the point, God instructs Isaiah to have a child and name him Maher-shalal-hash-baz, which means "the spoil speeds, the prey hastens."[3] This baby is the son of Isaiah the prophet, who "went to the prophetess, and she conceived and bore a son" (Isa. 8:3). Unfortunately, we don't know anything more about this "prophetess" and whether she, too, received a message from the Lord about naming her baby Maher-shalal-hash-baz. (Did she like the name, find it catchy?)

To sum up, the Old Testament has examples of women as prophets, as political and military leaders, as redeemer figures, and as strong maternal characters. It is not on the basis of their beauty (with the exception of Rachel and Esther) that they become players in the drama, and it is not because of their demure, "feminine" attitudes; it is for their accomplishments that they are cited. (Though the texts mention the beauty of women such as Sarah and Rebekah, their looks are not central to their stories, just as the writers mention men's looks without making that the central aspect for the men. For instance, Saul is said to be tall and handsome in 1 Sam. 9:2, and David, too, is called handsome, as well as ruddy and with beautiful eyes in 1 Sam. 16:12.) Why would stories of women leaders and colaborers with men in the drama of salvation be included in Scripture if we are not supposed to gain something from their examples? To what end would these texts have been preserved? Likely we are supposed to remember that God called and empowered women to significant tasks. Also, despite the less-than-ideal interactions between them after sin entered in, men and women still sometimes functioned together, as designed, to do God's work in the world.

Equally Redeemed

When we turn to the New Testament, the picture is much brighter. Christ came to "make his blessings flow far as the curse is found," to borrow from Isaac Watt's "Joy to the World." He came to pour his life into the things broken by the fall, to restore the relationship of human beings with God and also the relationships between people. In the stories and teachings of the Gospels we see Jesus extending grace to people, often unlikely and even unlovely people, and modeling a whole new basis on which human beings can interact: sacrificial love. The rest of the New Testament continues these threads, which are interwoven in the church—the saving grace of God in people's lives and the new type of relationships made possible by God's grace in the redeemed community. Once again, women, along with men, do God's work in the world.

Women Announce the Coming of the Word

Even before Jesus begins his ministry, God invites women's participation in the unfolding drama of salvation initiated in his birth. Before any man is consulted or involved, Mary is addressed by a messenger from God. At this crucial juncture, the impending birth of the most significant person ever born, God does not use a "man as spiritual head of the house" model, such as many Christians teach as God's way of doing things. And you would think God would want to do it right at the birth of the one and only Son of God. Rather, the angel is sent to Mary, and in an act of supreme faith, she agrees to be part of God's grand scheme, even though it will entirely change her life, and she makes this momentous decision without hesitation. In fact, there are few examples of such ready faith in Scripture, since people tapped by God for particular tasks often make excuses (Moses, Jeremiah), tell God to commission someone else (Moses), or ask for signs to ensure the promised outcome (Gideon, Zechariah). Mary, like Samuel and Isaiah, agrees unreservedly to God's request: "Let it be as you say." Mary agrees to carry the Word of God into the world.

Before the birth of Jesus, when Mary visits Elizabeth, her relative who is also carrying a miracle child, Elizabeth greets her with prophetic words. The text says Elizabeth is filled with the Holy Spirit, which underscores the fact that the words about to be uttered will be inspired by God. And she does, in fact, make some incredible observations. First of all, she recognizes that her much younger relative has been so blessed of God that she should feel honored to have Mary visit her. This is an unusual social reversal. Elizabeth also makes a prophetic comment about the identity of Mary's baby: that he is her Lord. This identification of Mary's baby with the Lord of the Old Testament is extraordinary, particularly given the reaction of even Jesus' closest friends during his adult ministry: they witnessed firsthand the miracles and teachings of Jesus, yet they had trouble understanding his identity. Elizabeth knew him when she had only a pregnant young woman before her.

Mary then responds with a song that describes the ways in which God has interacted with her personally as well as the ways God operates with people in general. God has favored a lowly woman as part of this pattern of showing mercy to the lowly and bringing down the haughty. She, too, in the tradition of Hannah, declares the stuff of history to be the acts of God—a prophetic role, to say the least. She also prophesies about the ministry that Jesus will undertake.

Finally, we are introduced to Anna, the woman Luke calls a prophet. She meets Mary, Joseph, and the baby Jesus in the temple at the time of Mary's purification. The text says that Anna had been a widow for over sixty years and lived in the temple day and night, waiting for the advent of the Messiah. When she sees this baby, she speaks to all those in the temple who have been waiting for the Messiah's arrival. Interestingly enough, it does not say that she spoke only to the women who were waiting for God's promises to be fulfilled, but to all who longed for the Messiah.

The birth of Jesus, then, is heralded not only by angels but by women who prophesy. One might ask why God would allow this at the crux of human history if God did not want women to speak out the Word of God! The prophetic discernment of the women in these stories comes from God and is approved by God. Especially in Luke's Gospel we see the women as mouthpieces of God, both at the beginning and at the end of Jesus' life: Elizabeth and Anna herald the birth, and the women at the tomb report back to the other disciples that Jesus is risen.

Jesus Traverses Social Boundaries, or Love Transgresses Human Categories

When Jesus begins his ministry, he demonstrates the generosity of God by his practice of interacting with a wide variety of people. Though he addresses his message to the rich at times and certainly tries to engage the religious elite of his day, he focuses his ministry on the masses of people and takes special care of the outcasts and the poor. This is not mere humility. He does not simply lower himself to interact with people considered to be on the bottom of the social ladder. Rather, in his ministry to the poor, the non-Israelites, the women, and the "sinners," Jesus shows his rejection of societal assumptions about the inferior value of people in those groups. Thus he refuses to abide by the normal patterns for interacting with them. As Jesus traverses social boundaries, he calls them into question. He refuses to measure people with the yardstick available in his culture. The outcast woman of Samaria at the well (John 4) is just as valuable as Nicodemus, a member of the religious elite (John 3). Jesus makes not only theological statements about the type of ministry he is pursuing, then, but also anthropological statements about the classes of people he is encountering. In other words, Jesus demonstrates not just something about himself (his humility) but also something about those people (their being objects of God's unstinting love).

When Jesus appeals to the woman of Samaria for water, she is surprised that Jesus transgresses gender expectations, that he would talk to her, a woman. Later in the story it says that Jesus' disciples "were astonished that he was speaking with a woman" (John 4:27). His conversation with her in John 4, not unlike the one he has with Nicodemus in John 3, is full of double meanings, unexpected turns, and most of all, the invitation of God to new life. He brings up her questionable marriage history, perhaps to show her that it will not be a barrier to her receiving this new life, and perhaps just to heighten her curiosity about him and his message. In any case, he does not focus on the sexual impropriety in her life, or allow it to define her, but instead discusses theology with her. He directs her attention to himself and, in fact, reveals his identity to her with unusual directness. She, in turn, runs off to evangelize her entire town, leaving behind her water jug, a tool and symbol of women's work.

In Luke 7:36–50, again Jesus refuses to allow a woman's out-of-bounds sexuality to determine how he interacts with her. While reclining at the dinner table of Simon the Pharisee, Jesus is approached by a "sinful woman" who creates quite a scene with her weeping and perfume. While she is washing his feet with her tears, the religious elite are despising her for her sexual experience and judging her in their hearts, as it was their privilege to do, they thought. Jesus, too, comes under their judgment for allowing her to touch him: if this man were a prophet, he would know "what kind of woman this is" (v. 39). Again, he risks his reputation to extend God's welcome to a woman. The others are offended by the very sight of this woman, who in their minds is equated with sexual sin and danger, but Jesus welcomes her touch. Apparently he is not afraid of her sexuality and so he doesn't reduce her to it. She remains a full person to him, and he invites Simon to see her that way as well: someone coming to him in gratitude for forgiveness.

In Mark 5, Jesus comes into physical contact with a woman and a girl who would have been considered ceremonially unclean. A good Jewish person, let alone a rabbi, would avoid this contact, but Jesus seeks it out, at least in the case of the girl. He enters the room where this twelve-year-old girl has died, and he touches her, speaks to her, and raises her up. The woman who was hemorrhaging would have been continually unclean, and to touch her would have made someone unclean for the rest of the day (Lev. 15:19–33), which means she was probably either divorced or never married. Not only is she healed because of her faith, but Jesus demands to know about her touch, though he could have let it go by simply making eye contact with her—if, that is, she had dared to look into his face. He values her voice enough to ask that she testify in public to what God has done in her, and this in a society that did not accept women's testimony in a court of law. More than that, he uses an affectionate term, "daughter," to commend her faith and to effectively welcome her back into human community. He declares her clean, showing that she can be restored to society and showing that his wholeness has been communicated to her, rather than her uncleanness being transferred to him.

The bent-over woman Jesus heals in the synagogue one Sabbath has suffered for eighteen years (Luke 13). In her case, it isn't her sensuousness that would put off religious men around her, but the fact that she is relatively old, crippled, and a woman. With these three strikes against her, she hardly seems worth risking the ire of the religious elite. But Jesus heals her anyway, though it is the Sabbath and they are in the synagogue. Just as much as the man that Jesus heals on the Sabbath in the next chapter (Luke 14), this woman is an object of God's love and Jesus' healing attention.

In all these cases, Jesus rejects traditional assessments of women: that is, that they are dangerously sexual or that they are insignificant because of their gender. Jesus doesn't treat women as sensual beings to be feared, but engages them in conversation. Further, he does not recoil from their touch, even when they are ceremonially unclean according to Jewish law, or socially suspect, as in the case of the sinful woman who washes Jesus' feet.

Discipleship Trumps Gender Roles

It is interesting that Jesus also refuses to affirm positive traditional roles for women, even when asked to. Most significantly, unlike the tradition of some sectors of the Christian church, he does not put his own mother on a pedestal and value her simply for her having borne him. In Mark 3, when she and Jesus' siblings come to see him, they cannot reach him because of the crowd. So they send for him: "Jesus, your mother and brothers and sisters are outside, asking for you" (v. 32). Rather than rush out of the house to see them, he comments to the crowd gathered there: "Who are my mother and my brothers?" And to those who sit around him, he says, "Here are my mother and my brothers! Whoever does the will of God is my brother and sister and mother" (Mark 3:33–35). He is asked to act like a dutiful son, but instead he uses the occasion to redefine family as all who are obedient to God. In other words, rather than give his mother or siblings special honor because of their blood ties, he extends God's welcome to those around him. At the same time, he is redefining his mother's and siblings' relationship to him. They too are being invited to be part of the family of God, through obedience, through discipleship.

Jesus teaches a similar lesson when someone in the crowd yells out: "Blessed is the womb that bore you and the breasts that nursed you" (Luke 11:27). Jesus probably understands that the woman is trying to give honor to him by saying that his mother must be proud of him, and honored on his account, but he responds with a surprising statement: "Blessed rather are those who hear the word of God and obey it!" He isn't putting Mary down, but raising the status of all the women in the crowd. After all, none of them could have the honor of being his mother, but all of them could be blessed on account of obedience to God. This is good news for them. Further, it speaks of a different valuation system: rather than being valued for the children they bear (in Mary's case, the Messiah), women will be valued on the same basis as men, on account of their discipleship, their doing the work of God. This is tremendously good news, even for Mary: she is depicted in the Gospels as a faithful disciple, not simply a traditional Jewish mother.

On another occasion Jesus is explicitly asked to endorse gender roles, but he doesn't. When Martha is busy with chores of hospitality (Luke 10), she asks Jesus to make Mary help. Instead, Jesus affirms Mary's sitting at his feet, learning, listening. It's not that hospitality is bad; in fact, in Luke 7 Jesus criticizes Simon the Pharisee for not extending him the common courtesies of hospitality. Martha, then, is doing a good thing. But Mary is commended because she has chosen something better; she has not let Martha's or anyone else's expectations of the nice, hospitable woman overshadow the need for active learning from Jesus.

In fact, we could say that Jesus not only refuses to endorse a traditional role for Mary but also affirms her assumption of a nontraditional one. With Jesus' explicit approval, Mary embraces the traditionally male role of learning from a rabbi. New Testament scholar Craig Keener observes that "Mary's posture and eagerness to absorb Jesus' teaching at the expense of a more traditional womanly role would have shocked most Jewish men."[4] By approving Mary's activity, Jesus redefines this role as a generically human one: human beings are invited to sit at his feet, to learn from him, to be his disciples. This is the highest calling.

In Luke 8:1–3 we learn that women not only sat at Jesus' feet but also followed him around the countryside. This would have been scandalous to onlookers, since adult coeducation was unheard of (as it was even in the United States until a little over a century ago), and it was probably uncomfortable for some insiders as well. Some Greek philosophers had women followers, but Jewish rabbis did not. Jesus welcomed women into his circle of traveling disciples despite the misunderstanding that he risked in doing so.

Furthermore, some of the women disciples are noted by name: Luke mentions Mary Magdalene; Joanna, the wife of one of Herod's stewards; and Susanna specifically, though he ends the introduction with "and many others" (Luke 8:2, 3). These three named women, as well as many other women unnamed in the text, followed Jesus. Another New Testament scholar, Richard Bauckham, observes that this naming of female disciples is parallel to the listing of the twelve named male disciples; out of a larger group that followed Jesus around, these are identified by name likely because of their still being known to the early church three or four decades later when the Gospels were written.[5]

Who were these women named in Luke 8? The general answer is that they were "women who had been cured of evil spirits and infirmities" (v. 2). They follow Jesus because they had been healed and freed. Mary Magdalene, whose name usually appears first in a list of female disciples, just as Peter's appears first in lists of male disciples, is introduced as a person from whom seven demons were cast out. Nowhere in the Gospels is she connected with prostitution, though for centuries the church has depicted her in this way. Her reputation as a "fallen woman" arose from conflating the footwashing stories (the "sinful woman" in Luke 7 and Mary of Bethany in John 12) and confusing the two Marys (of Bethany and of Magdala), with the result that Mary Magdalene, one of the most prominent disciples in the early decades of the church, has been demoted to the role of prostitute. (Indeed, the real question is not why the confusion happened in the first place, but why the church perpetuated it.) In any case, she along with Joanna, Susanna, and the others supports Jesus' ministry out of her means. This probably indicates that these were wealthy women past the age of having small children to care for, and had cast their lot with this radical rabbi even at the expense of their own social networks.

Not only are women named disciples, but many women are depicted as doing what disciples do. They witness Jesus' ministry, they follow him, and they serve him, which is what discipleship consists of.[6] In the end they also give witness to what they have seen and heard. After her conversation with Jesus, the woman of Samaria in John 4 rushes out evangelizing and comes back with many from the town; in the meantime the disciples have come back with some bread. She is doing theology and mission work while the disciples are making the church supper. The woman healed of the hemorrhage was required by Jesus to tell publicly what God had done for her, despite her desire to slink off, healed but silent. The texts regarding the sending out of the seventy or seventy-two disciples to open the way for Jesus' ministry do not explicitly describe the participation of women but also do not exclude the possibility that they too went out in Jesus' name.

Most clearly, however, at the tomb we see the explicit inclusion of women in the work of Jesus. All four Gospel writers describe the presence of women, named and unnamed, at the cross as well as at the tomb, something that can be said about very few things in the Gospels. At the tomb, the women are instructed, either by Jesus himself, or his emissaries, to "Go and tell." We have to keep in mind that the resurrection is the crowning act in Jesus' ministry; it vindicates all that he claimed about himself, it validates his teachings, and it forms the basis for Christian hope. The fullness of the gospel has been accomplished, and women are the ones entrusted to speak this truth first. In a culture that did not consider a woman's testimony valid in court, it is almost outrageous that women were the first witnesses of the empty tomb and were the people commissioned to tell the disciples (the disciples!) about it.

This commissioning fits what came before—the Old Testament female prophetic tradition as well as Jesus' welcoming women into his band of followers and his explicit endorsement of their public testimony—and is carried into the early church on the day of Pentecost. Not only were women in the upper room (including Mary, Jesus' mother, who had become a disciple), but they clearly evangelized on the streets of Jerusalem in foreign tongues; otherwise the defense Peter gives concerning their speaking makes no sense. Women's preaching necessitated an explanation, which Peter gave through the use of a prophecy in Joel: that in the latter days God would pour out the Spirit on women as well as men and that all would prophesy.

> In the last days it will be, God declares,
> that I will pour out my Spirit upon all flesh,
> and your sons and your daughters shall prophesy,
> and your young men shall see visions,

and your old men shall dream dreams.
Even upon my slaves, both men and women,
in those days I will pour out my Spirit;
and they shall prophesy. (Acts 2:17–18)

This, Peter claimed, had been fulfilled that day.

Furthermore, women had churches in their homes, we are told in Acts and John's letters. Male leaders' names are not associated with these communities of faith. For instance, in Acts 12 we learn about Mary, mother of John Mark, and the prayer meeting being held in her house, to which Peter goes upon his release from prison. A few chapters later, in Acts 16, Luke describes the first convert in Europe: Lydia. She is a businesswoman, a dealer in purple cloth, and the leader of a group of women praying down by the river on the Sabbath, where Paul finds them. (Without the requisite number of devout men to found a synagogue, women found other places to gather for prayer on the Sabbath.) Lydia hears Paul's message, embraces this gospel, and gets baptized, as do all the people in her household, after which she prevails on Paul's missionary party to stay at her house. Later in Acts 16, we are told that after the conversion of the Philippian jailer and his baptism along with his household, Paul and Silas again meet with believers at Lydia's house before leaving the city.

Though often credited with an anti-women bias, Paul demonstrates a more welcoming attitude to women than do some church people down through the centuries who have read his writing. For one thing, in his letters Paul greets women who were significant in the various churches: Apphia and two other leaders in Colossae (Philem. 2), Nympha in Laodicea (Col. 4), Euodia and Syntyche (Phil. 4), as well as a number of women in Romans 16, who, Paul says, worked with him in the gospel.

In Romans 16:1, Paul encourages the original recipients of the letter to greet Phoebe, whom he calls a "deacon" (*diakonos* in the Greek), the masculine nominative form of the word which is usually translated "servant." The fact that Paul used the masculine form of the word suggests that she held a particular recognized role of "deacon" or "servant" that carried the same responsibilities as when a man held that role. If Paul is not referring to a specific office that Phoebe held, we have to assume that he simply confused the endings, but that would be like using the wrong gendered pronoun (as in, Phoebe had his mission to fulfill). No educated person would do that, particularly not someone as articulate as Paul. When an English translation renders the word as *deaconess* it leaves the inaccurate impression that Paul is drawing a distinction of roles based on gender. (Fortunately this is less common in more recent translations.) In fact, Paul uses the term "deacon" in reference to a number of people: himself, Timothy, Tychicus, Apollos, Epaphras, and Christ himself.[7] These are all servants, as is Phoebe. Only a prior commitment to deny women's leadership would keep translators from applying the same term to Phoebe as to Timothy, since Paul himself uses the same Greek word. In addition, Paul refers to Phoebe as *prostatis*, a word used in other places to refer to those who are "over you in the Lord" (1 Thess. 5:12) or to designate church officials presiding over congregations (1 Tim. 3:4–5 and 5:17). Justin Martyr uses the masculine form of the word to denote a person presiding at communion.[8] Paul finishes off the introduction of Phoebe with instructions to the church in Rome to welcome her and provide whatever she needs, presumably for doing the ministry for which she was sent. Either that or he is appealing to them to get raisins for the muffins she is busy making!

The next item on Paul's list of people to greet in Rome is the missionary couple Prisca and Aquila. In Acts 18 we learn that Priscilla (Prisca) and Aquila made tents, and Paul not only worked with them but stayed with them as well. We also learn that they pulled aside the gifted preacher Apollos and instructed him in the full message of Jesus. It looks as if they are partners in their trade (tent making) and in their work of teaching people the gospel. Paul identifies them as people who worked with him in ministry and who have risked their lives for his sake (Rom. 16:3–4). The fact that her name appears first more often than not suggests that she was not simply Aquila's little helper, but may in fact have been the more dynamic personality of the couple. In any case, Paul is not reluctant to name women as coworkers with men, and in fact commends women as his own colleagues.

We find this again a few verses down when he mentions another ministry couple, Andronicus and Junia, his relatives whom he calls "prominent among the apostles" (16:7). For the first 1,300 years of the church, Paul's commendation of Andronicus and Junia was understood as an expression of gratitude to a man and a woman for their ministry. Junia was recognized as a woman by all exegetes from John Chrysostom in the fourth century to Peter Abelard in the thirteenth, and the name is in feminine form in virtually all the Greek and Latin versions of the New Testament as well as the Syrian and Coptic translations. However, a man named Aegidius of Rome (1245–1316) added an "s" to the name Junia so that it would look like a masculine name. He did this not because the ancient Greek texts of the New Testament demanded it (what biblical scholars call textual evidence), but because of his assumption that women could not be apostles.[9] Essentially he changed the text of Scripture because of his own theological commitments. At the time of the Reformation, Erasmus reaffirmed the female nature of the name, since he went back to the older Greek texts, as have all the major critical texts since then, until the early twentieth century. Recently, biblical scholar Bernadette Brooten's work on Junia has demonstrated that the masculine form "Junias" is nowhere attested to in Greek literature and letters, though "Junia" was a common woman's name.[10] Even the translations that are not attempting to be sensitive to inclusion of women have acknowledged this fact, and Junia, the female apostle, is now back in most English translations.

Other women mentioned in Romans 16 include Mary, presumably a Jewish convert as Mary was a Jewish name, who has "worked very hard among you" (Rom. 16:6). In this regard Paul employs a phrase he often uses to talk about his own labors in specific churches.[11] Then he asks to be remembered to Tryphaena and Tryphosa, "workers in the Lord," and Persis, "who has worked hard in the Lord" (16:12). Then come Rufus's mother, who Paul says was a "mother to me also" (16:13), and Julia and Nereus's sister who are simply noted by name, saints worthy of recognition. The point is, these examples show us that Paul not only recognized but celebrated the work of women alongside men in the spreading of the gospel.

Certain interpreters of Scripture, however, downplay all these words of commendation Paul gives to real women in ministry (not to mention women preaching on the streets on the day of Pentecost, the commissioning of women at the tomb, and other scriptural witness to women's leadership), because when they want to know what "the Bible says about women," they narrow their focus to two passages, 1 Corinthians 14:34–35 and 1 Timothy 2:8–15. For them these two texts are normative, which means that other things in Scripture have to be understood in light of what is said in these texts. However, to isolate a couple of passages and build a theology from them is never a reliable method of biblical interpretation. In fact, one general rule in good interpretation is that we take the clear things that appear in many places in Scripture and bring them to bear on the obscure or difficult text. We will look, then, at 1 Corinthians 14 and 1 Timothy 2, which are about how women are to behave in Christian assembly, but we will keep the rest of the Bible in view.

We also have to keep in mind that in his letters, Paul is addressing particular problems, and therefore the themes he discusses, the points he emphasizes, and the way he constructs his arguments are determined by the nature of the problems he is correcting. In his first letter to the church in Corinth, Paul addresses a number of issues, including the Corinthians' lack of clarity regarding spiritual gifts, both why they have them and how they should be used in public worship. In chapter 11, Paul instructs women on how they should appear (whether he speaks of head coverings or hair arrangement, no one knows) when they pray and prophesy in church. He asks them to be as culturally sensitive as possible, so that people won't be turned off to the gospel unnecessarily. But the entire discussion—which is a notoriously difficult one—revolves around women's self-presentation, *when they pray and prophesy.* He assumes that women will pray and prophesy in public worship, or he wouldn't have taken the time to give these instructions.

Later in the letter, in chapter 14, Paul is sorting out the apparently unruly worship practices in Corinth. Some people are speaking in tongues and no one can understand them. Paul reins them in: "But if there is no one to interpret, let them be silent in church" (1 Cor. 14:28). When it comes to prophesying, if someone is speaking but someone else receives a revelation, then "let the first person be silent" (v. 30). Right in the middle of the discussion about prophecy come these verses: "As in all the churches of the saints, women should be silent in the churches. For they are not permitted to speak, but should be subordinate, as the law also says. If there is anything they desire to know, let them ask their husbands at home. For it is shameful for a woman to speak in church" (1 Cor. 14:33b–35). Following these verses the discussion regarding prophecy resumes.

The question is how are we to handle these apparently contradictory verses, since, as noted above, only a few chapters earlier Paul gave instructions about how women should dress or arrange their hair *when they pray and prophesy?* In addition to Paul's prior endorsement, we have to keep in mind the whole range of women in the biblical record who did, in fact, speak in the company of God's people, often at God's invitation. The women in the biblical stories surveyed in this chapter cannot be forgotten as we endeavor to interpret 1 Corinthians 14:33–35. When people do try to make these verses normative, when they interpret this passage to be a universal prohibition on women's speech for all time and in all places, they have a great deal of biblical material that they must answer for.

How else have people interpreted the passage? The many suggestions offered seem to fall into a few broad categories.[12] First, it may be that the worship space resembled synagogue arrangement, in which women and men would be seated in separate areas. Paul, then, would be requiring women to stop engaging in disruptive speech, that is, asking for clarification from their husbands across an aisle, which obviously would make it hard for others to focus on the teaching. This assumes that women would be less educated and would have had less access to religious things, and therefore would be at a disadvantage in understanding what was being taught. Others have suggested that the women were particularly exuberant with their new Christian freedoms, and so they were the ones who were abusing the gifts of tongues and prophecy that Paul curtailed earlier in the chapter. Still others assert that Paul is simply attempting to uphold Jewish patterns of family relationships in which the husbands, more trained to read the Hebrew Scriptures than were their wives, have a teaching role. Others suggest that, given the Jewish nature of the passage, it doesn't represent Paul's view, but is simply a quote of what others say about women in worship. In other places in this letter Paul does quote the Corinthians' position before critiquing it, but this case does not fit that pattern since there is no counterargument. Finally, many scholars do not believe that Paul wrote it at all, since in some manuscripts verses 34–35 appear at the end of the chapter, which makes it look like a later addition; also, in their current location, these verses break the flow of the argument about prophecy, which is then resumed after them.

How do we know that Paul is not laying down a rule for all churches for all time? First of all, we have his stated assumption in chapter 11 that women will pray and prophesy in public worship; in other words, he has already affirmed their vocal participation in public worship. We also have the gratefulness he expressed regarding the labor of women for the sake of the gospel in Romans 16, and particularly the titles of leadership with which he names Phoebe (see above). Other verses in 1 Corinthians 14 use the word "all" (vv. 23–24, 31) or "each one" (v. 26) implying that women did, in fact, speak in tongues and prophesy. In addition, the appeal to "the law" in these verses is problematic for two reasons: first, because Paul is fundamentally opposed to making Jewish law binding on Christian behavior (see Gal. 2:11–14, where he opposes Peter to his face for making Gentiles live like Jews); second, because the law of Moses does not say anywhere that women have to be silent or subordinate. This prefigures, rather, rabbinic Judaism, which developed in the centuries following the destruction of the temple in Jerusalem (70 CE). Preeminent Pauline scholars, such as Gordon Fee and C. K. Barrett, suggest, for these reasons, that the most likely conclusion is that Paul didn't write it, or, if he did, that he meant only disruptive speech in the Corinthian context. Otherwise it is a contradiction to his own words elsewhere.[13]

The other text used by critics of women's leadership to "prove" that Paul was against it is 1 Timothy 2:11–15.[14] When we approach this passage we have to ask, again, what problems Paul is addressing in this letter and how we should understand his admonitions here in light of the rest of what he says and the broader scope of Scripture. The pastoral problem Timothy faces in Ephesus, and which Paul addresses, is heresy that poses a serious threat to the church. In fact, in the first chapter, Paul mentions two men by name who "suffered shipwreck in the faith" (1:19). The nature of the heresy we can only surmise by Paul's writing against it, but it appears to be related to the traditional religion of that city, the worship of Artemis. The huge temple to Artemis in Ephesus, the ruins of which can still be seen, demonstrates the prominence of this goddess cult there, as does the two-hour chant "Great is Artemis of the Ephesians!" (in Acts 19) when Paul was trying to introduce Christianity in that place. We have to keep this in mind as we approach the text at hand.

First Timothy 2 begins with instructions regarding public prayer, both what they should pray for and how they should pray: they should pray for everyone, including their leaders, so they can live quiet, peaceable lives. The men should pray with holy hands lifted up, free from argument and anger, and the women should pray with sound judgment, free from a focus on fashion and beauty (no pearls, braided hair, or expensive clothes, in particular). Paul is not suggesting that different things are required of men and women by God; rather, he is addressing the problems each group brings to public prayer.

The next section (1 Tim. 2:11–15) deals with the demeanor of women as they learn. Here are the instructions Paul gives:

> Let a woman learn in silence with full submission. I permit no woman to teach or to have authority over a man; she is to keep silent. For Adam was formed first, then Eve; and Adam was not deceived, but the woman was deceived and became a transgressor. Yet she will be saved through childbearing, provided they continue in faith and love and holiness, with modesty.

The first verse enjoins a quiet attitude, or a calmness while learning, and probably should not be rendered "silent" since it is from the same root word used in verse 2 about having quiet lives. The false teachers have made big inroads with some of the young widows (see 1 Tim. 5), and they may have been talking back to Timothy and other teachers with the vigor of the newly converted. The instruction here may simply be that they need to listen quietly to the gospel again—in fact they need to submit themselves to it, or to the messengers delivering it. The submission in view here is either to the teachers or to the teaching itself, but not to husbands, since this is a passage about public worship, not marriage. Along with this submission to the gospel or to its teachers is a restriction on the teaching of these women; they should not be allowed anywhere near the teacher's seat, because of their false doctrine. As in many letters, the crux of the matter is heresy versus gospel, and here it seems to be no different. Paul makes one more restrictive statement: that women should not have authority over or, more likely, gain the upper hand over men or dominate them. (Paul does not use the normal word for authority, *exousia*, but a strange word, *authentein*, that occurs only this once in the New Testament and rarely anywhere else in other Greek literature. Therefore his precise intention is difficult to discern.) In any case, it fits the picture of women who have been influenced by false doctrine not being allowed to usurp a place of authority.

How do we know that this approach is a fair one to take? Not only does it fit with Paul's endorsement of women's speaking in other passages, but it is the best way to make sense of the next set of verses. In verses 13–14, Paul gives two reasons for his restrictions: Adam was created first, and Eve was deceived, neither one of which fits his normal emphases. "For Adam was created first" is a strange reason, in any case, for keeping women quiet. Usually Paul likes to underscore their interdependence and mutuality in verses such as: "For just as woman came from man, so man comes through woman; but all things come from God" (1 Cor. 11:12; see also 1 Cor. 7). And when it comes to the fall, Paul nowhere else mentions Eve; instead, "Adam" is his shorthand for the culpable party. In Romans 5, for instance, it is Adam's sin that brings sin and death into the race, contrasted with the work of Christ for the redemption of the world. Also, Paul certainly does not believe women are the only ones capable of being deceived, since earlier in the letter he names men who fell for the false teaching. Despite the way the Christian church has used this text to promote ideas of female inferiority (especially the deceivability of women because Eve was deceived), that is not a good interpretation of Paul's intention here.

Rather, Paul uses a line of reasoning in this text that is unusual for him because of the specific heresy he is combating. The false teachers apparently advocated the idea that Artemis (or some conglomerate mother goddess) created women first, so Paul corrects this with a reminder that in Genesis, Adam was created first. Based on women's supposed priority in creation and their direct connection to the great goddess Artemis, the false teachers also promoted the idea that women were morally superior to men. In the face of this claim, Paul wants to establish that Eve was susceptible to temptation, not because he wants to demonstrate women's inferiority, but to call into question their ideas of women's superiority. In this discussion, then, Paul is not demeaning women or putting them in a lower place, but trying to get those with a hyperelevated view of women to realize they are no better than men. It's a leveling of women with men, not a demotion of women to a status lower than men.

Finally, Paul writes of women being saved through childbirth. Even those who claim to be biblical literalists rarely take this verse at face value, because nowhere else in Scripture is salvation linked to producing offspring. Even in Paul, the cross and the resurrection form the center of discussions about salvation. To be saved, or kept safe, through childbirth is a strange assertion in any case, but particularly in a discussion of worship, unless, again, we think of the goddess theology that pervaded Ephesus. Even after their conversion to Christianity, these women, who would have faced the possibility of dying every time they gave birth, may have continued to pray to the goddess to protect them in childbirth as a way of covering all their bases. Paul would simply be reminding them that they don't need to keep praying to Artemis for protection in childbirth, because God will care for them through it.

To read the passage as Paul's answer to a goddess-related heresy that got women fired up about their superiority and emboldened them to argue with Timothy makes sense of all the verses. Even the instructions regarding appearance may have been related to how women appeared in the temple of Artemis.

However one conceives of the heresy being combated, though, one thing is clear: Paul is addressing the heresy of that place and not writing out a church manual. How do we know that this is not setting down a universal rule against women's speech for all time? For one thing, as already noted, we have Paul's endorsement of women praying and prophesying in worship (1 Cor. 11) and his gratefulness for the ministry of actual women expressed in Romans 16. In addition, in Galatians 3:28 he depicts the redeemed community as one based not on social hierarchies but on the equal footing believers have in baptism. When we look at the rest of Scripture we see women called and empowered by God as teachers, prophets, evangelists, and leaders of various sorts, which should warn us against thinking that women cannot do these things. The stories of actual women cannot be overlooked as we consider passages such as this one in 1 Timothy 2.

Secondly, we could ask why the call for women's silence in 1 Timothy 2:11–12 is considered universally binding by some interpreters when those same interpreters do not consider other verses in the passage binding at all. For instance, most non-Pentecostals ignore verse 8, about men lifting holy hands, because they don't approve of anyone lifting hands in worship, and most Christian groups affirm modesty but reject Paul's instruction in verse 9 that women come to worship without jewelry, braided hair, or expensive clothes. In fact, many women (and men) wear their most expensive clothes and jewelry to church. These same groups may or may not think that women are more deceivable because of Paul's linking them to Eve's deception (v. 14), but they certainly do not treat the "saved through childbirth" idea as literally applicable. So the beginning and the end of the passage are not deemed applicable, but the verses in the middle about women's place are taken as universally binding, through time and across cultures. This inconsistent treatment of verses in the passage should call into question the use of this text as the cornerstone for Paul's view of women.[15] Even "traditional" or "take the Bible literally" folks don't think most of this passage applies today.

It should also raise questions about how these determinations are made. Why is the prohibition against jewelry easy to dismiss but the prohibition against women's speech easy to retain? It appears that this approach is informed throughout by cultural values: people buy into the notion that women should "look nice" so they ignore the restrictions on dressing up for church, but they also buy into women's subordinate place in society, and so they affirm restrictions on women's speech. In this case they are attempting to use Scripture to justify an ornamental view of women, something that the Bible does not support.

In contrast is Galatians 3:26–29, sometimes called the "Magna Carta of the church," in which Paul argues for equal standing in the redeemed community on the basis of our baptism. When we come up out of the water, the significant thing about us is not the social designations that defined us previously, but our being in Christ. This is part of Paul's over-all theological emphasis, the breaking down of walls in the redeemed community, and is therefore a better starting place for any discussion of Paul's ideas about women. It says:

> For in Christ Jesus you are all children of God through faith.
>
> As many of you as were baptized into Christ have clothed yourselves with Christ.
>
> There is no longer Jew or Greek, there is no longer slave or free, there is no longer male and female; for all of you are one in Christ Jesus.
>
> And if you belong to Christ, then you are Abraham's offspring, heirs according to the promise.

In the letter overall, Paul goes to great lengths to show that following the Jewish law is completely unnecessary for Christians. Being in relationship with God is not achieved through following Jewish law and marking their bodies as Jewish, but it is through Christ and washing their bodies in the water of baptism. Galatians 3:26–29 means this: Believers come into Christian community on the same basis: through Christ they are children of God, and offspring of Abraham. Since Abraham represents faith in God outside the law, Jews and Gentiles are put on equal footing through this same faith. One group is not superior to the other in terms of salvation, or access to God. In the redeemed community, the distinction between slave and free has also become irrelevant; they are welcomed equally into the fellowship and affirmed as brothers and sisters. In baptism, male and female believers are marked equally as being in Christ and in the family of God, in contrast to circumcision, which marked only men's bodies. This is a radically different community in which something other than human ways of categorizing people is foundational. And for Paul, the ex-Pharisee, this rejection of privilege based on these human distinctions is remarkable.

The question is, how does this spiritual equality get worked out in concrete terms in the new community, the family of God? When it came to service in the body of Christ, certainly Gentiles as much as Jews were empowered by God for ministry and affirmed by Christian communities in their leadership. And we have examples in the early church of slaves assuming leadership even in congregations in which their owners worshiped. When it comes to the third pair, "male and female," most Christians affirm the spiritual equality of people in both groups, but many shy away from granting equal participation in the life of the family of God. However, as F. F. Bruce observes: "If a Gentile may exercise spiritual leadership in church as freely as a Jew, or a slave as freely as a citizen, why not a woman as freely as a man?"[16] Paul seems to attach no theological significance to gender difference, or social differences of any kind, though his training would have pushed him in that direction. The social and even biological categories that define us are not determinative for relationships in the church. To make the distinction between Jew and Gentile theologically significant is anathema to Paul; perhaps to make distinction between male and female would be equally so. Perhaps it would be like preaching a different gospel, a gospel of freedom for men and social constraint for women.

Significantly, the lists of spiritual gifts in 1 Corinthians 12 and Ephesians 4 are not gendered. The sense of the passages is that God gives gifts and people should use them, without regard to rank and custom, for the building up of the one body. What if women bury their talents in the ground? How will they give account at the last day? What will the churches have to say for themselves if they have encouraged women to sit on their gifts, to never use them because that wouldn't fit comfortable cultural mores for women?

Conclusions

Looking at Scripture we have seen that women figured in the drama of salvation in a variety of roles. In ancient Israel, women not only gave birth to prominent children in the line of promise but also challenged kings and protected their families—even their entire people—from destruction. Some of them spoke with God and were entrusted with speaking for God. Though stories of women leaders do not predominate in the Old Testament story, still these women's lives demonstrate that God called women to and empowered them for all sorts of prominent roles even in a heavily male-centered culture.

We have observed that Jesus affirms discipleship as the highest calling for women as well as for men. In Luke 8 we learn of specific women named as followers of Jesus, and in that passage and in other places in the Gospels we hear of a larger group of women who followed Jesus and heard his teaching. He risked the repudiation of his message by having women in his group of traveling followers. Jesus not only treated women with the same respect that he gave men, inviting them into the relationship of discipleship, he preached a message that explicitly called men and women to live sacrificially for each other. In all his interactions, but perhaps most clearly in the foot washing, he set the pattern for how his followers are to live: significantly, they are not to "lord it over each other" as Gentiles do—those outside the circle of followers—but to express the attitude of Jesus, one of sacrificial service based on a clear sense of his own identity.

Paul affirms Christian service as the highest calling, even to the point of encouraging people to refrain from marriage so they could devote themselves more fully to ministry (1 Cor. 7). He approves of women performing all sorts of ministry, including having churches in their homes, engaging in evangelism, and specifically taking on leadership tasks such as praying, prophesying, teaching, evangelizing, and exercising oversight. Through his greetings we find that he appreciates the labor of women who have worked with him in ministry and, in fact, his words present a picture of people in the redeemed community doing the work of God in the world together.

What follows from a recognition that women are created equally in the image of God—equally fallen, equally redeemed? What follows from recognizing that women and men are welcomed into discipleship on an equal basis, and that their identity is to be staked on their baptism before anything else? What would change for individual Christian women, and what would change in the church if we took these things seriously?

At a deep level we can and should ask, what does being created in God's image, equally fallen and then also equally redeemed, mean for the whole female person? What does it mean in terms of where women derive their identity, in terms of how they construct their concept of their physical beings, in terms of how they think about vocation, callings, and aspirations?

3

SUPERMODELS FOR JESUS?

Christian Women and Body Image

"I am fearfully and wonderfully made," says the psalmist, and most of us would agree in a general sort of way: everything God made is good, and we know God declared humanity very good. But many women who look in a mirror, particularly a full-length mirror, trying to decide what to wear, are not in the frame of mind to believe their bodies are wonderfully made or very good. In fact, many women, even Christian women, despise their bodies.

Why is that? Why can we affirm something from the Bible as being generally true—our whole selves, including our bodies, are good in God's eyes—but we can't accept it on a personal level? Clearly there is no one answer to that question, given the complex interplay between personal experience and societal values, but a critical look at the portrayal of women in culture can shed light on the factors that influence our concept of our bodies. In the section that follows we will look at some of the ways the society at large communicates ideas about female bodies and female sexuality, about thinness and eating disorders, and about femininity and personal fulfillment. Then we will ask: what sort of messages regarding physicality have we received from our churches? Have religious institutions helped critique the damaging portrayals of women (and men) in the media or have they reinforced cultural ideals regarding female bodies and femininity? What aspects of the Christian gospel would speak to this issue?

One caveat before we begin: This chapter is not denying the need for healthy body weight; obviously, as people in this society have turned to junk food and sedentary lifestyles, the rate of weight-related health problems has risen. Some churches have begun, rightly enough, to encourage people to avoid gluttony in order to care for their bodies. But the fact remains that millions of women, those overweight and those at perfectly healthy weights, have a very difficult time feeling at home in their own skin. The discussion that follows, then, deals with women's ideas about their bodies and with the cultural ideals for women's appearance that influence women's body concepts. It seeks to answer the questions: How have women developed negative assessments of their bodies, and what can the church do to help women agree with the psalmist: "I am fearfully and wonderfully made"?

Women's Appearance and the "Male Gaze"

Obviously it is difficult to live in this society and not be bombarded with messages about our bodies. We are, after all, a media-saturated society. For instance, Americans watch, on average, four hours of TV a day (about one-quarter of their waking hours), not to mention the time spent playing video games and watching DVDs in any given twenty-four-hour period. In the commercials, programs, films, and games, we are presented over and over again with young, ultrathin women who seem to be happy and successful. The content of female success? The ability to be pleasing to men: pleasing to look at, "hot" (that is, sexy and exuding a desire to be desired), perhaps witty and feisty, but generally playing a supportive role. As women absorb this way of measuring feminine success, they form the habit of seeing themselves only as they assume men will see them, and valuing themselves only for how sexually attractive they can manage to be. Feminist scholars have termed this the "male gaze," which many women have internalized.

Whenever I have introduced this concept to a group, invariably someone will respond with the observation that women are often each other's worst critics. Many women seem to be more afraid of other women's judgment than of men's; they want to be thin or have perfect hair or find the right clothes in order to impress the women around them. This does not suggest that we are free of the "male gaze"; rather, it shows that we have internalized it, since we're still measuring ourselves against each other based on what men in this culture (supposedly) want from women. And this sense of competing with each other means that women often see other women simply as objects, which undercuts their ability to see each other as full human beings or recognize the potential for relationship. Imagine how different it would be if women were to appreciate each other on the basis of different rules: take, for instance, hands. Rather than small, dainty, and perfectly smooth hands with long nails—symbols of weakness and passivity—we could admire all sorts of hands, even large, strong hands, for the work they do, for the care for children and elders, and for their usefulness and beauty. Or hips: what if women weren't competing for the smallest jeans, the narrowest hips, or the flattest buttocks? What if the natural curves that suggest a woman's capacity to bear new life into the world were accepted with delight? But women compare themselves, not according to standards they have themselves devised, but according to ideals of beauty and femininity set for us by a male-dominated culture. We look at ourselves and other women through the lens of the male gaze.

The habit of judging ourselves on the basis of the male gaze is partly the result of the barrage of messages from beauty and dieting industries: without the help of beauty products a woman's face, hair, skin, abdomen, breasts, buttocks, thighs, you name it, will be too rough, too fat, too flat, not flat enough, too limp, too full, too shiny, not shiny enough, etc. Women are taught to think, as Christian writer Michelle Graham says in her book *Wanting to Be Her: Body Image Secrets Victoria Won't Tell You*, "My fill-in-the-blank isn't fill-in-the-blank enough."[1] All we have to do is buy more and more "beauty aids" or pay cosmetic surgeons to "fix" our "beauty trouble spots" and things will be fine, right? No, actually, because the multibillion-dollar beauty industry depends on keeping us insecure and addicted to their products.

In addition to "beauty experts" who instruct women directly about how they should want to present themselves, marketers throw at us countless images of svelte, half-undressed, young women selling everything from beer to long-distance telephone service. In hundreds of ways (each day, if they watch their four hours of TV), girls and women are presented with a standard of feminine desirability that they cannot attain, and all too often they develop a deep disdain for themselves because of their perceived failure to measure up. Boys and men, in the meantime, are taught to desire cosmetically, surgically and/or digitally enhanced images of female sexuality. How could all of this not influence how women construct their identity?

The objectification of women by reducing their value to the sexiness of their bodies has been the focus of feminist comment since the 1960s. In fact, the first mass demonstration in the modern women's movement was a protest at the 1968 Miss America pageant; some women held up posters depicting cows wearing 4-H–style ribbons to underscore the insult of having women judged like animals at a fair. In her *Killing Us Softly* films, sociologist Jean Kilbourne examines how women have been depicted in TV and magazine advertising in the past thirty years. She shows that in the seventies, many ads featured women with childlike and subdued expressions, often in humiliating poses and always in submission to men or lower than men if both sexes were pictured. By the nineties, women were gaunt to the point of looking skeletal, often made up to look bruised around the eyes, and in vulnerable poses.[2] Ads with supine women are all over the place: women are depicted as passive, as prey, as wanting to be ravished. In contrast, very few ads feature men lying down, or being vulnerable in any way.

In the face of these ads and the flood of books and magazines that promote hyperskinniness, there has been a steady countercurrent of material that critiques the culture of thinness. For instance, in her book *The Obsession: Reflections on the Tyranny of Slenderness*, Kim Chernin argues that body size ideals are constructed by cultures and vary even within a culture through time. There is nothing intrinsically beautiful about a particular body type; rather, bodies are deemed attractive or not according to cultural standards. She asks readers to consider the full-figured Renoir women, for example. (Though scholars discuss some universally appealing aspects of feminine beauty—large, nicely set eyes, for instance—ideals regarding body type seem more changeable across cultures, and seem linked to status. In a society where having enough to eat is a privilege, then larger female bodies may symbolize wealth and opulence. In our society, thin bodies are associated with wealth.) Not only is our obsession with the superthin, supermodel version of female bodies not universal, it is, she suggests, damaging to women. Rather than allowing themselves to relax into the fullness of adulthood, women are instructed to keep themselves small, childlike even. Dieting creates or helps to maintain a childish look for women so that men who are afraid of mature women's bodies and minds won't be threatened by them. Men who define masculinity by their role as protectors need their women to be, or at least to appear, vulnerable and helpless. Why is it, Chernin asks, that we want adult women to be cute and pony-tailed, like perpetual teenagers?[3] Even in language referring to adult women, speakers and writers often employ the term "girls" as if they are children and not adults.

But it is not simply a fascination with a perpetual childlike look that this obsession with dieting expresses. Rather, thinness fits a broader set of expectations for women: that they should take up as little space in this world as possible. They not only try to be thin, they work at appearing smaller than they are. "Makes you look 10 pounds thinner" is a standard marketing line for women's clothing, and "feminine" or "sexy" are the adjectives used to sell little high-heeled shoes that make women walk in choppy, unnatural steps and leave a tiny footprint—an apt metaphor, perhaps, for this entire phenomenon. Or consider women's gestures, which, in order to be "ladylike," are supposed to be gentle, controlled, and never too expansive. Men, on the other hand, are encouraged to take up space as if the world is theirs to fill: they can bulk up physically; wear big, nonbinding clothing; stride around in comfortable shoes with large gum soles; and flail their arms to make their point. Furthermore, as linguistics professor Deborah Tannen has argued, men tend to fill conversational space, since they are taught to feel entitled to dominate verbal interaction, while women tend to concede conversations to the men in a mixed group. In fact, women are considered assertive and domineering if they don't allow men to dominate verbally. What this means, then, in the end, is that being thin is part of a larger message about women learning their place relative to men in the world; it is about women following cultural instructions to stay dependent and unobtrusive. Social critic Naomi Wolf puts it well: "A cultural fixation on female thinness is not an obsession about female beauty but an obsession about female obedience."[4] Thinness is about keeping women weaker and quieter, more submissive and contained.

In addition, Susan Brownmiller, in her book *Femininity*, observes that it is not only an idealized female form but a highly sensualized version of the female body that is used in the public square.[5] In other words, the normal human functions of various parts of women's anatomy are hidden under the weight of their potential sexiness. Take eyelashes for example. Men and women have eyelashes for the good purpose of keeping harmful particles of dirt or small bugs out of their eyes. For women, though, eyelashes have become a site of sex appeal. They need to be long, thick, rich, full, dark, and any number of other words cosmetic industry advertisers have employed to make eyelashes all about buying beauty products. Legs are another great example. Men and women (at least those fortunate enough to have been born with them and who have not somehow lost them) have two legs for the primary purpose of personal locomotion. For women, however, legs have become measures of sensual appeal; they need to be thin, shapely, shaven, tanned (if one is Caucasian), and smooth. None of these attributes increases their usefulness in moving the body from here to there, but the attributes have become more important than function.

Even when it comes to star female athletes, the power, strength, and skill of their bodies are not as important as their sexiness quotient. For one thing, we could observe how little coverage women athletes and women's sports receive in premier sports publications such as *Sports Illustrated*.

Less than 10 percent of its articles deal with women, and women athletes are featured on the cover of this weekly publication as rarely as once a year, as in 2002, for instance. But the release of the swimsuit issue has become an annual media event, spawning videos, talk show appearances for the models, and doubled sales of *Sports Illustrated* for that week. Apparently even in a sports magazine, the athleticism of women who have trained for decades to be great at their sport cannot compete with models in semi-pornographic poses wearing micro bikinis. Pictures of sweaty, strong, competitive women in the heat of a game, true counterparts to the action shots of male athletes, are rarely published. It is telling that in the past few years the governing bodies of numerous sports (including beach volleyball, soccer, and tennis) have requested or even in some cases required women athletes to dress in more "feminine"—that is, skimpier and skin-tight—uniforms. And then there are the huge differences in figure-skating costumes: men are covered from wrists and neck all the way to the skates, whereas women don minimalist outfits that show off their skin—how does it feel to do a winter sport in a bathing suit? Why, some women athletes ask, can't they be valued for their skill, their strength, or their heroism just as male athletes are?[6]

Some of you reading this may be thinking that women have always been valued for their beauty: Helen of Troy, for instance, supposedly inspired the launch of a thousand ships with her beauty. Cleopatra might come to mind, or Shakespeare's sonnets to beautiful women, or the beautiful, dark lover in the biblical *Song of Songs*. While this is true, the landscape is different now with the intrusion of thousands of "this is how a woman's body is supposed to look" images delivered to our living rooms via TV and magazines. Never before has a society been so saturated with images, so bombarded with the appearance of idealized women in every state of dress and undress. In nonimage-based societies, a woman may feel comfortable being compared to other real women in the neighborhood, but some of the women interviewed for Graham's book, *Wanting to Be Her*, were afraid of how their bodies compared with the bodies of famous actresses and supermodels. These media-produced women are unlike women in one's own village or neighborhood since they have access to professional makeup artists, expensive hairdressers, personal trainers, and fabulously expensive clothes, not to mention cosmetic surgery and the digital enhancement of their images. Besides, some famous women of the past were considered exceptions: their beauty was of mythological proportions, and their appearance was never considered normative.

Some of you may also be thinking that this image fixation is hard on men, too, since the media also portray how men are supposed to look. It is true that idealized male bodies and faces appear in the media, but the pressure for conformity is not the same. For one thing, a wider variety of body types is acceptable; men can be something besides bone thin. For instance, in the TV show "King of Queens" the man has a beer gut and the woman is very thin. Men can also be older and yet still considered attractive. A man graying at the temples with creases in his face can still be the star, can still fall in love, because these things can be viewed positively—strength, wisdom, reliability—whereas for a woman these things mean she can no longer have love-interest roles. Rather, she will be cast in grandmotherly roles, even if she is heavily into Botox, plastic surgery, and abrasion treatments for her face.

More importantly, the media do not apply as much pressure on men regarding their looks because men are rarely valued only for their looks. Men's success (in the media and in the real world) is measured much more by their achievements: they save the woman, save the day, make the discoveries, make the money, unravel the mysteries, overcome the "bad guy," or solve riddles. If they look good along the way, so much the better, but the job does not demand that they fit a particular image of maleness. So if a man compares himself to film stars and finds his appearance lacking, he can trust that other attributes, such as being smart, witty, courageous, or simply economically stable, will help him succeed since women are taught to value these things in men. But men (and women) have been taught to value a woman primarily for her looks, so if she doesn't measure up in that arena, it is much more difficult for her to be successful.

What It Takes

Consumerism

The fixation on appearance, as noted above, intensified in the last couple of centuries for a number of reasons. We could cite the rise of factories when clothes began to be ready-made in standard sizes instead of made for individual bodies; the invention of the camera, which resulted in the huge proliferation of images; and the growth of the advertising industry in the late nineteenth century. Many scholars have noted that advertising, in order to create desire for products, required a new unhappiness with self on the part of consumers. Americans, who, in the early nineteenth century, had viewed themselves as citizens in a great democratic experiment, increasingly came to see themselves as consumers by the end of that century. This was especially true of women, who were targeted by advertising appeals because of their duty to buy whatever was necessary for the running of their households, and because of their roles as domestic ornament. They needed to buy things to look the part of "angel in the home." Now the beauty and thinness industries have grown beyond the wildest dreams of those nineteenth-century folks, yet the tactics remain the same: keep the focus on appearance through the creation of an unnatural and unattainable body type and beauty ideal.

The result? Every year Americans spend billions of dollars on cosmetics, dieting, and cosmetic surgery, and most of this spending is done by women. Women not only spend more money on these things, but they also spend a much higher percentage of their income on apparel and accessories.[7] This is partly due, of course, to the reality that women still make considerably less than men do: according to a US Department of Labor report of women's earnings in 2006, women between 45 and 64 make on average 73 cents to the male dollar, though this figure is somewhat higher for younger white women and lower for African-American and Hispanic women in any age group.[8] Women make less money but are expected to spend more of it on their appearance. In particular, being thin consumes a great deal of women's money, when one adds up the books, magazines, powders, pills, special diet foods, and surgeries, as well as the gym memberships, personal trainers, and home exercise systems that cost hundreds of dollars, not to mention the chic workout clothing. It looks as if our economy needs women to keep on obsessing about their appearance. Economist John Kenneth Galbraith once observed that "Behavior that is essential for economic reasons is transformed into a social virtue."[9] This is exactly what has happened with being thin, since the weight-loss and diet-food industries have helped create a climate in which being chubby is viewed as a moral failing, and eating high-calorie foods is "sinning" or "giving in to temptation." Just think of how often chocolate is associated with the word "decadent." Fatness is associated with laziness and badness in this culture and viewed with inordinate disgust, whereas being fit and trim suggests self-control and discipline, even if it is really about an out-of-control obsession with appearance, or an eating disorder and/or an addiction to spending money on beauty and thinness products. Some might object that society's disdain for fatness stems from health concerns, but if it were merely a health issue, we wouldn't view overweight people any differently than we view those who tan obsessively: people who engage in practices known to involve health risks.

Narcissism

Besides the expense of trying to fit a cultural ideal for beauty and thinness, doing so requires the sacrifice of hours, days, and weeks of a woman's life. While men are off making scientific discoveries, starting music bands, or working for political causes, women are encouraged to focus their time and energies on their appearance. If you want to look like Miss America, for instance, you may have to exercise five or six hours a day, diet to the point that you may not be able to think clearly, and quite possibly undergo surgeries such as breast implants, a nose job, and perhaps even a staple in your stomach. During the big-hair era in my high school, I had friends who spent an hour a day on their hair, and if it didn't turn out right, they would simply start over and devote another hour.

The goal of the "beauty industry" and some of the weight-loss industry is not beauty or even health, it is narcissism. We are encouraged to think about ourselves *all the time*. This is not a Christian virtue! It diverts women's energies and attention from being active members in God's new creation to a narrow focus on the self. Dieting in particular can render women immune to the pressing issues of our day; when a woman is thinking all the time about food—either eating or not eating it—about whether she has pushed the needle on the scale up a pound or not, or about whether she can fit into smaller-size pants, she may not have any passion left to care about war, genocide, sex trafficking, global warming, or destitute refugees who have moved into her own city. And she won't be likely to agitate to make society function in a more compassionate and just way. Naomi Wolf observes that dieting is "the most potent political sedative in women's history."[10] We will not be standing up for the rights of the dispossessed (which may even include ourselves) if we spend all our leisure time and much of our money on our own appearance.

Passivity

The narcissism and consumerism that the quest for beauty encourages certainly can lead to passivity with regard to anything in the world outside of this quest. On the other hand, the beauty quest may be fostered by ideals for women that are inherently passive. Therefore, it is not surprising that in 1920 women won the right to vote *and* in that year the first "Fall Frolic" was held in Atlantic City, which quickly became the "Miss America Pageant." Women's political gains were met with an attempt to keep them in the one sphere of public life that wasn't threatening to men: the ornamental, sexy, and/or beautiful. A *New Yorker* cartoon from that era depicts a man standing next to a line of buxom women in bathing suits with this caption: "Ah, proud to be an American." A woman's real contribution to this country, according to the cartoonist, is to look sexy, to be a sexual object for men. Keeping the focus on their ornamental or sexual value obscures women's capabilities in all other areas of human life: intellectual, musical, artistic, and political. To the extent that women believe the cultural messages that their value is in their body, they also may be unable to recognize or exercise their own capabilities.

Since the 1920s, *New Yorker* cartoons have changed as women's place in society has changed,[11] but the advertising industry often subverts the gains women make socially or politically by conflating ideas of female strength with female sexual power. A woman might be pictured as a professional carrying a brief case, for instance, but the focus on her legs as she walks away from the camera suggests that the important thing about her is still her sexiness. In addition, the expanded power to make choices that resulted from the women's movement of the 1970s was met with advertisers who turned it into merchandising appeals. For instance, the long-running slogan for Virginia Slims cigarettes was "You've come a long way, Baby," linking women's social progress with the freedom to smoke. More recently the marketing of exercise videos often suggests that having abs of steel is the kind of strength a woman should aspire to. The message to women over and over again is that their greatest power is in their consumer choices and their greatest service to humanity is looking pretty and thin, a passive calling indeed. In the end this means a narrowing of women's lives, a reduction of their place in the world.

What It Results In

Self-Hatred

Not only are the beauty ideals ridiculously self-obsessive, they are also impossible. For instance, twenty years ago American models tended to be around a size eight, whereas now they are a size zero. In 2006 two Latin American models died of malnourishment, and in the same year Madrid authorities imposed a required minimum body mass index (BMI) on models who wanted to walk in Spain's biggest fashion show. (This BMI was lower than the World Health Organization's benchmark for a minimally healthy weight).[12] What's disturbing is that all the starving, the excessive exercise, the surgical "improvements," and finally the digital enhancements give us pictures of women that seem normal, even enviable to us, when actually they represent abnormality and/or unreality. The logical extreme of this phenomenon, of course, is the digital "creation" of women, images that have no relationship at all to flesh-and-blood human beings. It is no surprise that so many female Americans report contempt for their bodies, or certain parts of their bodies, given the incessant presentation of waiflike models with narrow, boyish hips, much like the Twiggy ideal from the 1960s (except with bigger breasts, since breast implants have become such big business). In the popular book *Reviving Ophelia*, author Mary Pipher notes how comfortable girls are in their own skin until they reach puberty, when suddenly their inability to measure up in the sexual attractiveness department makes them hate their bodies. And since they absorb the message that physical appearance is the only important aspect of being female, if they don't feel that they measure up in this area, then they not only hate their bodies, but hate themselves completely. Even the women who seem to fit the cultural ideals have been conditioned to have disdain for their physical selves, and those who do not fit this ideal are in an even worse bind.

It would be hard to overestimate the degree to which this obsession with thinness dominates women's lives. Over the last three decades a sociologist, Jean Kilbourne, has produced a series of films critiquing the portrayal of women in advertising. In her most recent film, *Killing Us Softly 3*, she cites studies showing that a fairly high percentage of American women said they would give up five years of their lives if they could be ten pounds thinner.[13] After seeing the film, a student commented to me, "Hey, I'd give up ten years!" though she fell well within the range of healthy body size. We teach our young women to value slenderness and sexiness more than life itself!

Eating Disorders

Not surprisingly, then, about 20 percent of female college students suffer from eating disorders and over 60 percent have "disordered eating," which includes binge-eating, refusing to eat in order to lose weight, misuse of diet pills and laxatives, and engaging in excessive exercise.[14] That such a distressingly large percentage of young women struggle with food can be linked to several factors, but a cultural obsession with thinness is certainly one of them. An associate professor of medicine at Albany Medical Center, Dr. Sharon Alger-Mayer, was quoted in the *Boston Globe* as saying, "Being exposed to an environment with a lot of emphasis on thinness can put someone with a predisposition to eating disorders in a very high-risk situation."[15] That media images affect the attitudes and behaviors of girls and women should not be surprising given the fact that TV ads depicting people smoking were banned in order to reduce smoking.

Obviously there are other factors that contribute to the development of eating disorders, including, as Alger-Mayer observes, a genetic predisposition to them as well as a social environment that pushes people in that direction. In discussing the causes of anorexia nervosa, for instance, one of the most prevalent eating disorders, counselors have observed that some girls and young women who refuse to eat enough to sustain their bodies are rejecting female adulthood; perhaps they see it as too complicated, too sexualized, too dangerous to be a woman. Some have seen too much violence against women in the media or among their relatives, or they have been the victim of violence already. One student in this category told me that refusing to eat enough stemmed from her desire to die, but not through blatant suicide.

Others seem to use the rejection of food as a way of expressing control in that area of life, since they feel powerless in others. Controlling caloric intake becomes a huge source of pride, and loss of control a tremendous fear. Others seem to be saying: "You want me to be thin, that's the only thing valued? I will be thin!" A student showed me a picture of an anorexic woman who appeared to be close to death, ribs jutting out and a skull-like face. But the student's comment? "I still wish I had thighs that thin." Girls and young women report being complimented on their thinness right up until the day they go to the hospital, their lives endangered.

Bulimia, like anorexia, affects far more women than men, but unlike anorexia it is easier to hide, at least for a while. It often begins as a "safety valve" to help keep the body from absorbing the calories from a huge meal or snack; it is linked fairly directly with a fear of becoming fat. Gradually, though, the pattern of binging and purging becomes an end in itself, and the bulimic person becomes consumed with these activities to the detriment of her health—it destroys the esophagus and teeth, among other things—and her relationships.

Paradoxically, even overeating and weight gain can be an attempt to hide from sexuality, to reject the dangers of being a woman. If she has been sexually abused, a woman may fear men's stares or male attention of any kind, and hide behind extra weight.

Violence against Women

In the fall of 2006, two school shootings made national news: one in Colorado and one in an Amish schoolhouse in Pennsylvania. In both instances the gunmen separated the girls from the boys, and killed some of the girls after molesting or threatening to molest them. Bob Herbert, of the *New York Times*, made this observation:

> In the widespread coverage that followed these crimes, very little was made of the fact that only girls were targeted. Imagine if a gunman had gone into a school, separated the kids up on the basis of race or religion, and then shot only the black kids. Or only the white kids. Or only the Jews.
>
> There would have been thunderous outrage. The country would have first recoiled in horror, and then mobilized in an effort to eradicate that kind of murderous bigotry. There would have been calls for action and reflection. And the attack would have been seen for what it really was: a hate crime.
>
> None of that occurred because these were just girls, and we have become so accustomed to living in a society saturated with misogyny that violence against females is more or less to be expected. Stories about the

rape, murder and mutilation of women and girls are staples of the news, as familiar to us as weather forecasts. The startling aspect of the Pennsylvania attack was that this terrible thing happened at a school in Amish country, not that it happened to girls.[16]

Why is it so much easier for us to see and name racial and religious hatred than misogyny? At least partly it is because, as Herbert said, we hear about it so much we don't even listen any longer. And it's not just that violence against women appears so regularly on the news, but that such stories dominate prime-time TV detective shows; movies that portray the victimization of women are perennially popular; music videos often blur the line between sex and violence against women; and shockingly, millions of American boys and men spend hours of their lives playing video games in which they violently subjugate and humiliate female characters. The extreme version of this, of course, is pornography, now so readily accessible, in which real women are depicted as things to be enjoyed; in hard-core forms they are beaten and raped for the titillation of the male viewers. The violence done to women in pornography shows the complete dehumanization of the women involved: no one is thinking about whether the person likes jazz music or cream in her coffee or if she had dreams for her life. She is completely an object to be used, and used up, for strangers' sexual pleasure.

But all of this gendered violence in the media is more than a bad habit. It depicts as well as feeds the fantasies of millions of men who still believe, consciously or unconsciously, that they have the right to dominate every female on earth; but since they can't achieve that in their interaction with flesh-and-blood women, they enjoy playing it out in games, or watching it in videos and movies. How does all this relate to body image? Herbert again:

> A girl or woman is sexually assaulted every couple of minutes or so in the U.S. The number of seriously battered wives and girlfriends is far beyond the ability of any agency to count. We're all implicated in this carnage because the relentless violence against women and girls is linked at its core to the wider society's casual willingness to dehumanize women and girls, to see them first and foremost as sexual vessels—objects—and never, ever as the equals of men.

The reduction of a female human being's value to her sexual attractiveness comes at a terrifically high price: dehumanization, which in turn makes more probable all manner of violence. Over and over again in history we can observe that after a group has been dehumanized, anything can be done to them with impunity.

Cutting

With ideas like this firmly embedded in women's consciousness, it should be no surprise that they resort to violence against themselves: it feels right. When women engage in cutting, they are, at one level, simply agreeing with society that it is acceptable, perhaps even desirable, to harm women's bodies. Counselors working with young women who cut suggest a number of factors that contribute to the behavior, including but not limited to sexual abuse in their past, a lack of other avenues through which to release negative emotions, and the need to feel external pain in order to mask internal pain. But the striking thing is that cutting is "catching" on many college campuses, so that young women who know someone who cuts are more likely to engage in it themselves. They see violence against women in the culture around them, they meet someone who models how to do it, and they try it for themselves.[17]

Underlying it all is the negative assessment of their bodies, ranging from disappointment to all-out hatred, which they have already experienced for several years before they get to college. They may believe that they are worthless since they can't look like supermodels, so they deserve to be in pain. They may have experienced a boyfriend's disgust at their bodies or received blows to their bodies from those who should love them and respect their bodies.

Churches' Responses

If cultural ideals and practices have been damaging to women's experience of themselves in their bodies, how, we might ask, is the church responding? Most conservative churches have not noticed the degradation of women and violence against women that pervades the culture. When pastors enumerate evils in our society, the list rarely includes the points that Herbert made above. Most evangelical churches espouse some level of male domination and therefore have no critique to offer of its deleterious effects in society. Unfortunately, many churches perpetuate the idea that male predatory behavior is somewhat inevitable, with "the guys just can't help themselves" warnings to young women regarding sex. They implicitly teach that women have to be responsible for male sexuality.

All too often churches buy into cultural ideals about thinness, beauty, and femininity as well. For example, one denominational youth Web site posted a suggestion for an activity for girls for a special youth event: put on makeup together while hearing Bible verses. For this girls' lock-in (an overnight event at the church) it instructs: "Plan to have girls go through all the steps of putting on makeup in the morning, using each step as a reminder of how to be a beautiful young woman of God." It suggests starting with 1 Samuel 16:7, in which Samuel, impressed by the appearance of the young men, wants to anoint one of David's warrior brothers to be the next king. God reminds Samuel that though people look at the outward appearance and consider it important, God does not; God looks at the heart. But this powerful message is subverted by the rest of the activity, since putting on makeup is all about the outward appearance. In fact the whole event trivializes Scripture, associating, for instance, the application of lipstick with the verse, "May the words of my mouth and the meditation of my heart be acceptable in your sight, O God." In the context of this event, what the girls would probably absorb is: "May the color of my lips be acceptable to you, O God, not to mention attractive to boys in the youth group." In addition to promoting a shallow use of Scripture, this activity assumes that all the girls in the youth group wear makeup, and ingrains the message that each girl *should* wear or want to wear makeup. It appears to be a complete confusion of the beauty myth and Christian discipleship.

Many Christian magazines spread this confusion as well. The most complete interweaving of Scripture and cultural values about beauty has to be *Revolve*, the New Testament in magazine format, targeted to teenage girls. Right next to the truly liberating words of Jesus are sidebars with tips on makeup and attractiveness to boys, and pictures of thin, smiling teenage girls who fit stereotypes of suburban junior high school cool. The intentions may be good—to get teenage girls to read the New Testament—but not only does the format domesticate the text, it pushes the erroneous message that the Bible promotes our society's ideas of beauty and thinness, not to mention gender relations.

On the contrary, as we saw in the previous chapter, women figure prominently in biblical texts as they exercise strength, quick wittedness, and active devotion to God. Significantly, only Old Testament stories include details about personal appearance, and the texts point to men who are attractive perhaps as much as they highlight the beauty of women: Joseph is described as "handsome and good-looking," which is apparently why a married woman lusts after him (Gen. 39:6–7); Saul is so handsome that "There was not a man among the people of Israel more handsome than he," and he was head and shoulders taller to boot (1 Sam. 9:2); David was "ruddy, and had beautiful eyes, and was handsome" (1 Sam. 16:12); Daniel and the rest of the young men mentioned in the book of Daniel were trained in the King's palace only if they were handsome, well educated, and wise (Dan. 1:3–4). Clearly these men, however, are judged in the texts for what they do, not simply what they look like, and the same holds true for the women. Even Esther, whose beauty is an integral aspect of her story, in the end acts to save her people through prayer, fasting, and just plain bravery.

In an informal survey I conducted with female college students, I asked the students to share what their churches had said about body or body image. Most of the responses centered on how they were to dress. One reported that the girls were always told by male youth leaders what they shouldn't wear, though guys could wear whatever they wanted. Along the same lines, others observed that many more instructions were given about how a girl was to dress than a guy. (This entire approach assumes, of course, that women are completely unaffected by the sight of men's bodies, so what a man wears is not worthy of comment.) Others were warned that they had to wear dresses or God would be offended. One young woman told of how a female youth leader had made a comment in an eyebrows-raised sort of way about this fourteen-year-old girl's, ahem, curves, which made the student ashamed of having a big chest, as if that somehow made her bad. The only message that came through was that their bodies were sexual, and sexually dangerous to men.

Some groups within Christendom have gone to the extreme of forbidding the wearing of fancy clothes, makeup, or jewelry. The women may not cut their hair, which must be long but never loose, so they pull it back in buns or braids and wear bonnets, scarves, or smaller, ornamental head-coverings. They wear plain, loose-fitting, long skirts in dark colors so as not to draw attention to their bodies. Looking from the outside one might be tempted to interpret this positively: that these women are so secure in their own physical beings that they don't need patterns or colors or jewelry to enhance their appearance. However, the proscriptions regarding women's dress are given by men, on account of a generally negative assessment of human physicality (these bodies are not worth adornment), and a particularly harsh interpretation of women's bodies (they represent sexual temptation and are a distraction from things spiritual). In these Christian groups, and even in others where the teaching is somewhat more subtle, the women have often been taught to live in their bodies as if they are guests in a house they don't like. Through the instruction they receive, they are shamed into devaluing their physical selves.

Of course, some religious groups, both inside and outside Christianity, impose dress requirements on men as well, either to promote modesty or to identify them religiously. So in Amish circles, for instance, neither men nor women wear shorts, and people of both sexes cover their heads. Similarly, in Orthodox Judaism men wear the yarmulke (*kippah*), which parallels the women's head scarf, and in Arab cultures men wear a turban, the counterpart to women's *hajib*. However, women's dress requirements are usually more onerous and more stringently enforced.

At the other extreme, in other churches women have had confirmed (or simply not critiqued) the idea that the only important thing about them is their body or their face, so they devalue everything *but* their physical selves. All their talents, intelligence, sense of humor, wisdom, and even their spiritual awareness or longings are ignored. Nothing figures into the calculus of value except whether or not they have abs of steel and a beautiful face. Recently I heard of a children's worker who did a whole lesson on applying makeup with eleven-year-old girls, complete with the following moral to the story: "God doesn't want you to be ugly."

Both of these options, devaluing and overvaluing appearance, tend to have the same result: a negative view of self.

Helpful Messages Churches Could Give

Critique of Cultural Ideas about Women

Rather than simply accepting how the culture treats women, it would be healthy for the church to critique the violence against women in the media. This might include getting people to think not only about nudity in film but also about demeaning portrayals of women. It might require reflection on the video games and MTV programming in which sex and violence against women are all rolled up together. It might include discussions about the problem of domestic violence and the ways in which Christians' language about submission has fostered and also covered over this evil.

It would also be helpful for churches to critique ideals about thinness, beauty, and feminity, rather than simply reflecting the culture. As noted at the beginning of the chapter, a Christian woman's estimation of her body's worth should not be measured in how well she matches cultural stereotypes of beauty or sexiness but in God's declaration that her being is good. The problem, of course, is that idealized female (and male) forms are what seem good to us, since we are constantly bombarded with images of what "desirable" people look like. It's no surprise that many Christians equate these cultural forms with "how God designed us to be" and thus add religious impetus to their striving after the perfect body. But of course, this is simply a confusion of what our particular society values with what God wants.

The church should critique the idol of thinness. Despite the messages from TV, movies, and women's magazines, all women were not created to be a size six (or zero!). Thinness does not necessarily please God, notwithstanding all the aerobics and Tai Chi classes offered in church basements. It is not that exercise classes in church or anywhere else are inherently detrimental to women's body concept. It's just that the motive for signing up is often an obsession with body size and shape, not with health and fitness per se. The ultrathin ideal of femaleness needs to be critiqued, maybe even from the pulpit, so that women can live in thanksgiving for the real female bodies given to them by God.

Femininity needs to be critiqued as well. That femininity is promoted in church shows a confusion of culture with Christian instruction, and this confusion has negative implications not only for the women involved but also for the church itself. Femininity, as noted above, involves an artificial view of the body in which appearance or self-presentation trumps function; this in and of itself might not be problematic if the mechanisms for attempting to look like supermodels weren't harmful to women's health. But femininity, especially as it is promoted in churches, goes beyond body image to a certain view of the female self. It often involves a constriction of the self in which a woman makes her gestures small and demure, makes her voice soft and pleasant, and makes her life choices fit into someone else's plans. Femininity, then, involves constructing an inauthentic self to please external audiences; how, we may ask, is this Christian? How can anyone reject her full human self, created by God, just to please the people in the church, just to meet the social requirements of a particular culture or religious group?

In this culture femininity involves female weakness, or the appearance of weakness, and dependence on a man. The sweet, ladylike woman will need a man's protection, which in turn will mean that masculinity is defined in terms of the ability to lead and to protect, physically and financially. Ironically, the instruction given to women about how to be feminine includes ploys for appearing helpless when they are the ones actually calling the shots, as well as strategies for surreptitiously teaching the man how to play his role.[18] (That so much energy is devoted to instructing women how to be "feminine" suggests just how unnatural it is.) But again the question must be raised: what is Christian about teaching a woman to be dependent, or telling her to feign weakness? What does wedging oneself into a narrow definition of femininity or masculinity have to do with being a disciple of Jesus? In Christian circles, shouldn't the personalities and gifts given by God be so highly valued that everyone is encouraged to live into them fully?

Furthermore, though gender roles may be fine to live by as long as they are freely chosen, they may also subtly foster male domination and female abdication of full adult responsibility for a woman's life, neither of which fits God's design of human mutuality described in Genesis 1 and 2.

Speaking of "Flesh"

Since part of the impetus to devalue our physical beings comes from equating our bodies with sinfulness, perhaps it would be helpful if churches talked more biblically about "flesh."[19] In ancient Hebrew thought, flesh and the nonmaterial aspects of being human were not separable; in fact, a person was not thought to *have* flesh but to *be* flesh. A human was not a spirit caught in a body, but an animated body. In the Hebrew Bible, "flesh" is not sinful, only finite in comparison with God, and frail or susceptible to temptation.

In the New Testament the Greek word translated "flesh" is often used of Christ to emphasize that he was truly flesh and blood, a real and whole human being, even in his resurrection. This usage is found in the Synoptic Gospels, Hebrews, and Peter's letters. In John, "flesh" is used sometimes to refer to the limitation of being human, or to the sphere of salvation rather than the sphere of God (John 1). Even in 1 John, when the phrase "desires of the flesh" is used, the problem with these desires is that they focus on the earthly or the transitory, instead of the eternal realm of God.

Paul, however, is responsible for about two-thirds of the uses of the term "flesh," and he employs it in a couple of ways. Sometimes he uses it to refer to the human race (Rom. 3) or to normal human life that is not inherently sinful but simply limited and transient (Gal. 2; 1 Cor. 1). At other times, however, Paul uses it to designate not only that the flesh or body is vulnerable to sin (Rom. 8), but that it is the place where sin enters and resides (Rom. 6) and fights against the Spirit. It is significant that this is not a fight between our flesh and our spirits, as if our bodies are the problem and our spirits are all right. Rather, it is a struggle between human addiction to sinfulness and the Holy Spirit of God; it is the opposition of the realm of broken human tendencies, thought patterns, and goals to the realm of the purifying, life-giving realm of the Spirit. The problem is not that we are human—God made us human beings with human bodies on purpose—but that too often we choose the realm of existence that is vulnerable to sin instead of the realm of God's Spirit, God's life. In the end we could conclude that Scripture does not instruct us to view our bodies as inherently vile; the problem is not the meat on our bones but rather the broken human tendency to think in sinful patterns. We are called to reject sinful desires, but not to hate our bodies.

In fact, we are encouraged to share God's delight in the created world, in Genesis 1 as God declares good the whole complex, exquisite world in all its physicality. Psalmists also invite us to appreciate the beauty of the world and let it direct our hearts to God in awe and thanksgiving. And, of course, the psalm cited at the beginning of this chapter expresses delight in the poet's human body, and the wisdom of God in creating something so wonderful and complex.

> For it was you who formed my inward parts;
> you knit me together in my mother's womb.
> I praise you, for I am fearfully and wonderfully made.
> Wonderful are your works;
> that I know very well. (Ps. 139:13–14)

In addition to creation, another biblical theme counteracts the negative messages about body and physicality that the church has so long labored under: the incarnation itself. By entering into human flesh, God demonstrates that something physical can communicate spiritual benefit to us; it is precisely in and through the physical world that God comes and offers new life. In a similar way, we could say that God still uses the stuff of the material world to extend grace to us, first of all in the Lord's Supper, but also through the people around us, the natural world, music, art, and so forth. God addresses our minds, our spirits, and our emotions in and through our concrete experiences in this world.

Enjoying Our Physicality

To think biblically about our bodies would mean rejecting the assumption that we inhabit these bodies as a prison—as shown by comments such as, "I hate my body [or my fat bum, or my big nose]"—as if we can stand outside it, as if "the real me" is something detachable from my body. I am one unified whole, and my body is me, part of me, the place where I experience the delights of being alive in this world: it is *in* my body that I feel spring breezes on my arms, listen to beautiful music, feel the power of the surf, see the various shades of leaves in the fall, feel the exhilaration of skiing above the tree line on fresh snow, enjoy the challenge of a hard game of soccer, feel the soft face of a child through a kiss, taste a gourmet meal. Instead of reducing the body to sexuality, so the only time we talk about the human body in church is to warn against sex, could there be messages about enjoying our physicality in other areas of human life? Can we remember together that we are fearfully and wonderfully made, which includes being made in such a way as to enjoy the good gifts of God in this world in thousands of ways?

Exercise, then, could be reconceived as a means of enjoying our physicality, rather than a tool for squeezing our bodies into cultural ideals. Obviously it can be a means to keeping our muscles strong and our hearts fit, which is arguably part of our stewardship of what God has made and shows appropriate honor to the temple of the Holy Spirit, as Paul calls our bodies (1 Cor. 6:12–20).

Beyond Image, to Be Loved

In this society that worships images (not to mention image), we need to explore some alternative ways of understanding beauty, attraction, and deep appreciation of the other. It does not seem healthy to settle either for a body-denying antisensuality or for a body-idolatry that accepts cultural ideals for thinness and beauty and invests them with religious significance. Perhaps we can learn to see appearance for what it is: only a part of human appreciation of the other.

We may be attracted to some people visually at first and then come to love deeply in ways that embrace many aspects of their humanity. You might come to love how a person thinks, for instance, or that person's sense of humor or generosity. Or you might initially find someone attractive on the basis of appearance only to find out that you have nothing in common, or that the person is too mean or selfish for a substantial friendship. Sometimes the appearance of another person is not the first thing that draws you into a friendship. Perhaps through time and a deepening of the relationship, the person's face or eyes or smile, or the way he or she laughs, becomes precious to you. The result is the same: you can delight in the appearance of the other as part of a total experience of another human being in a friendship, romantic or otherwise.

Visual appreciation, then, is only a small part of human delight in another person's beauty. Someone who loses a loved one, for instance, may be very happy to have pictures of the person, though looking at the images draws out the longing for the person's full presence. We want to hear the person's laugh, smell her or his hair, touch the skin. Bereaved people talk of feeling almost physical pain at not being able to embrace a spouse who has passed away, not being able to caress that beloved hand, or experience a tight hug. We enjoy (and then miss) the full presence of another person.

Being Fully Known

George MacDonald observed that most people, even in marriage, never come to know another person very deeply; far too many people stand, as it were, on the shore of the ocean of the other person's life and never do much more than wade. Christians, of all people, should be encouraged to risk entering the mystery of the other person's life and to risk opening themselves up to the other. There should be no more slavish reduction of each other to cultural standards of beauty, sexiness, or thinness; no more slavish restriction of the self according to cultural notions of femininity. The church should be standing against these things, never promoting them, since we acknowledge that God made us. God made us in our delightful diversity: with different body types, with different gifts, with different callings. The church should be helping us construct identities and relationships based on the idea that God created us with delight, and God invites us to explore the fullness of our redeemed humanity.

Part Two

WE'RE IN THIS THING TOGETHER

4

THE GOOD, THE BAD, AND THE DOWNRIGHT STRANGE

Marriages in the Bible

After graduating from college, naturally I began receiving news from my alma mater, including the annual list of donors to the college (and, yes, a plea for me to give money as well). As the years went by, I noticed a curious thing: half of my college friends—the women—were disappearing. Many of them had married, and as the annual donor listing came, I was struck by the realization that all the single women were listed with the title "Miss" followed by their first and last names, such as Miss Anna Roth, but all my female friends who had married had become invisible, as in Mr. and Mrs. James Doe. Was it just convention that a man's name could denote two people, or did women really disappear when they got married? In what way did this convention perhaps point to a frightening reality for married women: that they had simply been subsumed into the life of a man? I began to muse about the way in which women function in marriage, as well as in other relationships. Was becoming invisible a Christian requirement; was it actually a Christian thing to do at all? What, if anything, did the Bible have to say about how a marriage should be structured?

Biblical Underpinnings of Christian Marriage

When we look to Scripture we can find some general guidelines about how families should live together (with love and respect, for instance), but further than that the picture is murky. In other words, Scripture does not require any one particular family arrangement. Take, for instance, the fact that the most explicit descriptions of family life in Scripture involve extended families living together, replete with multiple wives and other female sexual partners for the head of the clan. Certainly what has come to be known as the "traditional family" is not derived directly from Scripture. As popular writer Rodney Clapp observes: "The 'traditional family' is not a family lifted out of the Bible's patriarchal period, its united kingdom period, its exilic and postexilic period, its early or late New Testament period, or any other period."[1] Each historical period highlighted in biblical narratives had its own set of assumptions about how marriage and family life should be organized, whether it's the polygamy and concubine system of the monarchy, or the slave, wife, and children paying deference to the *paterfamilias* in the New Testament. We have no single picture of how a marriage should be structured—and certainly no picture that resembles typical twenty-first–century family models; rather we are left to investigate how the main teachings of the Bible speak to marriage in particular and family life in general.

Another general observation we could make is that in Scripture the family is not depicted as God's special instrument to save society. In the Old Testament God works with the nation of Israel, and in the New Testament the church is to be the place where people are encouraged and equipped to do the work of God in the world. Sometimes we hear the sentiment that we need to save the family, or through strong families save the nation, but to "save the family" is not our primary calling as Christians. Rather, we are to bear the presence of God to a hurting world, in community with our brothers and sisters in Christ. Having said that, I would hasten to add that marriage *can* be a locus of significant ministry (and certainly of great delight), and our children *can* bring many blessings to us and to others. In other words, I don't intend to imply that marriage and family are unimportant, but I want to remind us that they cannot bear more weight than God designed them to carry.

We will turn now to a more specific examination of Old and New Testament teachings regarding marriage and family.

Old Testament Foundation

A good starting point for a discussion of marriage between two Christian people is a consideration of the creation stories in Genesis 1 and 2, since, as noted earlier, Jesus himself appealed to the creation narrative as God's design for marriage. We find in these chapters theological statements that undergird marriage: that the man and woman share essence, function, and substance.[2] First of all, we have the statement that human beings are made in the image of God. They share the same essence. The most significant thing that we learn about them is something that they have in common, and this something, their being image-bearers, sets them apart from the rest of creation.

The second foundation for marriage in this passage is the joint commission that God lays on Adam and Eve as a couple. They are to carry out God's work in the world together. God does not give more authority or power to the man but jointly entrusts them with the tasks of filling the world with new life and seeing to it that everything works harmoniously. In God's design, then, there is mutuality; not only do they share in essence, since both are made in God's image, but they share in function, since both are called to care for God's world together.

Finally, in Genesis 2 we see that Eve also shares the substance of Adam, having been taken from the rib. Eve, as noted earlier, is not some sort of divine afterthought who was only almost as good as Adam or almost a human being; she did not occupy a place somewhere between the animals and Adam in glory, authority, or likeness to God. Rather she is on his level. Adam's euphoric utterance after he awakes underscores the beauty of the equality he sees: at last, a partner, "bone of my bones." She is not an add-on to his life but truly a companion, an equal, a partner comparable to him. The model in which the man's dreams and aspirations fill center stage, and in which the woman tries to fit her life in and around his, is called into question by the very passage so often used to claim its legitimacy.

Another Old Testament source with hints about how things should go in families is the book of Proverbs. In the first chapter, the son is instructed to remember the teaching his mother and father gave him; this implies that the parents shared authority and respect. At the end of the book (chap. 31), the ideal wife for King Lemuel, according to his mother, is a woman who runs a huge household—kings' households are often that way—and engages successfully in a variety of business ventures. Modern readers might bristle at the tireless industry exhibited by the wife while the husband sits at the city gates, but in its cultural context the passage shows a high regard for this woman; after all, they are publicly acknowledging her accomplishments.

When we turn to the rest of the Old Testament, however, we might notice that the depictions of actual marriages are not typified by mutuality and equal regard. We have stories of polygamy, in which one woman is favored over the other(s) and the women often compete for love and for success in childbearing. For example, the sisters Leah and Rachel were forced by their father's intrigues to compete for the affections of Jacob, and pressured by the dictates of their culture to compete in the bearing of sons. Here we have the good (Jacob loves Rachel enough to work for her for fourteen years), the bad (Leah always feels unloved), and the downright strange (the sisters make deals with each other about who sleeps with Jacob, and both decide he should produce children through their female servants; Gen. 29–30). Perhaps the tragedies that arise from polygamy are described to underscore the fact that it flies in the face of the design stated in Genesis: a husband and wife are to cleave to each other. God's ideal for marriage does not seem to include room for extra wives.

In addition to polygamy, other problematic aspects of marriages are depicted in the Old Testament. Wives don't seem to have much say in what happens to them, so both Sarah and her daughter-in-law Rebekah are put in harems when their husbands fear for their lives; concubines have even fewer rights than wives. The Levite's concubine (discussed in chap. 2) was apparently completely at the mercy of her master and their host, though these men lacked mercy and threw her out to a violent crowd (Judg. 19). Women were married off or ripped out of marriages for the political advantage of a father or husband. In addition, men such as David and women such as Gomer (Hosea 1–3) have sexual relationships outside their marriages. King Solomon was linked to so many women he couldn't possibly know whether any given sexual encounter was inside or outside marriage: 1 Kings 11:3 informs readers that "among his wives were seven hundred princesses and three hundred concubines." None of these examples fit God's ideal set out at the beginning of Genesis; rather, they underscore the brokenness of male/female relationships after the entrance of sin on the scene. The dysfunctional family interactions found in biblical stories display the imperfect ways that people interact in this world, and not the design of God.

The laws governing marriage in the Old Testament also do not reflect the mutuality suggested by Genesis 1 and 2. The laws give men virtual ownership rights over their wives; even the last of the Ten Commandments forbids coveting the neighbor's wife or his slaves, ox, donkey, or anything else belonging to him (Exod. 20:17). Women seem to be bartered in marital arrangements where money is exchanged either to pay a father for the loss of her labor (bride price) or to pay a groom's family to accept a new member (dowry). Men were permitted multiple wives and endured a less severe punishment for sexual activity outside marriage, whereas women could have only one husband, and their virginity at their wedding and faithfulness in marriage were much more closely guarded. This is common in many ancient cultures as means of protecting paternity rights.

These laws seem to suggest that God favors men, but is that really the case? If we return to the example of Jesus' response to the question of divorce (Mark 10:2–12), we learn that not everything in the law reflects the preference of God. The religious leaders try to trap Jesus with the question: "Is it lawful for a man to divorce his wife?" They are essentially asking him, "How do you interpret Deuteronomy 24:1, which refers to a wife that 'does not please him because he finds something objectionable about her'?" As Jesus so deftly points out, divorce was not God's intention, but was permitted by God because their hearts were hard. God's intention, Jesus reminds them, is found in Genesis 2, which he quotes for them: "For this reason a man shall leave his father and mother and be joined to his wife. . . . Therefore what God has joined together, let no one separate." This bit of legal material in Deuteronomy 24:1, then, points not to God's design but to God's concession to human weakness. It underscores the broken nature of human relationships after the fall, and the way that God works with people in their culture. Given the male-dominated nature of the cultures of the ancient Near East in which Israel existed, what laws would offer protection to the vulnerable and yet make sense in that culture?

New Testament Foundation

The New Testament offers readers only a handful of examples of actual marriages. Mary and Joseph work together to obey the divine instructions they each received regarding the coming of Jesus, though Joseph doesn't believe Mary until he hears from an angel himself. In a similar way, Elizabeth and Zechariah also followed the plan communicated to Zechariah by the angel, including naming the baby John. In Ananias and Sapphira we have another picture of a husband and wife working together, though this time on an evil scheme to withhold money from the Christian community (Acts 5). Finally, we have a somewhat more developed picture of the marriage of Priscilla and Aquila, who shared their tent making and their ministry labors (Acts 18). With only these few, sparsely narrated examples, we have to look at the teachings of the New Testament and ask how they apply to marriage.

In the New Testament, we find the call for mutuality is made on a number of bases. First, we have the ministry of Jesus, both the example he sets in his treatment of women and his teachings about discipleship, and especially women as disciples. Then, the New Testament writers promote a message of salvation that is not gendered; in other words, they conceive of all human persons as sinful and in need of the grace of God, which comes through Jesus' death and resurrection. In keeping with the teachings of Jesus, they affirm that love is the quintessential sign of discipleship and mark of Christian community. All of this has a bearing on how we understand the most intimate relationship two Christians can have: marriage.

Jesus' Mission and Example

Christian theology has always affirmed that Jesus came to bring redemption into all the areas of life on earth where sin brought brokenness and destruction. As discussed in the first part of the book, alienation entered human experience when sin entered the picture: alienation between humans and God; alienation between humans and the rest of the created order; and, central to a discussion of marriage, alienation between human beings themselves. The mutuality suggested by God's jointly commissioning them for work in the world is disrupted by the new reality, that of male domination and female subjugation. In Genesis 3:16, the woman is told that her desire shall be for her husband and he will rule over her. Here is clearly one devastating instance of the brokenness of humanity after the fall. The coming of Jesus, though, ushers in a new era in which the alienation can begin to be overcome; now people can be restored to a loving relationship with God and a loving fellowship with other people; the mutuality that typified human relationship in the garden is available again in the redeemed community. It is not accidental that the two greatest commandments focus on these very things: learning to love God fully with everything we are, and learning to love those around us. Jesus teaches about both of these in his life on earth and also models for us how to live them out. It is worth considering his interactions with women as a starting place for a discussion of how people in the redeemed community should interact.

For instance, we have the healing stories. Jesus risked the anger of the Jewish elite by healing at least one woman on the Sabbath (and she was older, to boot) and by breaking uncleanness laws by touching the daughter of Jairus though she was dead. He made public the healing of the hemorrhaging woman, whose touch also would have made him unclean. Mary Magdalene was explicitly welcomed as one of Jesus' followers, after being exorcised of seven demons, and the other women mentioned in Luke 8:1–3 who followed Jesus around had also received healing from him. The healing of the daughter of the Syro-Phoenician woman ends with Jesus publicly commending the woman's faith, in stark contrast to the lack of belief of the people around him. Jesus took pains to highlight the faith of women, to raise their status in society, and to welcome them as disciples.

Jesus' practice of teaching his female disciples right along with the male ones suggests that he respected women as full, rational human beings. He addressed the intellect of women, not only as he instructed female disciples who followed him, but also in private conversations in which he discussed theology with women. For instance, he engaged the woman at the well (John 4) in the same type of conversation, full of double meanings, that he had had with Nicodemus, a highly educated member of the Jewish elite (John 3). She accepted Jesus' words and was entrusted with his revelation of himself as the Messiah. Martha and Mary also are complimented by Jesus' willingness to offer them some of the grandest theological promises he made: "I am the resurrection and the life . . ." (John 11).

Jesus also refused to treat women as sex objects or stigmatize them on the basis of sexual transgressions (even when asked to), thus refusing to participate in a powerful form of male domination over women. After all, if women are viewed only as objects of male sexual desire, or if they are to be blamed for male temptation, they are dehumanized and need not be treated with respect, let alone justice. In contrast, in Luke 7:36–50, Jesus extends welcome to the "sinful woman" who washed his feet despite the Pharisees' disgust. In the end, the judgmental males are judged by Jesus' words, just as they are in the story of the woman caught in adultery in John 8.

Unlike many preachers, even in our day, Jesus incorporated positive examples of women and women's work into his teaching. For instance, he compared the kingdom of God to a man planting seeds and a woman working leavening into a lump of dough (Luke 13:18–21). He also depicted God's persistent love with a couple of parables: a shepherd searching for the lost sheep and a woman sweeping her house looking for the lost coin (Luke 15:1–10). He addressed them with words and images that were part of their daily lives. At the same time, however, he did not endorse confining women to roles traditional for them in that culture. Jesus' parable of the widow and the unrighteous judge in Luke 18:1–8 underscores his rejection of male domination. In this parable the widow pleads her case, but the wicked judge does not want to give her what is due. Through her persistence the judge, who has no intention of giving her justice, finally relents simply because he is worn down. The misuse of power by a man is highlighted by the parable as well as the victory of a vulnerable woman. Widows symbolized the most vulnerable element in society and were often treated dismissively and spoken of derisively. Jesus, however, commends them by casting a widow as the positive figure in this parable and elsewhere by highlighting publicly the generosity of another widow, who gives her last coins to the temple, in contrast to the proud, who put in many coins but don't sacrifice much in their offering.

We could line up countless further examples of how Jesus interacted with women simply as those who need God's compassion, just as men need it. He never acted in ways that implied women were less important (as if they weren't made in the image of God), or more sinful (as if they were more responsible for the fall). Jesus simply loved, healed, spoke with, and befriended women as well as men. Even at peril to his ministry, Jesus welcomed women into his circle of disciples, allowing them to follow him around the countryside and provide financially for his missionary expenses (Luke 8:1–3). More than that, he offered them forgiveness on exactly the same basis as he offered it to men. His message was that any person, man or woman, adult or child, Jew or Gentile, whole or diseased, comes a sinner to God but can leave forgiven.

What does all this have to do with marriage and family? It demonstrates God's estimation of women as equally valued, equally called to discipleship, and as we saw in the women's commissioning at the tomb, equally called to do the work of God in this world. In this the followers of Jesus resemble Adam and Eve in the garden, who were commissioned at the beginning of things. Jesus' welcome of women (and all other types of marginal people) was not simply a strategy to get the message out, it *was* the message: God extending grace to fallen humanity. At the end of Jesus' earthly life the curtain was finally torn—this symbolic gesture of God announced that all can approach God on the same basis: no more priests as intermediaries, no more priority to Jews, no more priority to men. God leveled the playing field to welcome all.

The negative attitudes toward women played out in Old Testament stories by sin-damaged men are not perpetuated by Jesus, but challenged by him, the one who pictures God for us in concrete ways. In his band of followers Jesus worked to reverse the effects of the fall, not simply in his treatment of individual women during his ministry and not simply through the act of redeeming women in precisely the way he redeemed men. He did it by requiring that his followers imitate him with lives of love, love for God and love for others. The most basic characteristic of a disciple was the same for women and men: sacrificial love for others.

The Demand of Christian Love

In the redeemed community, then, people are called to love one another; in fact, they are to be known for their love for others. Jesus summed up the totality of what God expects of us with the commands to love God fully and to love those around us sacrificially. In John's Gospel, Jesus is quoted as saying that we should love each other as Jesus loved us, a pretty tall order. We should love each other with the kind of love that involves kneeling before the other in humble, even humiliating, service. It is telling that the footwashing story (John 13) ends with Jesus asking those present whether they understood what his actions meant; clearly they didn't, because it went against what their culture told them was appropriate. Perhaps the same could be said of Christians in our culture; we don't understand the story and certainly don't apply it to the relationship between Christians called marriage. If we took it seriously, we would not be asking questions about who is the boss, or who has the power and authority in our relationships. These questions might strike us as being as inappropriate as James and John's request that they enjoy power and authority in Christ's kingdom. To ask the question is to show how little they understand Jesus' mission, in which service and sacrifice connote true greatness. Finally Jesus spells it out for them: people who are not his followers may typify their relationships with "lording it over" the other, but in Jesus' rule, the norm is sacrificial love. Could he get more explicit than that?

It may seem ironic that just when he is lifting women up, treating them as full human beings (and he may have been the only man ever to do that for them), Jesus calls them all—women as well as men—to sacrificial service. Why free them only to enslave them again? But it is a different thing entirely to be in relationships of mutual service and love than to work while others take their leisure. When one makes sacrifices *for* the other when no sacrifice is made *by* the other, it can result in drudgery and a deadening in the relationship. The call Jesus made to all his followers, to imitate him in humble self-sacrifice, makes loving service rich and joyful, and, significantly for women, safe. He did not (and does not) demand the obliteration of the self for another or for Christian community, but requires that one's full personhood be engaged in loving relationships. Theologian Elizabeth Johnson observes that "Neither heteronomy (exclusive other-directedness) nor autonomy in a closed egocentric sense but a model of relational independence, freedom in relation, full related selfhood becomes the ideal. The vision is one of relational autonomy, which honors the inviolable personal mystery of the person who is constituted essentially by community with others."[3] Paradoxically, in this "relational autonomy," we are both redeemed individuals and members of the community of the redeemed.

To push it even further, according to New Testament writers, a Christian's primary identification is with the other followers of Jesus, the sisters and brothers in Christ, rather than with one's biological family.

Jesus himself decentered the family with his question in Mark 3: who are my mother and brothers? He answers his own question: those who are obedient to God are his brothers, sisters, and mother. This new family membership claimed a higher allegiance than one's biological kinship network, a radical claim indeed in a society where "family members were virtually shackled by patriarchal control."[4] As Jesus predicted, his movement brought struggle within families, as some members embraced the gospel and others did not, and it is in this context that Jesus uttered his hyperbolic warning that if one does not hate father, mother, or spouse, one cannot be a follower. If family stands in the way of one's being a disciple, one must turn away even from very deep familial ties and choose Jesus and the community of the redeemed. Jesus wasn't asking his disciples to disregard a fundamental commandment, that is, to love the other as we love ourselves, and he wasn't expressing anti-family sentiments, but he was requiring followers to remember where their highest loyalties lie: not with family or nation but with Jesus and the community of the redeemed. His teaching does not impede healthy families, then, but keeps biological family from being of paramount importance, or an all-consuming focus.

The Rest of the New Testament

As in the Gospels, the writers of the Epistles enjoin sacrificial love as the core of Christian ethics, so the question is, how do we apply this to the most intimate of Christian relationships: Christian marriage? For instance, consider Philippians 2, where we are called on to exhibit the same humility with one another as Christ did when he condescended to be born in human likeness. Does this passage apply to all Christian relationships, or should we make an exception for marriage, allowing men to forgo this humility when it comes to the persons they are supposed to love the most? Or what about 1 John 3, which states that the greatest expression of love is to lay one's life down for a friend? How can one do this while simultaneously imposing one's will on another person? You can't convincingly say, "We are going to do things my way because I am the head of this house," and in the next breath say, "but I am ready to lay my life down for you." It is nonsensical because these are opposite orientations: "doing things my way" means a selfish focus on my own desires or an arrogant assumption of my own superior judgments about your life, and "laying down my life for you" means a selfless focus on the other person. To put these two together would be something like this: I am willing to do everything in my power to make your life better, to help you flourish in all areas of life, as long as it doesn't interfere with my plans for myself.

Clearly there is no justification for disregarding biblical calls to humble love when we talk about Christian marriage. Since the bond between two Christians in marriage is a subset of the web of relationships in the body of Christ, it is clear that all the admonitions about how Christians are to treat each other would apply to marriage. When Mark and I were planning our wedding, we chose as our wedding text Colossians 3:12–17, which says:

> As God's chosen ones, holy and beloved, clothe yourselves with compassion, kindness, humility, meekness, and patience. Bear with one another and, if anyone has a complaint against another, forgive each other; just as the Lord has forgiven you, so you also must forgive. Above all, clothe yourselves with love, which binds everything together in perfect harmony. And let the peace of Christ rule in your hearts, to which indeed you were called in the one body. And be thankful. Let the word of Christ dwell in you richly; teach and admonish one another in all wisdom; and with gratitude in your hearts sing psalms, hymns, and spiritual songs to God. And whatever you do, in word or deed, do everything in the name of the Lord Jesus, giving thanks to God the Father through him.

These seemed like very desirable practices for two Christians to follow as we constructed a life together, but the pastor was concerned that this was not a wedding text, whereas the next set of verses were. (Col. 3:18 begins one of the "household tables" that describe the hierarchies that pertained in Paul's era with children, slaves, and wives in subservience to the father-master-husband in the house.) The pastor came through with a wonderful homily, but the point is, we don't often remember that the whole New Testament contains challenge and instruction regarding how we are to interact with one another in love, in the larger body and in our homes, which are subsets of that Christian community. The gospel demands that all of us love and respect and honor each other in the body of Christ and in our homes. How could it be otherwise?

Rejecting the hierarchical model of marriage that is still so comfortable in this culture in favor of a love relationship shaped by Jesus' definition and demonstration of love would be truly countercultural. It certainly would be more inviting to those who are watching from the sidelines; they would know we are Christians by our love, not by our culturally defined "traditional" marriage. It would also simply be obedient, since all Christians, whether male or female, are required to imitate Christ in his humility and radical love. What Paul says in Philippians 2 about humility and putting the other before the self may rightly be translated into practice by a quip my husband heard in a talk by popular author and speaker Tony Campolo, that the only argument Christians should have in marriage is: "I want to do it your way." "No, I want to do it YOUR way!"

Even the Ephesians 5 passage, frequently cited as a text that proves marital hierarchy, is primarily a call to mutuality and sacrificial love. It follows a set of instructions (in vv. 15–20) enumerating how people in the redeemed community should conduct themselves, including such things as using their time wisely, refraining from drunkenness, and being filled with the Spirit. As in Colossians 3, here the believers are encouraged to sing and enjoy fellowship together and also to give thanks in everything. Then Ephesians 5:21 says, "Be subject to one another out of reverence for Christ." The question is, does this refer to everyone in the body of Christ, since it follows verses that refer to all believers, or does this refer to husbands and wives, the subject of the verses that follow? Some English translations, including the New International Version, append the "be subject to one another" passage to the verses about Christians in general, and insert a paragraph break after it. However, the Greek text did not have paragraph breaks, so this is merely an interpretive move of the translators. And in this case it appears to be wrong.

How do we know? "Be subject to one another out of reverence for Christ" (v. 21) is clearly the topic sentence for the paragraph about wives and husbands, since in the Greek the following verse does not even have a verb. It simply says, "Wives to husbands." Subject yourselves, or submit yourselves, to each other—that's the main idea, and everything that follows in the paragraph is an explication of that main idea. Apparently translators who are uncomfortable with a verse that calls for mutual submission between husband and wife attempted to downplay it by removing it from the discussion where it clearly belongs, and joining it to the previous paragraph about how Christians should treat each other in general. But even if we see it as part of the general instructions to Christians, it still applies to marriage, since all general instructions about how Christians should treat each other apply to Christian people in all their relationships, including marriage. Either place you put it, the verse still calls men and women as Christian people to mutual submission; it's just that letting it serve as the topic sentence, as it was designed to be, grounds the discussion of marriage more explicitly in the general Christian theme of sacrificial deference to one another.

So the husband and wife are called on to be subject to one another (NRSV), or to submit to one another (NIV). In verses 22–24, women's part of the submission is discussed, and in verses 25–33, men's part of submission is highlighted. Women are encouraged to respect their husbands and submit to them as the church does to Christ. This is an interesting image since the church is meant to be out in the world doing the work of Christ; the church's submission is in carrying on the work of Christ, not in a passivity sheltered from the world. The church submits to the One who went through the fire already, the One who sacrificed himself for the church. It is safe for the church to submit to Christ because he won't ask for any sacrifice that he hasn't already made. And the wife, too, acts in ways that will help her husband thrive, in a submission that is also safe because of what is required of her husband—that he lay down his life for her. She is to defer to him as the head, which has been interpreted by traditionalists to mean the husband is the boss of the family. Others have suggested that this is descriptive of Greco-Roman households—the *paterfamilias* as the boss of the whole operation—but is not prescriptive any more than the discussions of slavery mean that we should hold slaves. And, of course, when the role of the husband is described in the following verses, there is no call for him to rule over the wife, or even act as her protector. Still others have suggested that the word *kephale*, translated "head," should be understood to mean "source," so that the parallel is between Christ as the source of the church and the man as source of the woman (in creation) or source of the family (the one who founds the marriage). In any case, the sense of the verse has to fit the entire passage, and this passage is not about ruling over, but about mutual giving. We see this most clearly when we look at what is required of men.

Men, as their side of the submission, are called to love their wives and lay down their lives for them, as Christ did for the church. No matter what we think about the term "head" in the previous verses, we have here fairly clear instructions: the man is to lay down his life so that his wife can flourish. His being the head cannot mean following his own selfish desires at her expense—even at times when they are at loggerheads over a decision—because the call on his life is to give it up. This is no different, of course, than the observation in 1 John 3 that the love we should have for each other is the kind where we lay down our lives for a friend. All Christians are to act in this way, not just husbands, but the instruction here may be to them specifically since it was such a shocking readjustment of their thinking about marriage. To first-century Greco-Roman sensibilities, the man of the house was to be obeyed by slaves and children and respected by his wife. In the best case he was a benevolent dictator and in the worst case a cruel tyrant, so the call to love one's wife with a love as sacrificial as Jesus' was completely unheard of. It is the same radical call that Jesus placed on all followers—to love one another as he loved them—but specifically applied to men in the marriage relationship. The point of comparison between the husband and Christ is to highlight the self-sacrificing love of Christ, which should be imitated by the husband. This is not about the husband's authority over his wife, since all the instructions to the husband in this passage are calling on him to love as Christ did, laying down his life for the church (Eph. 5:25), or tenderly and carefully as he loves his own body (vv. 28–29).

Many people have observed that women are called on in this passage to respect their husbands while husbands are called on to love their wives, and they take this to mean that there is something in men that needs respect and something in women that needs love. However, the text is more likely addressing a problem women had with submission, that is, that they had trouble respecting their husbands, and a problem the husbands had with loving their wives. In each case, they need the instruction because of their own lack, not because of the nature of the other person. In other words, on the one hand, it is not hard to imagine that a woman would find it hard to respect a man she was forced to marry and whose laziness or indulgence in alcohol had a direct bearing on her standard of living. On the other hand, men were never required to love their wives in Greco-Roman marriages; the most required of them was to provide food and shelter and to refrain from beating them. Men may have had a very difficult time hearing that not only did they have to restrain any violent tendencies and show kindness to their wives, but they also had to love them. Furthermore, since we are all called to love one another, clearly women must do much more than simply respect their husbands. They must love them in order to be obedient to the central commands of Jesus and the instruction of the apostles.

In any case, in this passage and others that deal with household structures (in Col. 3; in 1 Pet. 2 and 3), the writers have two overriding concerns: that everyone live according to the law of love modeled for us in Christ, and that every effort be made to promote the gospel. The instructions seem to be: live within the structures of society in such a way as to honor God and draw people to Jesus, but let the gospel redefine the roles within that structure. This does not mean that the structures themselves are right and good; for example, slavery is not good, but the New Testament writers are realists. Since slaves can't change the system and can't escape it, the instructions are concerned with how they can best function in the system: best in terms of personal dignity and best in terms of the gospel, when it comes to non-Christian slave owners. Paul offers a huge hint, however, at how Christian love should subvert the whole system in his letter to Philemon. Basically his message is this: now that your runaway slave has become a Christian, you should welcome him as a Christian brother. The gospel has a radically leveling potential in its call for a slave owner to love his runaway slave as a brother and for husbands to love their wives enough to lay down their lives for them (Eph. 5).

For Paul, the church is the primary family, and the biological family is a subset of it.[5] They are not two mutually exclusive entities but are organically related. Promoting the gospel was so important to him, and Jesus' return seemed so imminent, that perpetuating earthly families seemed a distraction. Hence his call for celibacy in 1 Corinthians 7. When Paul did engage in specific instructions to families, it was in the context of the larger project of promoting the gospel: Christians should keep in mind that if they are perceived as socially lawless, people will be offended and on that basis will be closed to the gospel. The family, then, is part of the greater body that is at work promoting the work of Christ in the world.

In our situation there is no real danger of Christianity being perceived as something that makes women lawless and insubordinate to their husbands. In fact, as some argue, we have the opposite problem now: we have so aligned our Christianity with conservative mores regarding women that we turn people off to the gospel. As they reject traditional roles for women they think they have to reject the teachings of the Christian faith. John Stackhouse, for instance, suggests that culturally accepted hierarchies were important for the acceptance of the gospel in the New Testament era, but in our day these very stratifications have become a hindrance to spreading the gospel.[6]

The Mutuality of Using Gifts

Mysteriously enough, God has chosen to carry on the work of Christ in the world partly through us, the church; we participate in the new creation as God calls and empowers us. Not only are Christians commanded to love each other, as well as their enemies, but they are instructed in numerous places in the New Testament to use the gifts given them by God. Interestingly, these instructions are given without reference to gender or to marriage. Are women really justified in thinking that this call on their lives dries up when they get married and have children?

A couple of passages list some of the gifts that Christians might have, and significantly, none of these lists link gifts to marital status or even gender. "The gifts he gave were that some would be apostles, some prophets, some evangelists, some pastors and teachers, to equip the saints for the work of ministry, for building up the body of Christ" (Eph. 4:11–12). This passage does not say that some *men* are teachers and preachers and some *women* have the gifts of nurture or hospitality. We have another list of gifts in 1 Corinthians 12:4–11:

> Now there are varieties of gifts, but the same Spirit; and there are varieties of services, but the same Lord; and there are varieties of activities, but it is the same God who activates all of them in everyone. To each is given

the manifestation of the Spirit for the common good. To one is given through the Spirit the utterance of wisdom, and to another the utterance of knowledge according to the same Spirit, to another faith by the same Spirit, to another gifts of healing by the one Spirit, to another the working of miracles, to another prophecy, to another the discernment of spirits, to another various kinds of tongues, to another the interpretation of tongues. All these are activated by one and the same Spirit, who allots to each one individually just as the Spirit chooses.

Later in the same chapter Paul gives another list, this time of offices: apostles, prophets, teachers, those who do deeds of power, those with gifts of healing and gifts of leadership, and those who give assistance. Again, nowhere in this list are the gifts linked to one gender or the other. Furthermore, the distribution of gifts and talents is not done according to our ideas of social propriety. Inconveniently enough, God invests people with gifts according to private divine decision and not according to what our church culture deems appropriate. See Acts 2, for instance, in which women are out on the streets prophesying in foreign tongues. Peter had to give some sort of biblical defense for this outpouring of the Spirit that didn't fit social expectations at all. The message seems to be: here are some gifts, here is a church and a world in desperate need of God's grace, so use the gifts to do the work of God together.

It is God's business, then, to decide who gets which gifts, and it is our job to use those gifts and to encourage others to use what God has given them. If it is a responsibility of Christians in the body of Christ to help one another to employ the gifts and talents given them by God, how much more should Christians united in marriage do this for each other? As mentioned earlier, a Christian marriage is not an entity unto itself, but a piece of Christian community rooted in the larger fellow-ship of the church, a piece of the whole mosaic, if you will; therefore the gifts of each person are still necessary to that body. In the case of a married couple, neither person's gifts or talents are more important than the other's. Neither person's life plans cancel out the other's. Nei-ther person's dreams and ambitions absolve the other from the need to use his or her gifts to participate in the new creation. The question for Christian couples is not "How will the man use his gifts and how will the woman support him?" but "How will we work together so that both of us are good stewards of the gifts entrusted to us by God?"

Sometimes this call to mutual use of gifts is rejected on the basis of some spiritual-sounding, but spiritually unsound, arguments. Contrary to some popular teaching, nowhere in the New Testament is the husband called the priest of the family. The two functions of priests are: represent-ing the people to God and representing God or communicating God's grace to the people. Husbands are not pictured as the ones who have to represent their families before God, and neither are they the special conduits of God's grace to their wives and children. As the writer of Hebrews explains, we have no more need of intermediaries since Christ, our great high priest, has opened the way to God for each person (Heb. 4:14–5:10). The good news of the gospel is that each of us has equal access to God—after all, the veil in the temple has been torn—and each of us now is also called to bear God's grace to the other. This is what we affirm with the phrase "the priesthood of all believers": each of us can go to God directly and each can and should bear the love and grace of God to others. Let's not throw away some of the more powerful affirmations of the Protestant Reformation here and make husbands a new set of priests to control their families' spirituality!

And we should note that even before the Reformation, men did not hold these functions in families; we have, after all, a long line of examples in Scripture in which God speaks directly to women, even married women. Remember the description of Samson's mother from chapter 2, who heard directly from God, and Mary, who also heard from God? Remember Deborah and Hulda, each married, but each a prophet in her own right? God doesn't need husbands to be spokesmen for him in their families. Luther observed that mother and father together are "apostles, bishops, and priests to their children, for it is they who make them acquainted with the gospel."[7]

Further, the husband is not the arbiter of gifts in the family, deciding whose gifts matter and whose are to be buried, or whose are to be used when, as if both people weren't answerable to Christ directly. Romans 12 calls each of us to assess our own gifts and use them well. Jesus' parable of the talents warns us that we have a responsibility to use wisely that which has been given to us because we will be answerable to God in the end. Would the returning master of the household be mollified if the excuse for burying one's talent was, "I got married," or "My husband didn't want me to . . ."? What would the returning master say to the husband who encouraged his wife to squelch her gifts, whether from misunderstanding his role or from sheer insecurity or selfishness?

Finally, a self-sacrificial love—something husband and wife are both called to—would say, "I want you to use your gifts, to bless people, to honor God, to flourish personally, no matter what that means for me." Recently I attended a sixtieth wedding anniversary party for a couple in our church. When asked to give tips to all of us "youngsters" on how to have a good and long-lasting marriage, the man said, "We always considered each other equals. No one was more important than the other one; no one mattered more. We are equal in God's eyes and so we treated each other as equals." The woman commented, "I have had a lot of wonderful friends in my life but Gus is my best friend." This was a tender moment; it was a testimony of two saints of the church who have endeavored to follow Jesus' example of love, who have valued each other's lives and the gifts God has given to each of them. If spouses love each other, wouldn't each want the other to use his or her life in the most compelling way for the work of God in this world?

Conclusions

The hierarchical model of marriage assumed in many conservative church circles as the only Christian way to organize relations between a husband and wife is simply not the only way. It is not uniquely Christian, and, in fact, one could ask whether a hierarchical arrangement is particularly Christian at all. How does one affirm the equality of the woman and man in Genesis 1 and 2, their sharing in the image of God and their co-commissioning to do God's work together, if one person has the upper hand? How does one simultaneously act like the boss and lay one's life down for the other? Can we take seriously Jesus' equal treatment of women and his call for his followers to engage in lives of humble service, if one person holds veto power in any important decision in a family? What are we to make of the Old Testament and New Testament women described as prophets, disciples, missionaries, businesswomen, hosts, and leaders of house churches if we assume women can play only supportive roles in men's dramas?

To reject a derivative and dependent status for women is not to reject biblical principles. As we have seen, Scripture tells us the woman was designed to act in partnership with the man in the project of human life, including marriage. That some of the marriages in the Bible do not depict this partnership says more about human brokenness than about God's design, and this means we don't find helpful patterns to emulate in our modern marriages. In fact, the title of this chapter may be misleading, since we find mostly bad and downright strange marriages in the Bible, and not much of what we would judge healthy and good.

Further, if we're looking in Scripture for passive women who fit our stereotypes of nice, godly women, we may also be disappointed. Aside from the women who are victimized, biblical narratives depict women as active participants in various events, based on their own rather than their husbands' or fathers' faith. This suggests that it is a godly thing for a woman to consider her life in light of creation and redemption and to look for the vocation God's love draws her to, rather than to assume that she must simply accompany the man she marries through the dreams of his life. Though some women may choose to do the latter, it doesn't mean that is God's design for marriage or even necessarily a good thing for the women involved. What about all those women who get twenty years into marriage and suddenly realize that their husbands have used their gifts and pursued their dreams while they themselves have buried their talents in the ground? This looks less like God's plan than the pressure of human culture, and that is the focus of the next chapter.

5

MISTAKING THE INDUSTRIAL REVOLUTION FOR THE GARDEN OF EDEN

The Myth of the "Traditional" Marriage

Recently a student described something we sang in chapel as a "traditional" song; it happened to be from the 1980s, and I was struck by how flexibly this word is used. "Traditional" can mean something twenty years old, as in the case of that worship song, to someone who has no sense of when something came into being or what came before it. In other words, a tradition may be only a few decades old but be assumed to have always existed. In common usage, the "traditional" thing feels completely timeless, without beginning, even though it actually marks only the beginning of what we know.

This sort of ahistorical thinking is typical in our society and may not matter all that much when it comes to clothing or architectural styles, but when it comes to marriage the implications are serious. This is because so many people, both secular and religious, assign normative value to the version of marriage they consider traditional; in other words, they think it is not only how marriage has always been structured but how marriage *should* be organized. In many Christian circles the traditional version of marriage is not only considered right but is assumed to be what God wants for people in marriage, despite its lack of historical longevity or cultural breadth.

In current discussions of marriage the term "traditional" is often used in a misleading way. Mostly it is used to imply that marriages were always a certain way—"the Christian way"—until the feminist movement came along in the 1970s and ruined everything. The reality is, however, that marital expectations and practices vary across cultures even among Christians and between the wealthy and the poor within any given culture. Anthropological data, for instance, show tremendous variety when it comes to almost any aspect of marriage practice, including mate selection (whether marriage partners are chosen by clans or families or just the parents, or most recently, the people involved); the location of the couple after marriage (most often women seem to move to men's clans in traditional societies, though sometimes men move to women's clans); which direction monetary obligation goes in arranging a marriage (whether a bride price is paid by the groom's family to the bride's father, or a dowry is paid by the bride's family to the groom); the division of labor; the ease or relative difficulty in dissolving a marriage; the taboos regarding extramarital sexual relations; and the practice of acquiring multiple spouses, most often expressed in males' prerogative to have a number of wives, though in some cultures women would have a number of legitimate sexual partners.[1]

Further, these varied practices have changed over time, even across the many cultures and centuries in which the biblical texts were written. Most notably polygamy, which figures prominently in early Old Testament stories, disappears from view in the New Testament. But we tend to read our own ways of doing things back onto our ancestors, and so we assume that our version of traditional marriage is something lifted straight out of the Bible. For instance, I have had students claim that the marriages depicted in Genesis show God's design for the man to be the protector of his wife. When they look at the data, however, they are hard pressed to find a single story in Genesis in which that is even remotely true, while there are a number of stories in which women are used to save the hides of men. The pull of the traditional marriage seems to be very strong, so strong that we read it right back into the biblical texts.

In the social sciences the same phenomenon pertains. Anthropologist Stephanie Coontz observes that we lay our assumptions over historical data even when we talk about ancient hunter/gatherer societies; to think that women "stayed at home" while men went "off to work" on the hunt is misleading, since in a modern hunter/gatherer society studied in the 1960s the women provided the bulk of the food for their families. While the men hunted, the women walked on average twelve miles a day and carried from fifteen to thirty-three pounds of food to their families. Women with children younger than two walked the same distance and carried the same loads, along with the child in a sling.[2] And yet, because the men are off hunting, at least some of the time, we picture the women as passively "staying at home" while their husbands are out "providing" for them. The realities are covered over by the ideals we impose on them.

The questions are, then, where did our ideas about traditional marriage come from and how do those ideas maintain such a powerful grasp on people in conservative churches?

A Short History of the "Traditional" Marriage

Before the Industrial Revolution in the late eighteenth and early nineteenth centuries, there was no "traditional family," if by that term we mean the husband going off to work while the wife stayed home. There was no place for the man to go off to, in fact, since before the Industrial Revolution 90 percent of the population in this country lived on farms.[3] In the agrarian model, everyone worked and everyone's labor was integral to the family economy. The man might sell or trade his corn at the market, but the woman might sell or trade her butter, churned from milk that she labored to retrieve from the family cows. The man might spend the winter fixing farm utensils and the woman might spend hers making cloth and sewing the clothes that the growing children needed to keep warm as they walked to school, but they would be gathered at the same fire as they did their respective tasks. No one was said to "work" while the other "stayed at home." They *both* "worked" and "stayed at home."

When children came along they were expected to learn the skills necessary to keep a farm family economy going, and they spent much more time at home than at whatever meager schooling might be available to them. This meant that each parent mentored the children of his or her sex into the jobs that would be expected of them as adults. Both parents were personally involved in and, in fact, critical to their children's preparation for their future.

The same was true in family businesses. When a family ran a store or relied on a cottage industry, shoemaking, for instance, rather than farming, the work of wife, husband, and children as they grew would be necessary for the livelihood of the family. Each one's skills and hard work counted in the equation. Even centuries earlier in the guild system that grew up in cities in the Middle Ages, master craftsmen were expected to be married because a wife's work was integral to the household economy.[4]

With the development of factories and a market economy in the early nineteenth century, however, production began to move outside the home to a significant degree. First, textile mills and food factories began to replace work that had been the responsibility of women in the home, and soon factories expanded throughout the economy. Not only did this change the location where various products were made, but it also changed the basis on which the economy functioned. Now people were paid in cash for the work that they did away from the home, rather than for the materials or foods produced at home.

When that happened, people's assumptions about marriage and family, and even masculinity and femininity, changed dramatically. Masculinity became linked to earning money and providing for one's family financially; in fact, ideally he would earn enough money to have a wife who stayed home rather than having to go out to work in a factory or take in laundry. Having a wife "at home" was a significant marker of having achieved middle-class status, since in the lower classes both men and women have always had to work. (This underscores the link between the development of capitalism and of the "ideal" Victorian household.)

This new concept of masculinity demanded that femininity be defined in new ways. In the growing middle class a woman was valued no longer for her work but for her ornamental quality; her passivity rather than her productivity began to be prized. Not surprisingly, this is the era in which a caricature of female form became fashionable: the tiny corseted waist and the huge bustles to accentuate hips. It is significant that it wasn't until this era that much was written in this country about "The Woman Question," which became an American obsession in the nineteenth century.[5] When women's work was valuable to the family, people didn't wonder what women were for, or what they should be, or how to define their value. It was only when their work and their place in the family became devalued that these questions arose. By the end of the nineteenth century, middle- and upper-class women had been assigned a new function: they were to be the consumers who helped fuel a rapidly expanding market system.

As the home ceased functioning as the locus of family productivity, it too had to be redefined and assigned new value. Despite the amazing amount of work still done there, by someone, if not the wife, the home was now idealized as a sanctuary from the harsh realities of life in a market economy that men faced each day at work. In *Christianity and the Making of the Modern Family*, theologian Rosemary Radford Ruether observes: "Language borrowed from monastic communities and evangelical crusades would invest the family with new salvific significance as a place of refuge from the fallen world. Ideal women, segregated in the idealized home, would assume a halo of angelic purity and suffering love."[6] A new understanding was created to accommodate a new economic reality for the middle class. Femininity, then, came to be measured by how well a woman could be the "angel in the home," who would influence her husband for the good with her cheerfulness and with a heart untainted by the grasping, greedy world. Instead of husband and wife working to make ends meet, as in the agrarian model or in the lower classes, the wife existed *for him*, her only duties were to make him happy and produce heirs to inherit the money he was making.

In this cash-based economy, the paid work of the man suddenly became much more valuable, rendering domestic work increasingly devalued and even invisible. In upper-class families the wife still had the responsibility to ensure that the household ran smoothly, which meant oversight of servants and the procurement of goods. In middle-class families in which the women did not earn money, the reality is that their labor contributed a great deal to the family economy. Many women still made their own soap, baked their own bread, made clothes for the family, and washed these same clothes on washboards that demanded quite a bit of physical labor just to pull the soaked, heavy garments out of the tub; the wife was also the family teacher, doctor, counselor, and purveyor of religious life. Women did all this in addition to having many babies, which translates into many sleepless nights, coping with children's illnesses and dealing with deaths of infants and children. Women not only bore children but, as ideal mothers, were also supposed to raise them, without much help from the husband if he was employed away from the home, such as working long hours at a factory each day. Bringing up children became the province of the mother, rather than the shared responsibility of both parents as in earlier generations, when both prepared their children for the future.

The ideal of the so-called traditional family—father off at work, mother home with a growing family—does not represent how things always were; it is a product of nineteenth-century industrialism and the development of the middle class. Even in this country, which had a fairly sizable middle class in the twentieth century compared with many other places, the majority of families never embodied this model. Farming families still shared domestic space more fully, and immigrant families and families in the lower classes arranged their lives according to their own cultural ideals or economic realities. There is, then, no one correct version of how men and women structure marriage; for there to be one right model, it would have needed to be historically and geographically universal.

To choose the "traditional" model of marriage is like choosing to wear Amish clothing: it may help mark the boundaries of a particular

Christian community, but is a historical artifact, not something pre-scribed in Scripture. In fact, it is a serious thing to equate this structure with God's will or the Bible, because if we do, we are implying that people in other cultures are not as pleasing to God as we are. If, for instance, grandparents, other relatives, or whole villages in rural China raise the children, while the younger adults grow food, can we really suggest that they are less pleasing to God? Or if we assert that the "tra-ditional" model is God's will, are we ready to say that people in social classes where "staying home" was never an option for women fall short of God's will somehow? This sort of belief gives God's imprimatur to *our* American way of doing things and names our economic privilege as the design of God.

The Lure of the Victorian Marriage

In the nineteenth century, middle-class white Christians embraced the new ideals for home and wifehood described above wholeheartedly, it seems, and invested them with spiritual necessity. If the man sub-jected himself to the secularizing and tempting world of business, then someone needed to be the Christian anchor in the family. This job fell to the woman. Women, it was now assumed, were spiritually superior, because for one thing they made up the majority of churchgoers in Christian traditions of virtually every stripe in mid to late nineteenth-century America; indeed, it may have been this very preponderance that led to the characterization of the woman as the "angel in the home" who was to exert a sanctifying influence over the husband and children. Men, on the other hand, were assumed to be susceptible to the allures of the secular workplace, the "dram shops" as bars were called, and loose women. They needed wives who helped them be moral, or even Christian.

Since then conservative Christians in the United States have tended to teach that the middle-class Victorian model for marriage—the bread-winner husband off to work and the wife at home with the children—is *the* Christian way to do things. The work of Barbara Ehrenreich and Deirdre English, *For Her Own Good: Two Centuries of the Experts' Ad-vice to Women*, demonstrates that the lure of the Victorian family has been afoot in American culture for 150 years, with experts of all kinds trying to compel us to believe that women staying home with children and refraining from paid labor out in the marketplace is the "natural" way. When the church tolls the same bell, it is not exhibiting a biblical, countercultural standard, but joining in the chorus of expert advice that argues that women's domesticity is "natural." It simply adds religious justification for this stance. Christians who advocate women's staying at home because they are women simply mirror cultural ideals that still hold sway among middle-class Americans.

This pattern intensified after World War II with the need to move Rosie the Riveter back home and get her shopping to boost the economy. As observed earlier, this set up has never been a reality for most families in the United States (not even in the 1950s), but to notice this makes people uneasy because it calls into question the link between God's will and this particular family model. But call this model into question we must. Lewis Smedes, theologian and ethicist, calls cultural practices such as marriage structure and assumptions regarding roles "folkways," and he observes: "For when folkways of the group are translated as divine command and internalized as the will of God, they bind the conscience. . . . Thus folkways that posture as divine rules are anti-Christ."[7] When people think God is especially pleased with *their* way of doing things, it may be time to examine their assumptions.

What is so alluring about the Victorian model of marriage? A wide-ranging study done a few years ago about marriage among conservative Protestants offers a few clues.[8] The researcher, sociologist Sally Gallagher, studied the pronouncements about marriage and child raising made by prominent people such as James Dobson and Pat Robertson, and she interviewed a few thousand rank-and-file evangelicals, Pentecostals, and other Protestants. She found motivations for privileging this model that are described in the sections that follow.

The Victorian model of marital relationships is important for some evangelicals because they think it marks the boundary between them and "the world." They feel that by following this model they distinguish themselves from the world in a way that God desires. Of course, for many this boundary marker is in name only in day-to-day life. In other words, they are hierarchalists only nominally because, despite the language of male headship, most evangelical families, according to Gallagher's research, engage in a form of mutual decision making anyway: "The practice of family is most often a blending of symbolic headship and pragmatic egalitarianism—the language of husband's headship and authority is alive and well, but mutual decision making and a pragmatic division of labor characterize most households."[9] In other words, at the micro level many evangelicals practice mutually respectful and loving marriage. However, her research did not address the macro level, where inequality still arises: when it comes to whose education to further, for instance, or whose career to pursue—whose calling to flesh out in the world—it still winds up being the husband's, in the majority of cases.

For some who actually practice it, a traditional model is attractive because of the rigid roles for husbands and wives in marriage; it lends clarity to their expectations of each other. The appeal of much writing on marriage, both inside and outside Christian circles, seems to be that it gives people clear directives on what they're supposed to do as husbands or wives, as mothers and fathers. This resembles the pull to legalism in any area of Christian practice: once there is a clear list of things to do and not do, one can simply try to follow the script. This obviates the need to wrestle with gray areas or to negotiate things.

In addition, many conservatives see the need for a traditional marriage setup because of the moral weakness of men and their need for women to help them be moral. (Some current traditional marriage material reads very much like Victorian writing on the subject.) Pundits such as James Dobson teach that men are sexually weak and naturally irresponsible, but their "social liabilities disappear" through marriage. Dobson writes: "What a woman does for a man, then, is to harness the sexual energy that was unbridled and threatening to society—and focus it on protecting and providing for a family."[10] According to Dobson, unless men engage in a "benignly patriarchal family," they will never grow up, and women will have no security in which to engage in reproduction. "From this perspective," observes Gallagher, "abandoning the notion of husbands' headship would abandon men to psychological immaturity and the dangerous drives of their biology."[11] For Dobson, the husband's headship in the home includes the responsibility of deciding how family work is structured; he will allow his wife to have a job outside the home—almost as if he is her parent—but only if there is financial necessity.

Ironically enough, given the assumptions about men's inability to control their own sexuality without wives to help them, some of the women and men Gallagher interviewed expressed the view that one of the main reasons for adhering to a man-as-head-of-house model was that men are emotionally stable. Women, they said, are less rational, and more emotional, and need men to be the foundation of stable marriages.[12] One wonders whether all these people are really unaware of the millions of relatively successful single-parent families headed by women.

Some of the people Gallagher interviewed also expressed a fear about the loss of order that would ensue if no one was in charge; they seemed to assume—as many Christians do—that the only viable structure for a marriage is hierarchy and that everything else will be interpersonal anarchy. (See chap. 1 for a discussion of the theological implications of this view.) In the mid nineties my husband and I went to a presentation some friends gave in an effort to raise the financial support they needed to join a Christian marriage and family ministry. At one point they flashed on the screen a list of causes of divorce that they would be contending with, including infidelity, pornography, alcoholism, domestic violence, abandonment, and egalitarian marriage. (As they used to say on *Sesame Street*, one of these things is not like the others!) For them, egalitarian marriage seemed dangerous because without someone as the ultimate authority there would be instability and marital breakdown.

This presupposes a governmental model of marriage or a business model. For instance, students have explained to me that they believe in a "president, vice president" picture of marriage: "I would always consult her when making a decision and see what sort of advisory comments she would make, but the decisions would be up to me." Or people assume that a marriage must be run by the highest-paid member, the CEO, with whom the buck always stops—ignoring the fact that even in business there can be partnerships. But the real question is: why would the most intimate of human relationships be made to mirror political or business ventures? Wouldn't friendship be a better starting place for thinking about a lifelong commitment of love?

Some evangelical women also reported feeling good about a hierarchal marital setup because they felt loved and provided for; they had a sensation of security that was probably linked, even if unconsciously, to the idea that if one follows the script everything will go well. But perhaps most importantly, in training themselves to submit to the desires of another person they believe they are learning to submit to God.[13] The irony here, of course, is that if both partners are Christians and are learning deeper obedience to God, the model of mutual submission would be more effective for the spiritual development of both individuals. What would a husband learn about submission to God or about humility if he is the king of the household?

Finally, Gallagher observes that mainstream evangelicals, those who affirm male headship in marriage, also reject egalitarianism out of fear of theological liberalism and androgyny. First, people such as James Dobson and Tim LaHaye attempt to link biblical feminism with liberalism, one of the worst slurs in their mouths. Gallagher observes that these authors have been so successful in linking Christian feminism with theological liberalism that feminists' "views are characterized as teetering on the edge of biblical relativism's slippery slope."[14] The argument assumes that feminist Christians disregard Scripture or have a "low view" of the Bible, though in reality biblical feminists embrace Scripture, even delight in it, finding there a standard of love to which they can call people. When traditionalists make this kind of attack, they have succumbed to a temptation common to us all, which is to confuse one's own interpretation of Scripture with "what the Bible really says." When biblical feminists disagree with their interpretation, traditionalists assume feminists are rejecting the Bible, whereas feminists are only denying the validity of a particular interpretation.

The other approach Gallagher notes that some employ to argue against evangelical feminism is to equate egalitarianism with androgyny. She notices that no matter how carefully evangelical feminists articulate the difference between egalitarianism and androgyny, their arguments are cast by opponents as requiring identical roles and gender identities.[15] Homeschooling advocate Mary Pride exemplifies this fear of androgyny when she asserts that women, stepping outside their God-ordained role into paying jobs, drive men to homosexuality. Therefore, in Pride's opinion, "feminism is a one-way path to social anarchy."[16] In order to avoid this social chaos, she advocates women "staying at home" and having many children, which is a likely outcome for those following her advice: she teaches that marriage is not for companionship but for procreation, and only those who are selfish or lack sufficient trust in God would use birth control.

As an aside, her advice, much like the writing in the mid to late nineteenth century regarding women and family, is an attempt to bolster the Victorian breadwinner-and-housewife model of marriage while the same time redefine the woman's role in it. In the Victorian era, the woman's job was to create a haven for the beleaguered husband; she was the doting housewife. In our era, the rhetoric revolves around her duty to protect the children from the evils of the larger society; she is the "stay-at-home" mom. In the end, though, the effect is the same: to keep women in the home with a social justification that looks like a religious duty. Women's roles, then, are differentiated clearly from men's roles, which means that those who subscribe to this model can feel safe from androgyny.

Fear of androgyny seems to be at play in the work of Wayne Grudem and John Piper, *Recovering Biblical Manhood and Womanhood*.[17] They argue that women have the same essence as men and are equally valued, but they have restricted function in marriage and in the church, a position with echoes of Barth. Gallagher comments: "In a move reminiscent of segregationist arguments for separate but equal treatment, gender-essentialist evangelicals have begun to argue that men and women each have authority that is exercised in different ways."[18] These gender-essentialists use the same arguments about "separate but equal" that have already been shown to be destructive in another area of human categorizing: race. Popular author Rebecca Merrill Groothuis observes: "Regardless of how hierarchalists try to explain the situation, the idea that women are equal *in* their being, yet unequal *by virtue of* their being, is contradictory and ultimately nonsensical."[19] As in the discussion about race, this distinction doesn't work; instead, it points ultimately to an assumption about the lesser personhood of one group, which justifies its lower status.

The question is: why would people affirm equality of essence between men and women, but work so hard to maintain gender roles, especially roles that lead to social inequality? Here we come to the crux of the matter: many people believe that preserving gender roles will protect people's sexuality, or, put another way, that maintaining social difference will protect sexual difference. The social options, they feel, are limited to rigidly defined male/female polar opposites on the one hand, or a complete loss of sexual boundaries on the other. Androgyny, then, is feared as a loss of sexual boundaries; that is, people think that the rejection of traditional gender roles will mean sexual sameness. They fear that the erosion of social differences will result in hermaphrodism, in which individuals are sexually complex and, without the guidelines of sex roles, confused about how to maintain a steady sexual identity, or will result in women becoming "masculinized."

But does sexual sameness necessarily result from a rejection of rigid sex differentiation? Considering that in our society couples arrange their marriages with varying degrees of commitment to gender-segregated work, for instance, and different models of decision making, it is clear that people do not have to play rigid gender roles in order to protect their sexuality. Definitions of masculinity and femininity, in any case, vary dramatically in the United States, depending on region, class, ethnicity, and religious affiliation. Furthermore, the characteristics or roles dubbed "masculine" by our society, such as strength or forthright speech, are arguably human characteristics that have been narrowly assigned to only half the race. The same is true of "feminine" characteristics, such as tenderness or relationality. When a woman exhibits strength she is not becoming masculinized, but more fully human; when a man displays tenderness, he is not becoming effeminate but also more fully human. Fear of androgyny, then, can keep people from expressing their full humanity.

Fear of androgyny also exerts pressure on women to accept unjust treatment. To work against negative stereotypes of women or unequal treatment is often perceived as a repudiation of being a woman. For instance, when I was in seminary, if I observed that I wanted to be treated like a person for once, someone would invariably make a comment such as, "You just don't enjoy being a woman," as if there was something wrong with me, or as if I was rejecting something God had given me. But that was not the point; I was simply tired of being asked to embrace some sort of subjection to men in order to prove I was glad God made me female. (The irony here is that sexism *does* make a woman enjoy being a woman less.) Lewis Smedes put it this way:

> Males may assume that their gender will not get in the way of their being treated as persons. Women have often not been granted this assumption. So when women say, "Treat me as a person and not as a woman,"

one can understand what they want: they want respect for their status as responsible human beings. Religiously, they are deserving respect as equal bearers of God's image. Femaleness is an adjective to personhood. To assign persons roles that they as individuals do not personally choose to accept, and to do this on the basis of gender, is to make sexuality basic and personhood secondary. That evil would be less severe if both sexes were in equal positions to deal out power and privilege. However, the deck is stacked when males grant each other treatment as persons and treat females merely as females.[20]

It is the injustice of sexism, of being treated as second-class, that bothers many Christian women, not femaleness itself, just as racism bothers people of color, and not their race itself. Women who say they want to be treated as people are not antifemale but against the subjugation of women. They are also not antimale just because they make a critique of male privilege; they are simply against that privilege. In this context, a friend observed to me recently, "Humans of all cultures, regardless of sex, don't take too well to second-rate-citizen treatment, particularly if it is a function of something they have no way to change."

Conclusions

We have examined the limited history of the "traditional" marriage, and allowed its cultural and temporal specificity to call into question that model as "the one right way to do things," or "the Christian way to do things." We have also looked at some of the reasons that evangelicals hold on to this structure, many of which are based on fear: fear of male sexuality, fear of female emotional instability, fear of social anarchy, fear of feminism, fear of androgyny.

Is fear an appropriate starting point, or should we begin to make important decisions, such as how we structure our lives together, on some other basis? Perhaps we should ask different questions, such as: How can we construct a marriage that promotes the flourishing of both people? How can we encourage the widest use of who we are for God's work in the world? In short, how can we love the other person most fully?

The next chapter will look at ways in which people have arranged their lives to balance domestic and professional work in the marriage overall, rather than in one person's life or the other's.

6

TWO HEADS ARE BETTER THAN ONE

Marriage as Partnership

Increasingly, the old argument that "someone has to be head of the family" has been falling on hard times. Marriage mores have been changing in the culture at large and even in conservative Christian circles. As noted in chapter 5, Sally Gallagher found that many evangelicals practiced more mutuality than they said they believed in. Family therapists Jack and Judith Balswick observe that modern marriages, even among Christians, tend to be much more egalitarian and for the benefit of both people than in previous eras.[1]

And yet people still construct, or think they have to construct, marriages that privilege men's dreams and giftings. This chapter will discuss the internal barriers to egalitarian marriage and also the benefits of working toward mutuality in our relationships. Then we will consider how shared parenting can work and examine some of the socioeconomic impediments to a good work/family balance for most Americans, and particularly women.

Learning to Think outside the "Traditional" Box

Even if Christians have come to see that Scripture does not demand a Victorian model for marriage, the biggest question many have about a mutual-regard or egalitarian marriage is: can it work? Doesn't someone have to make the final decision? The answer is a resounding *no*. In any other healthy friendship one person is not "the boss"; rather, the relationship moves forward through a process of mutual give and take. For instance, what if you had a friend who suddenly started making all the decisions, such as where you would go to eat, what films you would see, and which other people would be invited along? You would think that the friend either had become a benevolent dictator who simply wanted things his or her way or had assumed the role of a wise parent who claimed to know better than you what is best for you. It's likely that neither one would be comfortable with the friendship. In the case of the dictator, it would be hard to tolerate the arrogance; in the case of the wise parent, you might disagree that a peer could really know what is best for you. Aside from situations of removal from harm, can someone ever really know what is best for another adult person? Can we actually take into account all the external and internal factors that come into play for another person as he or she makes a decision? Even if we could, is it our right to override the desires of another person with our agenda? It doesn't seem so. The use of power in a friendship destroys intimacy to the degree that it is used, because one person does not have the freedom to fully express herself or himself. If we understand the importance of both autonomy and commitment in friendship, we should be able to see the value of this balance in the friendship between people who are headed toward or already in a marriage.

So let's ask the question in the other direction: Can people have an intimate and loving marriage if there is *unequal* power in that marriage? Can there be trust if one person has the ultimate veto power? As Carl Jung said: "Where love rules, there is no will to power; and where power predominates, there love is lacking. The one is the shadow of the other."[2] If God created people with all their complex aspirations and delights, their talents and personalities, then surely these should be explored in marriage, not suppressed through playing gender roles or exercising power one over the other. Asking the same person to give in on every important decision will inevitably result in that person being gradually diminished. Family therapists Jack and Judith Balswick observe:

> Assimilation in marriage, where the personhood of one spouse is given up, is not Christian. . . . In Christian marriage each partner is subject to the

other: each is to love and be loved, to forgive and be forgiven, to serve and be served, and to know and be known. A marriage in which one partner, the husband or the wife, is asked to give up his or her personhood for the sake of the other denies God's expression in and through a unique member of the creation. The relationship is remarkably more fulfilling when both persons are expressed equally through their union.[3]

In other words, mutuality is not only more theologically sound—couples living out the love required of Christ's followers—but it is more emotionally rich and enjoyable.

This is due, paradoxically perhaps, to the fact that it is precisely in a relationship of mutual self-sacrifice that one can be most fully known. The selfishness that characterizes male chauvinism (*It has to be my way because I am the man*) and some forms of secular feminism (*I am not going to give an inch because men always walk all over women*) can be overcome, allowing for deep intimacy. In a relationship of Christian mutuality, the destructive sacrifice of the self, what the Balswicks call assimilation, is rejected in favor of a healthy giving and receiving in each direction between the marriage partners. In other words, it is safe for a woman to engage in self-sacrifice if her husband is committed to laying his life down for her as well; it is safe for a man to be vulnerable if his wife is vulnerable with him, and both are committed to the health and growth of the other. They give themselves *to* the other, but don't give themselves *up for* the other. Both people live out their individuality as fully as possible, being honest about their needs and desires, not papering over them in an attempt to appear submissive or spiritual.

It sounds pious, perhaps, for women to say they will follow their men anywhere and sacrifice anything for them, but if they do it at the expense of who they are and what they need at each juncture, there will be no way for intimacy to thrive. In fact, the self-abnegation (or self-abdication?), the burying of the self in the name of femininity or of "Christian submission," is not Christian at all. Lewis Smedes observes: "Total self-giving, generous as it may seem, is destructive of marriage because it saps a partner of the creative independence he/she needs in order to contribute himself/herself to the other person. In order to give one's self, there must be a genuine self to give."[4] God in Scripture does not call us to destroy ourselves or repress ourselves but to live in thankful wonder at the people that we were created to be. Marriage, according to the design in Genesis, was not set up to submerge the life of one person in the other, but for mutual flourishing. God calls us to mutual submission for the development of both people and the deepest intimacy possible.

Equal-Regard Marriage

A book came out a few years ago called *Halving It All: How Equally Shared Parenting Works*, in which the author, Francine Deutsch, interacted with hundreds of couples, looking at issues of domestic work and childcare in families. She discovered, for one thing, that some couples, ranging from blue-collar wage earners to executives, manage to split childcare and domestic tasks evenly between them. The keys seem to be flexibility and the desire to make family life fair to both partners. In fact, some of them did not set out to engage in "equally shared parenting," but it evolved as they worked together to create a good life for each other and for their children.[5]

An equal-regard marriage does not require one particular organization of work any more than shared parenting does. However, a marriage of mutuality may be more difficult to achieve in a setup with highly gender-segregated roles. The answer seems to be yes, but rarely. For one thing, mutuality is more difficult to achieve in these situations where tasks are assigned on the basis of cultural ideas about masculinity and femininity, since this setup often results in the tasks being unevenly distributed, with little room for negotiation.

For instance, let's take the hypothetical couple Tim and Tianna, who assumed when they got married that she should do all the work on the home front and Tim would earn the money. Tianna took responsibility for the cooking, cleaning, shopping, decorating, gardening, and whatever else came up. Things were fairly balanced until they had children, but then her work hours often extended long into the evening. Tim would come home from work tired and feeling entitled to relax; in fact, he thought it not unreasonable to expect to find dinner on the table when he got home. He couldn't see that Tianna had also been working all day and continued to do so while he sat reading in his favorite chair.

The question for this couple is: can they renegotiate their responsibilities to make the situation workable for Tianna? If they can, and the work freely chosen is not unevenly divided up, then it may be fine to arrange their lives this way, as long as they can resist the temptation to assign superior moral or spiritual value to this structure. They are making a social choice, not following a mandate from God.

But it is difficult to know whether the traditional assignment of chores has been freely chosen in any given marriage. Many women, especially in their teens and twenties, say that this is what they want, but they have never seriously considered the possibility of any other option. They have never been encouraged to dream outside the box; they have not heard that life choices are more complicated than a simple either/or—either a vocation *or* a family—though men always assume that they can have both these things in their own lives. Many women in evangelical circles have rarely been challenged to consider that their Christian responsibility in this world may include a huge range of things, that God has given gifts that it is incumbent on them to use. In fact, just the opposite has been communicated to them in countless ways: that their highest calling, or the only Christian calling for a woman, is to marry, have children, and "stay at home" raising them. To embrace this model may simply be taking the path of least resistance, rather than choosing a life trajectory based on gifts and responsibility.

A second model for a mutual-regard marriage is one in which couples choose to differentiate the work on the basis of the talents and preferences of the persons involved, rather than on gender. The premise is that some tasks are simply more odious to some and enjoyable to others. Cooking is a good example because for some people it is a chore that has to be done so that the family can eat, while for others it is a way to unwind at the end of a stressful day, a chance to be a little creative. But even assigning roles based on preferences can be too rigid for two reasons: first, there are always tasks that are unpalatable for both people and others that are enjoyable to both. How are those to be divided? Second, without the flexibility of trying new tasks, the people involved may never discover new things that they are good at or enjoy. Everyone in my family, for instance, is thankful that my husband discovered that cooking is therapeutic for him.

The third way of organizing life together in a mutual-regard marriage is simply to assume that either party can do any task. In his classic work *The Road Less Traveled*, psychiatrist M. Scott Peck suggests that in marriage, the wider the range of tasks that each person can do, the freer they are to love each other. When a husband is kept helpless in the kitchen and a wife is kept helpless about finances, a couple can find artificial security because each can feel indispensable. However, Peck observes, the healthier the relationship, the less each person is threatened by the capabilities of the other; the more each can do, the more they interact freely on the basis of love rather than out of a fearfully maintained dependence on each other.[6] This doesn't mean that all tasks are shared equally all the time, because it is natural that each person gravitates toward those he or she likes best to do, but Peck is arguing that no tasks should be off-limits to either person on the basis of cultural notions of gender or on the basis of personality.

Benefits of a Mutual Marriage

Freedom to Love Fully

As mentioned above, when concern for the health and growth of the other person goes in both directions, there won't be a competition for power in the relationship, and there will be safety for each person to be vulnerable and sacrificial in their love. People can learn a deep trust, since they know the other person will not take advantage of their weaknesses.

Deeper Communication

In any type of mutual-regard marriage, a deeper level of communication is required as the parties negotiate, and keep negotiating, how to divide tasks in their shared life together. This deeper communication is itself one of the benefits of this model. When my husband and I were first married, even negotiating housework took a bit of work, since these chores were not shared by our parents; without role models, we felt as if we were blazing a new trail. Then, when children came along, we began the ongoing discussion about who does childcare when, and who picks up which child from preschool or friends' houses or church. More significantly, as we each pursue our careers, every potential employment change requires a huge amount of deliberation about the implications for each of us as people and for our respective goals and callings. But in it all, the friendship that is our marriage has deepened.

Like many things in life, the goals worth achieving take effort. Sometimes the negotiation includes conflict as spouses try to create something that diverges from the model their parents lived out before them. One of the women Deutsch interviewed talked of going on strike, simply refusing to clean up after her husband, or refusing to cook one more meal while he relaxed after they both arrived home from work. They gradually grew better at talking these things out. In another case the woman described how she and her husband arrived at joint responsibility for parenting and housework: "I think a lot of this . . . had to do with my learning how to articulate my needs instead of just put[ting] them in the closet and wish[ing] somebody would pay attention to them without my having to say anything about it."[7] My husband and I used to joke that each of us wondered why the other person couldn't read our mind, as in, "Why doesn't he ask what's wrong, when clearly I am frustrated?" In the end, though, we learned to assume less about what the other person wanted, or what the other noticed in our demeanor, and we learned to talk more about everything.

Justice: Equal Value Placed on Each Person's Contributions

Both partners experience the well-being produced by the justice of an arrangement that does not assign more work, or more unpalatable work, to one person. When both people recognize that all work is human work and that the labor involved in the domestic side of life might logically be shared, since both people enjoy its benefits, they can assist each other with everything. This is particularly important if both spouses work outside the home, but it also applies in situations where only the husband leaves the house to work. This approach rejects the assumption that he gets to enjoy leisure in after-work hours while she has neither leisure nor any hours "after work" until children are asleep.

Not only jobs and domestic work have to be juggled, however; there are things such as finances that have to be worked through together in an egalitarian marriage. It seems obvious that the mutual respect and love demanded of Christians in a marriage would mean sharing equal access to finances. In other words, how could someone claim to be laying down his or her life in self-sacrificial love, and at the same time hold on to the purse strings as a means of wielding power in a family? If both spouses work outside the home, the one who makes more money is certainly not more valuable in the eyes of God and probably shouldn't posture as if divinely appointed to be the boss. Even more so, in a family arrangement in which one person's contribution to the family economy is unremunerated—as most child care and domestic work is—the income of the other should belong to both. A person's work is not intrinsically more valuable simply because there is a paycheck attached; they both are working to make the entire family economy function, and therefore the money that comes in should be available to both contributors to this family economy.

One of the great ironies of the feminist movement of the 1970s is that women struggled to break out of the traditional family structure, and at the same time argued for the value of women's unpaid labor. It was feminists who first complained that women's domestic work was so devalued after the Industrial Revolution as to be invisible to men and to larger society. Feminists were the only ones to argue for Social Security for women who had, in fact, worked, despite the way that society dismissed their labor as "staying at home." If raising children and tending to domestic tasks allows the productivity in other segments of the American economy, why, they asked, shouldn't women be protected by the government when they reach retirement age. (In fact, the question was a good one, since an alarming number of women who enjoy middle-class status during their spouse's working years find themselves in the welfare system when he dies or leaves.) The feminists' demand that women have a choice about their lives—whether to pursue a career as well as a family or to make their contributions as "housewives," as they were called then—sounded like a rejection of the family because the traditional family structure was called into question. However, feminists were not saying that domestic work was bad, but simply that women, as well as men, needed to have the freedom to make choices about how they organized their domestic and professional lives.

Fullness of Humanity Expressed

Rather than attempting to live up to societal ideals of the perfect wife or the perfect husband, or of femininity or masculinity, both people can be fully human with one another. Rather than letting some socially prescribed gender roles dictate how they interact, they can allow themselves and allow each other to blossom into the individuals they were created to be. It is strange to think, for example, that the man would always be the strong one in the relationship; what about his needs for comfort and encouragement, the times of weakness when he needs to be taken care of? It would be equally strange to assume that the woman is constantly weak and needing to be taken of. Rather, it is in the nature of being human that sometimes we are weak and broken, sometimes strong and able to give a lot, regardless of gender. The genius of Christian community in general, and marriage in particular, is that we help to carry each other during the hard times. Men don't have to pretend that they are the ones "in control" all the time, and women don't have to pretend that they need to be taken care of all the time.

Using a Broader Range of Gifts and Abilities

Each person can explore a range of activities, rather than assuming that a woman can use her gifts only in one slice of human existence. Both people encourage the other to use their gifts as they participate in God's new creation, in whatever ways their talents, their dreams, or their callings lead them. In A Time for Risking, anthropologist and global ministries professor Miriam Adeney challenges women to remember that just because they get married or have children doesn't mean they are absolved of the Great Commission. Jesus calls his followers to be salt and light in this world, and an equal-regard marriage is a place where women are asked not to bury their gifts but to use them as we participate in the new creation.

Benefits in Child Raising

If a couple has children, the benefits of egalitarian marriage increase for all parties. For one thing, the parents share the energy drain that the care of infants or small children demands. This may mean that they are both bone tired, but at least they are in it together. More than that, though, they share the wonder of watching the unfolding of the personalities of the small people who have come into their family. Rather than hearing second-hand of the changes in a child, or of the funny things that the child has done, each parent knows the joy of being there. Fathers as well as mothers can experience the deep joy of intimacy with the children when they both spend time caring for them. Once I heard a lecturer who advocated egalitarian marriages but admitted that she would hate it if her kids called out for her husband first in the night, or came running to him rather than her with their joys. Isn't that a selfish position, to want to be the central parent at each juncture? How did her husband feel, always being the second-string parent? Her need to be needed meant he didn't have as significant a relationship with the children as he might have had, and it meant the children didn't know him as well as they could have.

In contrast, friends of ours told how their daughter, when she was tiny, would stand up in her crib after waking in the morning and say, "Mommy, Daddy, Mommy, Daddy . . ." until one of her parents arrived. She wanted to see them both because she had experienced the involvement of both parents in her care. She, along with many other children in families of shared parenting, benefited in having the opportunity to form deep relationships with both parents, rather than just one.

Often, however, it is just when children come along that couples find it most difficult to retain mutuality in their relationship. The next section will explore some of the reasons for this.

Raising Children Together

Overcoming the Internal Barriers to Equal Parenting

For Christian women, at least a couple of layers of social pressure have shaped their thinking about child raising and perhaps formed in them an internal critique of shared parenting: there are the general cultural messages about how children should be raised and then there are arguments particular to Christians about women's place, women's duty. We will address biblical material first and then look at cultural prescriptions.

What Does the Bible Say about Motherhood?

Surprisingly little. Despite the implicit or explicit teachings of many churches and much Christian writing about family, the Bible does not teach that a woman's highest calling is to have babies. As mentioned earlier, the most prominent mothers in the Hebrew Scriptures are those in Genesis whose childbearing was central to their significance in the history of salvation, as was their husbands' fathering of these children. When it comes to creating the new nation of Israel, producing offspring is the main task set before both the women and the men. But other women in the Old Testament are not highlighted on the basis of being mothers. The prophets Miriam, Deborah, and Hulda come to mind (see discussion in chap. 2), or the wise woman of Tekoa and the valiant queen Esther. These examples call into question the idea that women are valuable to God or to the people of God simply because of the children they bear. Even Ruth's story turns on her love and commitment to Naomi, and in the case of the "wife of Manoah," who later gives birth to Samson, we know only that she understands the angel's message whereas her husband does not.

In the Gospels, only two women are introduced on the basis of the children they will bear, and these two, Mary and Elizabeth, have unique roles in redemption. Yet neither is simply a traditional mother: Elizabeth speaks prophetically, recognizing Jesus as "her Lord," and Mary becomes a disciple, casting her lot among Jesus' followers at his death, rather than returning to Nazareth (to raise her grandchildren or whatever). The mother of James and John appears a couple of times, but she, too, may have been a follower—hence her request that Jesus give her sons places of honor (Matt. 20:20–21). Otherwise, the women described or merely mentioned in the Gospels are disciples (Mary Magdalene, Mary and Martha, Mary of Clopas, Salome) or women Jesus healed or helped in some way. In Acts and the letters that make up the rest of the New Testament, women are known for their ministry in the broader Christian community, not their motherhood, with the exception of Eunice, the mother of Timothy. (See especially the list in Rom. 16, where women are commended for their efforts in spreading the gospel.) The Bible, then, does not teach by example or precept that the main purpose of a woman's life is to be a mother.

Further, when parenting is mentioned in the Scriptures, there is no prescription regarding how child rearing is to be done, and Scripture certainly does not say women should be "stay-at-home" mothers. In fact, the Bible gives no detailed instructions about who should administer care to children. There is no verse that says, "Children are the responsibility of women" or "children need their mothers in order to grow up well." These are maxims in our culture but not commands of Scripture. The closest approximation to these might be 1 Timothy 5:14, in which Paul instructs Timothy regarding unruly widows: "So I would have younger widows marry, bear children, and manage their households, so as to give the adversary no occasion to revile us." Lest we think that the phrase "manage their households" consigns women to the house in a way unique to their gender, we should compare it with 1 Timothy 3:4, where elders or bishops are directed to manage their households well, and further, 1 Timothy 3:12 specifies "Let deacons be married only once, and let them manage their children and their households well."

This means that despite the claims of some Christian leaders, the Bible does not promote one Christian way to raise children. Surely if God intended us to bring up children or structure our marriages in one particular way, then Scripture would give clear instructions about it. As it is, we apparently have latitude in these areas as long as we stay within the parameters of God's requirement to love.

Cultural Pressures regarding Motherhood

If Scripture does not demand that women be "stay-at-home" moms, we might well ask where this assumption comes from. In this case, we have seen that many of our assumptions about marriage and child raising come from middle-class Western industrialism. This means that adhering to the model in which women opt out of the paid labor force does not mark us as true Christians but simply shows we are products of our culture, as are millions of others who embrace the same marriage and childrearing ideals though they do not claim to have any Christian connection. In other words, there are many people, Christian and otherwise, who subscribe to the idea that women's primary job is to care for home and children.

We see this most clearly in the sheer number of books that continue to show up on the bookstore shelves about women juggling family and work responsibilities, while there is nearly total silence regarding men navigating those things. If we didn't assume that children were solely or mostly women's responsibility—if, in other words, we assumed children were all parents' responsibilities—then there would be a great deal more public dialog about men struggling with the domestic/professional balance. A New York University sociologist did interview research with college students over a five year period (1998–2003) and found that most of the men assumed that their future wives would work. However, they also assumed that if child care couldn't be worked out, their wives would and should stay home with children. To these men, it seemed natural to prioritize their own jobs and careers over their wives' careers, and it also struck them as natural for women to care for children. In contrast, the young women for the most part rejected the idea of reverting to traditional roles if child-care issues couldn't be resolved. For one thing, they want to share parenting and careers, and also they do not assume, given the rate of divorce in society, that someone will be there to provide for them financially, even if they wanted that.[8]

In many ways the message is not simply that it is "natural" somehow for a woman to raise children, but that doing so brings a woman her only true joy. This line may have been easier to promote in the centuries when colleges and universities were closed to women, since women's options were much more limited. There was a certain consistency to the cultural messages then: you women will not be allowed in the professions, so why should we educate you? Now, when the doors are legally open to women to pursue an almost limitless array of careers, we are saying in effect, You are free to get educated, but we really hope you'll be so kind as to forego all your interests, your training, and your dreams and focus only on your children. Many women, frankly, would enjoy their children more if they combined parenting with other things. Not only do women not necessarily feel elated at being home with children all the time, but thousands of women experience depression being the primary care-giver to small children.[9]

To see that this notion of women's "true calling" or "highest joy" is still lurking in American culture, we have only to look at the prevalence of the "opting out" trend stories, that is, stories about women leaving the workplace. Trend stories by their very nature rely on very little data, since they are attempting to name a trend that others have not yet noticed, and so in this case a handful of women may be portrayed as being typical of millions. Worse, the theme of these stories is often contrary to what the women themselves say. The journalists rhapsodize about the inexorable pull of some neotraditional version of motherhood or about the women's supposed sudden awareness of their personal limits, while the women themselves say that they were pushed out of the workplace by the lack of high-quality child care and by the inflexibility of their employers with regard to work hours. For instance, the *New York Times* ran a story in 2003 about Ivy League–trained lawyers and doctors who left their high-paying jobs to stay home with young children; the women interviewed gave up their jobs because the hours were unrealistic and because part-time work is usually mind-numbing, a dead-end in terms of promotions, and without benefits. These trend stories will continue to crop up, however, since they tap into an old set of assumptions about the differences between men and women, and therefore about parenting.[10]

Another side effect of this idea that women's highest calling, or only true calling, is home and children, is that any work women do outside the home is considered secondary: the man has a career and the woman, if she works, has a job, but her real work is in the home. Therefore when they both return from work, she begins the "second-shift" while he relaxes in front of the news. This may feel natural to them, that the woman would do "women's work" when they both return home, particularly if in their families of origin their mothers performed all the domestic chores. Although some pollsters report that men do much more caregiving for children and tending the home than they used to in two-income families, other reports are not so sanguine.[11]

Further, if the man has a career or a calling, and the woman merely has a job, then when it becomes necessary for someone to flex a bit with work, the woman has to do it. For instance, who adjusts when a child or ailing parent needs care, or who gives up a job whenever the other wants to move? Once a guest speaker at our church gave a sketch of her life, which went something like this: "We moved to X so my husband could take a church. I developed a ministry among refugees, but just when it was going well, my husband came home one day and announced we were moving to Y. It took me a while, but in Y I started a literacy program for disadvantaged young readers. Just when that work started thriving my husband declared that we were moving to Z. So in Z I had to begin all over again." There were four or five iterations of this kind; finally, she said, her husband died and she then became a national leader of women's ministries in her denomination. The assumptions running through that story were very troubling. Her husband seemed to act as if his job was the center around which the family turned, and her work held no significance at all. Furthermore, he respected her so little that he felt he could make unilateral decisions that had a tremendous impact on her life without even consulting her. This is, I hope, an extreme example, but the underlying assumptions about the relative value of women's and men's contributions to the society or to the new creation of God seem pretty widespread.

Straying from Coparenting

Even for those who intend to coparent, it doesn't always turn out that way. For one thing, some couples end up in an arrangement that looks fairly traditional because of the "woman-as-expert syndrome." When a couple has their first baby, often they are overwhelmed by the sense that they don't know what they're doing, since babies don't come with operating instructions and since the books, articles, and Internet sites designed to help new parents give such radically divergent advice. Many women, however, earned money during their teenage years by babysitting or were required to help with younger siblings. And, because of societal expectations that women will care for children, a young mother is more likely to have read some of those books, articles, and Internet sites. Add to that the unrecognized assumption in many couples' minds that mothers somehow know how to handle babies better than fathers do because they carried them in utero for nine months, and the stage is set for the man to feel insecure about his potential parenting skills. When the baby arrives, what happens? The mother, though she genuinely wants the father to be involved in caring for their child, assumes the role of expert, acting like she knows the best way to do things, which in the end discourages him from participation. To mitigate this, some friends of ours devised the "Daddy's world and Mommy's world" system, in which each parent had the freedom to make decisions about the baby when he or she was doing the caregiving, and they discovered that babies and young children are very resilient: they can be fed things in different order, can be bathed in a variety of ways, and can be dressed in clothes of dubious combination, and they still thrive.

Other new fathers may resolve to be highly involved in caring for their children, but they view it as helping out their wives, and therefore they expect appreciation for every little thing they do in caring for children. If a man compares himself to the guys at work and finds that he does more than they do on the home front, he may expect his wife to heap up the praise. However, if he were to compare himself with her, he might recognize that he doesn't do nearly as much as she does. I call this the "helping out" syndrome, when the father still assumes at some level that the work is hers and any little bit he does deserves a load of gratitude. People in the larger society very often confirm this sort of thinking; for instance, while I was in my first academic position, I was on a search committee for a new faculty member and we interviewed a candidate over dinner. On the way into the restaurant, one of my male colleagues asked me, "So, is your husband babysitting the kids tonight?" "No, actually he's spending time with his own children." That same year a local newspaper published a piece on Father's Day written by a man who fumed about the low expectations in this society regarding fatherhood. For example, when his wife picked up their daughter from preschool, the teachers made no comment; why, when he picked up their daughter, did the teachers remark on what a good father he was? He was disgusted by this double standard.

So even in cases where couples intend to share child care, they may not wind up doing it because of an inadvertent privileging of the woman's experience in dealing with small children, or because of a persistent assumption that men are just helping their wives out when they engage in child-care chores. Deutsch observed that good intentions were not always enough; ongoing communication and negotiation were necessary so that couples didn't revert to the patterns they grew up with.[12]

The reasons for straying from coparenting may be much larger, however: economic realities and other external barriers in our society. For instance, pay inequity often leads to men being the ones to keep their jobs, while women's lower-paying work is forfeited. The next section deals with some of the societal barriers to equal parenting.

Overcoming External Barriers to Equal Parenting

The latent and not-so-latent assumptions about women's "natural" responsibility to care for children have had enduring social effects: despite all the rhetoric about "family values," we have no political will to enact legislation that would benefit families. No other Western democracy has such backward laws when it comes to making it easier for women, as well as men, to create a good balance between their homes and jobs.[13] For instance, the United States lags far behind European nations with regard to parental leave after childbirth or adoption, which means that in no other Western country is a woman penalized as much as she is here for cutting back on hours after the birth of a child, or taking time out of the workforce. We have very weak maternity laws and virtually no provision for male parents to care for their own babies. In fact, in the 1970s a woman could be fired from many types of jobs for becoming pregnant: schoolteachers and flight attendants, for example. Now it is illegal to fire a woman for becoming pregnant, but employers are not required by law to hold a person's job during maternity leave, let alone to give paternity leave when a child is added to a family. Ours is also the only democracy without a law giving parents time off to care for a sick child, which means that millions of Americans have to choose between sending their children to school sick or staying home with them at the risk of losing their jobs or being unable to buy groceries at the end of the week. Contrast this with European countries: among the top countries in the world for productivity (gross domestic product-per-hour-worked), all have family-friendly policies. Their economies are strong and their family policies are incredibly generous compared with ours. In addition to this, in the United States, where workers generally get two weeks of vacation a year, the workweek is getting longer, but in the European Union, where workers get a minimum of four weeks of vacation annually, the standard workweek is steady between 35 and 39 hours. Part-time workers in the EU enjoy not only benefits but much higher job security and job satisfaction, given the wider variety of part-time jobs available. All of these comparisons put the lie to the oft-touted truism that if companies had paid parental leave, for instance, or otherwise caved in to the demands of families, the economy would falter.

We also lag far behind other industrialized nations in our laws providing for part-time work and flexibility in work hours. In poll after poll, American men and women express a desire for less rigid workplaces that allow them to better balance work and family time. Even from the perspective of the bottom line, employers would do well to take notice: the business firm Deloitte & Touche estimates that it saved $41.5 million by instituting flexible hours so people can adjust start and end times to accommodate school or child-care hours for their children. The money is saved in a much lower rate of employee turnover.

The fact that women earn less also contributes to keeping the family arrangements at status quo. Writer and political activist Faulkner Fox describes how she and her husband had agreed on a fifty-fifty parenting and domestic work setup, but the logical thing at various points drove them to an inequity that mirrored the society. He had a more structured job, for instance, and his job paid quite a bit more, so she took on full-time care of their baby. As the months passed, she wondered whether this setup, which in theory she and her husband did not endorse, would, in fact, become the pattern indefinitely, or whether they would find a way at some point to share parenting and domestic chores more equally again.[14] Deutsch interviewed other couples who made similar concessions and found that some broke out of this initial division of labor and achieved a better balance between work and child care for both partners, while others never managed to do so. That women face lower pay to begin with and then are penalized with lower status and lower-paying jobs for having taken time out for children means that it is difficult for many women to go back to work. Some families made what they thought would be temporary concessions, but which became the permanent pattern, while other families organized the parenting one way for a time (i.e., women as primary caregivers until after the children went to school), and then structured things differently as the woman reentered the workforce.[15]

In addition to lower pay, inflexible work hours, little opportunity for quality part-time work, and few benefits, there is the difficulty of finding high-quality child care. When we had our first child and were researching child-care options, a friend commented, "Having a baby is a piece of cake, but finding child care, now *that's* hard!" Unfortunately, many people in this country have had that same experience; it is difficult to find high-quality, reliable daycare, something that other Western countries have prioritized as a way to express their commitment to their children and to women, if women are still the primary caregivers. In a country where more than 80 percent of single parents work, and more than 80 percent of married women work, it is strange that there is so little political will to address the issue of public funding for child care. In her book *Not Guilty! The Good News about Working Mothers*, Betty Holcomb devotes a chapter to negative American attitudes toward daycare, despite the positive statistical data that should challenge these attitudes. For instance, she describes women who are regularly accosted by coworkers about the dangers of daycare, particularly after some daycare negligence or violence harms a child and makes the news, despite the fact that American homes are far and away the most dangerous places for children, statistically speaking.[16] And, contrary to trend stories, children who are cared for by people other than their parents do not turn into sociopaths or maladjusted adults at a higher rate than children cared for in their homes. In fact, Holcomb cites studies showing that children who have spent time in some child-care setting are more likely to develop interpersonal skills and confidence in peer settings.

Beyond assumptions about danger in child-care centers or the maladjustment that critics speculate will develop in daycare children, there is a deep-seated assumption about "women's place" that underlies any discussion of child care. Take, for example, the conflicting rhetoric about single mothers and welfare: pundits make pronouncements about how women should get off welfare and earn their way in the world, and then from the other side of their mouths, they say that we should not have public daycare because it will encourage women to abdicate their responsibility to raise their children. Thinking of child care as a temptation to women to leave their children, however, shows ignorance of the real-life dilemmas of millions of women who head single-parent families; these mothers want to provide for their families but also desperately want safe and enjoyable environments for their children's care.

And for any mother, the "women's place" mentality implicitly denies that women have anything of significance to contribute to society other than raising children. This is certainly not true with regard to the labor market where increasingly the work of women is necessary for the health of the economy.[17] Furthermore, the "women's place" approach assumes that what is good for women need not be taken into consideration, or that their frame of mind when caring for children doesn't matter as long as they are there. This is contradicted by the lives of many women for whom working, even part-time, is critical to their well-being, and in the end makes them better parents. Finally, the "women's place" approach also effectively defines child care as off-limits to fathers; there is no political will, therefore, to ask the questions about what is good for men or what might be best for children.

In the end, there are at least four reasons why it makes sense to share the care of children: it is good for the parents to be involved in the larger society by using their gifts; it is good for the advancement of Christ's work in the world for mothers and fathers to bear his presence into the many vocations; it is good for the children to have more than one or two adults who are significant in their lives; and it is good for those child-care givers who are childless or unconnected to the larger society or simply need the income or any other of a host of reasons.

There's Hope: The Reality of Shared Parenting

The reality is that, despite the trend stories about women leaving the workplace and the "common wisdom" about women who work full-time and then have to do the "second-shift" after they get home, this is not how it is for many couples. In countless households, the adults share all sorts of work in ways that benefit them all. In other words, contrary to what some people feared, in shared-parenting situations the mothers do not care less about their children, research has found, but the fathers participate more.[18] And the fathers' involvement goes much deeper than merely helping out a bit more on the weekends; it entails men as well as women making conscious decisions that prioritize family over work. Deutsch found that men who shared child care did sometimes have to adjust their career goals, or forego promotions—just as female parents do—but that none of them regretted it. All the men in her study who engaged in shared parenting found it to be profoundly rewarding. One man observed, "Now watching my children develop is just amazing. It's fantastic! It's really mind boggling! I can't imagine a parent who could miss that."[19] Others spoke of never really knowing their children until they cared for them and learned what every little expression meant, or every tone of their cry. In fact, Deutsch observed, "The intensity of attachment between these men and their infants was as strong as the bond we usually associate with mothers."[20] It is the time spent, not the biology of the parent, that determines the closeness with the child; in other words, it is through sharing the small things such as learning to tie shoes or climb up the stairs or devising little games together that intimacy develops. These things, Deutsch observes, "can seem pretty mundane to less involved fathers, but it is these seeming trivialities that connect parent and child, and parents to each other."[21]

This last point is an important one: not only did the men in her study experience deeper intimacy with their children, but they also expressed their enjoyment of a deeper bond with their wives as they shared the wonder of watching their children develop. It was a joint project, rather than the woman's project that he heard about or helped with. From the women's side things were better too. One mother commented: "There's a whole lot less conflict if you aren't always mad at your husband about how you're being a martyr."[22] Sharing work, including child care as well as other domestic responsibilities, makes that work part of the bond of intimacy rather than a source of struggle and separation between husband and wife.

Conclusions

Our society is changing; even the fact that women now make up more than half of medical students and more than half of law school students suggests that many young women intend to make different sorts of contributions to society than women did fifty years ago. As women's lives and aspirations change, the men associated with them will also have to think differently about their own lives and the families that they form together. As Gloria Steinem once quipped: "The feminist movement will have succeeded when a man asks if he can have a career and a family too." She was calling for something important: that men take just as seriously as women do the very real tension between the responsibilities of caring for children and the demands of a vocation. Creating a situation in which two people share equally in parenting may require them to examine their deepest assumptions regarding career/calling and family. In fact, Deutsch suggested that spouses should think in terms of familial vocation rather than personal careers, and thereby take into account the well-being of all members of the family when domestic and professional decisions are made.

This seems like a profoundly Christian suggestion: that we take into account everyone's best interests and preferences and make decisions on that basis. After all, we are the ones instructed by Paul: "Let each of you look not to your own interests, but to the interests of others. Let the same mind be in you that was in Christ Jesus, who, though he was in the form of God, did not regard equality with God as something to be exploited" (Phil. 2:4–6). As we commit to relationships based in that sort of humility and in a love that seeks the best for the other, we can share the work of life together, both in our homes and out in the world as we bear the presence of God there.

Part Three

WOMEN IN THE CHURCH AND THE WORLD
OR
WHY WATCHING TV IS NOT ENOUGH

7

SEEING THE INVISIBLE

Women in the Early Church

Some years ago, I attended a lecture by a prominent evangelical speaker who gave a litany of problems facing the church. Included in his comments was this question: Since women were happy being silent in the church for two thousand years, why do they all of a sudden need to be leaders? How silent were they, though, I wondered, and how happy with whatever limitations were placed on them? The speaker was assuming that women were content within the social strictures they faced throughout the history of the church; however, women's writing uncovered in the past thirty years has demonstrated that their acquiescence to societal norms had more to do with their feelings of powerlessness than with their delight in being kept subordinate. The speaker also assumed that restrictions on women's participation in church leadership have been consistent across societies and constant over time. This is simply not true; the historical record shows that women have enjoyed varying degrees of freedom to use their gifts in different settings, in different cultures, and at different times, as we shall see. Finally, it looks as if he mistook the statements of male leaders limiting women's participation in the ministry of the church for how things actually were; he assumed that women complied uniformly with whatever proscriptions were placed upon them. However, recent scholarship has shown that there have always been women who have been involved in the church in ways forbidden to them. Women have never been as passive as some male leaders have wanted them to be; hence the repeated injunctions regarding women's place. You don't, after all, have to keep saying "Be quiet" if no one is making noise.

The speaker mentioned above, though, is not alone in confusing the prohibitions against women's public ministry with how they actually functioned in the church. In the 1970s and 1980s, when scholars first focused attention on women's participation in the early church, for instance, they often regarded the negative instructions of the church fathers as adequate indicators of women's roles in that era. One scholar, in 1982, explicitly stated her intention "to explain the role and place of women in Early Christianity as it emerges from the writings of the Fathers of the Church."[1] This work was significant, not so much for what it showed about women's place, as for its outline of the various male leaders' desires regarding proper female roles in the church.

Increasingly, however, evidence is emerging that demonstrates women's actual participation in the life of the church. The following discussion, which will be by no means exhaustive, will highlight the activities of real women in the history of the church in the West, based on this new concrete evidence of women's active participation in leadership. Along the way we will note some of the attitudes of male leaders regarding women, as well as restrictions that were imposed.

Women in the First Centuries of the Church

In the Church of Saint Praxedis, a basilica in Rome built in honor of two female saints, a mosaic more than a thousand years old depicts four women. Praxedis and her sister, Prudentiana, appear on either side of Mary, mother of Jesus, along with a fourth female figure whose head is surrounded by a square halo. The square halo indicates that she was highly honored and still alive when the mosaic was produced. Inscribed vertically along this fourth figure is her name, Theodora, and above her is the word, *episcopa*, the feminine form of the word translated "overseer" or "bishop." The words *Theodora Episcopa*, or Bishop Theodora, appear again nearby.[2] This is an example of the growing body of data concerning leadership positions women occupied in the early centuries of Christianity. Books such as Ute E. Eisen's *Women Officeholders in Early Christianity: Epigraphical and Literary Studies*, and Kevin Madigan and Carolyn Osiek's *Ordained Women in the Early Church: A Documentary History* present data about the various roles that women played early on, including ordained positions of deacon, priest (presbyter), and bishop.[3]

Evidence for women's leadership in the early church falls into three categories: inscriptional, epigraphical, and literary. Inscriptional evidence, as the name suggests, includes mosaics and inscriptions such as the one in the Church of Saint Praxedis. Epigraphical evidence refers to the memorials of women leaders that have survived on gravestones and in churches where they served. Finally, we have references to and discussions of women's church leadership in letters, treatises, and journals, which constitute the literary evidence. Unfortunately we have only a few theological texts written by women before the Middle Ages, which means that the writing of most of these women, if they did in fact write, has not survived.

But scholars have not always had (or paid attention to) this data, which means that the history of women in the early church has been emerging only recently. The cultural blinders of recent centuries led generations of historians to assume that only men were leaders, partly because the church has so assiduously ignored the activities of actual women and looked only to the texts that restricted their involvement. As noted in chapter 2, women held leadership roles in at least some New Testament churches. We saw that Paul commended many women for their efforts as missionaries, as servants of the church (a term he also used to refer to himself and Timothy and other prominent male leaders), as "those who worked hard for the gospel," and even as an apostle (Junia). We noted that Paul expected women to pray and prophesy in public worship, hence his long discussion in 1 Corinthians 11:3–16 on how they should appear when they do so. And women's open-air prophesying was affirmed by Peter as a sign of God's blessing on the day of Pentecost. Despite these affirmations of women's ministry, it is striking that when the New Testament uses masculine plural words to refer to saints, the elect, or believers, and so on, the church has always interpreted them to mean men and women, but when the same New Testament writers use the masculine plural to refer to apostles, teachers, or bishops, the church has interpreted these words as referring only to men.[4] This type of literary convention in Greek and then Latin has helped hide the role of real women in the New Testament church and beyond.

As it became clear that women did hold offices in the early centuries, the first reaction of many scholars was to dismiss these women as having played different roles than men with the same titles. When historians uncovered cases where women bear titles of authority in the church or in society at large, one of three things often happened: it was assumed that the woman was married to an official with that status, that the title was merely honorary, or that the women were officials in their own right, but with less authority or competencies than male counterparts. Furthermore, these women were considered "exceptional," not people whose status is to be emulated. Each of these assumptions may tell us more about the historians than the actual experience of the titled women.[5]

Among church historians, it is now commonplace to observe that women were involved at every level of church leadership early on. Many have also argued that women had more latitude to use their gifts in the years when the church was a movement, before it became institutionalized. Thus when people's gifts were valued on the basis of empowerment by the Spirit rather than on some formal office of leadership, women could participate more fully. When church structure moved from house churches to bodies governed by a "monarchical bishop," the diversity in leadership was suppressed. This tendency was exaggerated further with the legalization of Christianity under Constantine (313), and later the elevation of the faith to the official religion of the empire (380). The redeemed community was no longer a fellowship that welcomed slaves, women, and other societally disenfranchised people on an equal basis (not that it had ever lived up to this ideal completely); now it came to look very much like a miniature of the empire. Women's participation in church leadership dropped dramatically when the church hierarchy began to resemble the political hierarchies of the empire, when the rich, powerful, and politically connected were the most likely to attain positions of leadership in the church. It seems clear that women played a larger role in the first centuries of the church than they did when the church became institutionalized along the lines of the Roman political hierarchy.

However, in light of the new inscriptional and epigraphical data, we can observe that women's leadership in ministry did not stop after the first few centuries. There is concrete evidence that women held offices in the church, over wide geographic areas and across centuries.[6] In some places, this was likely due in part to women's disregard for the strictures placed upon them, but also to varying degrees of openness to women's leadership that local leaders exhibited. Certainly the church was patriarchal, in the sense that it was run largely by men, and often by men who argued for the inferiority of women, but it has never been uniformly so. Clement of Rome, in 96 CE (or thereabouts), wrote in praise of "many women invested with power through the grace of God, [who] have accomplished many a manly deed,"[7] which shows both his awareness that women worked effectively for the gospel and his assumption that doing so made them attain something higher than femaleness, that is, manliness. Furthermore, this evidence undercuts the theory that women could find a place to express leadership only in heretical groups. The emerging Roman church was not uniformly exclusionary and, it could be noted, heretical groups were not uniformly welcoming to women. Even some gnostic groups, which are often touted these days as female-friendly, were in practice fairly misogynist.[8]

In the sections that follow, we will examine some of the roles and offices women held in the early centuries. Among other things, they were apostles, prophets, deacons and deaconesses, presbyters (priests), teachers of theology, bishops, widows, martyrs, and virgins, that is, women who had renounced sexuality and devoted themselves to the church.

Titles and Offices Women Held

Bishops

The mosaic of Theodora Episcopa mentioned above appears in a church built by Pope Paschal I, who was pope from 817 to 824. The woman in question was his mother, and according to papal records his father is mentioned with no church title, which means he had no church office. Theodora, then, was not the wife of a bishop. In addition to the designation *Theodora Episcopa* on the mosaic, there is an inscription on a reliquary tablet nearby which reads: "where the body of his most gracious mother, the Lady Theodora, the bishop, rests."[9] Unfortunately we have no information about the specific activities in her ministry, or how she rose to a position of authority.

Apostles and Prophets

A number of women were called apostles in the early church, beginning with Junia, in Romans 16:7, though, as noted in chapter 2, her female identity became obscured for centuries, beginning in the Middle Ages. The Samaritan woman, Mary Magdalene, and the other women at the tomb, though not called apostles per se in the Gospels, were designated as apostles by early church writers because they were purveyors of the good news. Interestingly enough, in the early noncanonical Christian literature (that is, the pieces of writing that didn't make it into the canon of Scripture), Mary Magdalene figures as a prominent disciple, or even the most prominent of Jesus' disciples. For instance, in *The Gospel of Mary*, Mary Magdalene challenges the grieving disciples to prepare themselves for the preaching ministry to which the Lord called them. After Andrew expresses disbelief that her message is from Christ and Peter asks resentfully, "Did he prefer her to us?" Levi observes that Jesus apparently did love her more. In the end the disciples are challenged by her faithfulness, and they go out and preach the gospel.[10] This extrabiblical material may not be technically historical, but it suggests the central role that Mary played in the early days of the church, and shows how the memory of her significance was carried into the second century when this writing was likely produced. (*The Da Vinci Code* notwithstanding, Mary's significance was based not on her ability to bear a baby but on something much more countercultural: she was commissioned as a disciple.)

Women subsequent to the New Testament era were also given the title "apostle" by the church, women such as Thecla and Nino. In the widely read book *The Acts of Paul and Thecla* (written in Greek sometime between 185 and 195), Thecla is described as a virgin engaged to be married, who chooses a life of celibacy after hearing Paul preach. She becomes one of his ministry companions and engages in preaching and teaching in her own right and performs sacramental rites such as baptism. Finally she faces the wild animals in the arena, and lacking anyone else to help her, baptizes herself before she dies. She is not called an apostle in the *Acts*, but by the fifth century Thecla was very popular, and she was then referred to repeatedly as an apostle. The fact that her account has survived in Greek, Coptic, Syriac, Armenian, Slavonic, Arabic, and five Latin versions testifies to the fact that her steadfast refusal of her fiancé and her parents' wishes for her, as well as her courage in the arena, inspired huge numbers of believers over the course of several centuries.[11]

Nino, too, was called an apostle on account of her preaching ministry. The author of the "Life of Nino" claims that she preached, converted people, and baptized people after she was brought to Georgia (in the Eastern Empire) as a prisoner of war. She is credited with converting the royal family of Georgia and is thus named "apostle" and "evangelist." The writer of her biography describes the preparation she had for this missionary activity: she studied with a female theologian, the best theological teacher in Jerusalem. In addition, she was ordained by the patriarch Juvenal of Jerusalem with this prayer: "I send her to preach your divinity and that she may proclaim your resurrection wherever it is your pleasure that she may go. Christ, be Thou her way, her companion, her haven, her teacher in the knowledge of languages . . . like those who in days past have feared your name."[12]

When it comes to prophets, Luke explicitly names Anna a prophet and depicts Mary's relative, Elizabeth, functioning as a prophet in her declaration that Mary was "the mother of my Lord" (Luke 1:42–43). In Acts 21:8–9 the four daughters of Philip are said to have engaged in prophesying. Christian historian Eusebius (ca. 263–339), in the face of a heretical group who wanted to claim them as its own, asserted that these four women were worthy teachers of the new covenant. He made no objection to their work on account of their sex; he just wanted to underscore that they were within the mainstream of the Christian

church. He also wrote of other women who were prophets, such as
Ammia of Philadelphia, without drawing attention to their sex. Other
writers mention Theonoe and Myrta, women who were prophets in the
orthodox tradition. (In addition, women were prominent as prophets in
some of the movements designated heretical.)[13] Apparently the office of
prophet gave way to martyrs and confessors in the third century, roles
that women as well as men played.

Teachers of Theology

From inscriptions and also literary sources we can observe that women
engaged in the public teaching of theology, in both monastic settings and
noneucharistic church worship. For instance, Marcella (ca. 325–410), a
wealthy widow in Rome, participated publicly in the theological debates of
her day. She also set up a school where male and female ascetics, theologians, and clergy gathered to learn and discuss theology. Many times she is
characterized as a student of the prominent biblical scholar and translator
Jerome, though she was a theologian in her own right before he arrived in
Rome and they became acquainted. She was so wise in her interpretations
of Scripture that after Jerome left Rome, clergy and other serious students
of the Bible went to her to learn what obscure passages meant.[14]

There are other women who functioned as theological teachers as well
in the 300s, women such as Proba, who recast some Bible stories using
lines from Virgil. Her work the *Cento* was used widely to instruct in the
Bible long into the Middle Ages. Another aristocratic, and therefore well-
educated, woman was Melania the Elder, who came into conflict with the
powerful Jerome and became the first of many wealthy Roman women
who went to Palestine to set up monastic houses there. Her granddaughter
Melania the Younger founded monasteries in North Africa and in Jerusalem, and devoted her life to the study of Scripture and to the instruction of men and women in the Bible. Two other women associated with
Jerome, Paula and Eustochium, moved to Jerusalem and set up a double
monastic house—one with a men's section and a women's section—as
well as a hostel for pilgrims who traveled to the Holy Land. This means
the two women were spiritual guides to many people of both sexes.

Macrina, the older sister of Basil the Great and Gregory of Nyssa,
taught Christian theology. After her death, Gregory, himself one of the
great writers of the church in the East, referred to her as a "second
Thecla," emphasizing her teaching ministry, and in another place he
called her a "Christian Socrates." He praised her as an outstanding ex-
positor of Scripture as well as a teacher of theology, philosophy, and
science. Eisen notes: "This example shows that even for an 'outstanding
representative of orthodoxy' like Gregory of Nyssa a woman's teaching

presented no problem and required no accompanying restrictions. In his literary work he clearly acknowledges Macrina's theological superiority."[15] The other brother, Basil the Great, is credited with the establishment of monasticism in the Greek-speaking eastern part of the Roman Empire, and Eastern Orthodox religious houses are still Basilian, acknowledging that debt. However, it should be noted that Macrina had already set up a religious community for women, and she persuaded Basil to give up his vain life and pursue a monastic vocation, which he began with four years under her guidance.[16]

Inscriptions highlight other women honored by husbands or monastic communities as "teachers," such as (another) Theodora in Rome. On her tomb, erected by her husband, the inscription includes the line: "She, the best keeper of the law and the best teacher of the faith."[17] In Macedonia, yet another Theodora was honored, this time by the monastic community of which she was the head, as teacher and spiritual mother. "The teacher Kuria" is mentioned in a papyrus letter.[18] This evidence suggests that the acceptance of women as teachers and leaders was more widespread and long lasting than had been thought.

Presbyters

Inscriptions also demonstrate that women were called presbyters, or priests, in the East until sometime in the fourth century and in the West longer than that. The designation presbyter on inscriptions occurs in the East (in Greece, Asia Minor, Egypt), as well as in the West (Sicily, Italy, Dalmatia), on eleven surviving inscriptions.[19] As with inscriptions bearing men's names, these women's names do not represent all the women who held this office. Literary documents such as the fifth-century *Acts of Philip* contain lists of ministers that explicitly name women presbyters.[20] Also, there are prohibitions that underscore women's activity at the altar: for instance, although the Synod of Laodicea in the fourth century forbade the sacramental activity of women at the altar, in 494 Pope Gelasius wrote in a letter to all the bishops in parts of southern Italy and Sicily: "Nevertheless we have heard to our annoyance that divine affairs have come to such a low state that women are encouraged to officiate at the sacred altars, and to take part in all matters imputed to the offices of the male sex, to which they do not belong."[21] Not only were women exercising sacerdotal functions, but clearly they were being encouraged to this activity by their own congregations and quite possibly by their bishops as well. The practice persisted, for in 829 a letter to the emperor from at least some of the bishops describes their efforts to keep women from the altar:

We have attempted in every way possible . . . to prevent women from approaching the altar, as it is forbidden. Since we have learned from a report from reliable persons that in some provinces, contrary to divine law and canonical ordinances women enter the sanctuary, shamelessly take hold of the consecrated vessels, hand the sacerdotal vestments to the priests, and—more monstrous, improper, and inappropriate than all else—give the people the Body and Blood of the Lord . . . we have attempted to prevent these things, so that they may not spread.[22]

This suggests that women's ecclesial and sacramental roles were disputed for many centuries, that acceptable practice was varied as well as changing, and that the changes were not necessarily linked to Scripture or apostolic practice but to the increasingly male-dominated social situation.

Deacons/Deaconesses

Probably many people who hear the word "deaconess" imagine a very different role from that of "deacon," since many modern churches assign completely disparate tasks to women and men respectively. However, in the first centuries of the Christian era this was not the case, since male and female deacons assisted with baptism and with eucharistic worship and engaged in ministry to the poor and sick. The second-century document *Didascalia Apostolorum* gives guidelines about the appointment of male and female deacons who would serve as assistants to the bishops. The female deacons were instructed to involve themselves in ministry to women, including anointing women being baptized (though men should still speak the divine names over those being baptized) and instructing the newly baptized women in the life of faith. In addition, the female deacons would bring communion to pregnant women, as well as to the sick in the congregation who were female.[23]

In fact, the very term "deaconess" is misleading because in written documents as well as inscriptions on graves and church memorials, women were referred to using the masculine form of the noun, and we have no examples of the female form being used until the fourth century. Women, starting with Phoebe in Romans 16, were simply referred to as "deacons," using the masculine form of the word. Then there were a couple of centuries in which the terms "deacon" and "deaconess" were used interchangeably for women; the masculine form, "deacon," was still applied to women as late as the sixth century.[24] This widespread and long-lasting use of the term "deacon" underscores the office rather than the gender of the person filling it; in any case, male and female deacons were ordained and considered part of the clergy, particularly in the East. The ordinations of the males and females were parallel, although the prayer spoken over women included the names of biblical women prophets: "O Eternal God, the father of our Lord, Jesus Christ, Creator of man and woman, who filled with the Spirit Miriam and Deborah and Anna and Huldah, who did not disdain that your only begotten son should be born of a woman . . . now also, look upon your servant" (*Apostolic Constitutions* 8.20.1–2). Even the Council of Chalcedon (451), in Canon 15, recognized that female deacons were ordained, though they weren't to be ordained until the age of forty. In the Emperor Justinian's *Novellae* (New Laws) articles sometimes included female deacons in discussions of the clergy and sometimes referred to them as distinct from the clergy.[25]

It used to be assumed that female deacons had to be celibate, either virgins or widows, but clearly this was not a universal rule, since some female deacons were honored by their husbands in their burials. Some, in fact, were part of complex families: Sophia, for instance, was called a deacon on her gravestone and also "the second Phoebe," in honor of the Phoebe in Romans 16.[26] Obviously the inscriptions do not inform readers of the precise activity of these women, but "they testify to the expansion of the office, especially during the fourth, fifth, and sixth centuries."[27] Archaeologists have uncovered gravestones, altar pieces, rood screens, and mosaic tiles in countries all the way from Western Europe to the Middle East which name women as deacons or deaconesses. Even the persecutor of Christians, Pliny, reports in a letter to Emperor Trajan in 111 CE the arrest of two female slaves who were known to fellow Christians as *ministrae* or deaconesses.[28] There is no description of what that role involved, though it had some official status.

Martyrs

Though we are beginning to hear more of modern-day martyrs around the world, the role of martyr in the early church may be less familiar to us than some of the other positions that women (and men) held in that era. Clearly, in the arena, women being martyred had the opportunity to publicly testify to their faith, and in this way participate significantly in the mission of the church. But more than that, "martyr" was an important classification of officially recognized heroes in the early church, and the stories of martyrdom developed into a new, incredibly popular genre of devotional literature. In addition, congregations began to celebrate the holy lives and courageous deaths of these women and men on the anniversary of the martyrdom of each, which became known as the feast day of that particular martyr. Through the stories and the feast days, the church remembered these male and female heroes and held up their faith for others to emulate.

For instance, in *The Martyrs of Lyons* (177–178) we can read of a woman named Blandina, whose courage and fortitude wearied those who were taking turns torturing her. At one point she is tied to a stake so that wild animals will make short work of her, but they refuse to touch her. The one reporting these events observes: "She seemed to hang there in the form of a cross, and by her fervent prayer she aroused intense enthusiasm in those who were undergoing their ordeal, for in their torment with their physical eyes they saw in the person of their sister him who was crucified for them."[29] Centuries later, the Roman Catholic Church would declare that only men could represent Christ, and therefore only men were fitted for ministry, but in these early years Blandina's cruciform dying reminded her biographer of Jesus.[30]

In another famous account, two young mothers, Perpetua and Felicitas, faced death on account of their faith. Felicitas, a servant of Perpetua, is scheduled for execution but, much to her dismay, given a reprieve due to the advanced stage of her pregnancy. After the birth of her baby in a prison cell, she meets the wild animals, glad not to have been disqualified on the basis of her childbearing. Perpetua, who wrote the main body of the narrative and who herself had recently given birth, claims that the Lord calmed her longings for her own new baby and dried up the flow of milk to her breasts. In a last-ditch attempt to get her to recant, Perpetua's father brings the baby boy to visit her, but her faith overcomes the regret of leaving her own baby behind. That both Perpetua and Felicitas faced martyrdom willingly despite their own young children is not a devaluing of motherhood but a testimony to the power of their faith.[31]

The stories of the martyrs are in part evangelism, intended to encourage readers to a similar courage, and in part they are theodicy, an attempt of the persecuted to make sense of and even experience some sort of victory through their suffering. But these texts also functioned to glorify images of women's strength and to demonstrate their powerful participation in the mission of the Christian community.

Widows

For the first three centuries of the church, the order of widows was the most numerous and prominent group of women in the church.[32] The question is, what was their role? Were they simply objects of charity, receiving from the largess of the Christian community, or were they workers in the church, contributing to its ministry? At the birth of the church recounted in Acts, providing for widows immediately comes to the fore, and Stephen and others undertake this first service job mentioned in the New Testament. When a woman enrolled as a "widow," it could be that she was showing her need to draw support and security from her local Christian community.

However, Anna, the prophet who was residing in the temple at the time of Jesus' birth, serves as a prototype for the widow role formulated later in the Christian community.[33] She was elderly, widowed, and devoted to prayer, fasting, and teaching. We have indications that in the second century this second meaning is intended when women enrolled as widows, since it is often clear that they are not supported by the church, but instead have some ministry function within it. Though the roles varied regionally, they had approved responsibilities in the redeemed community revolving around prayer and fasting, and also in a wide variety of other activities, such as caring for the sick, giving theological instruction, testing the deaconesses, and anointing women being baptized.[34]

Women in Early Monasticism

Choosing celibacy was another way for early Christians to testify to their faith with their lives. Women as well as men became hermits in great numbers; in fact, if we are to believe the estimates of the wandering monk Palladius, in the fourth century, about ten thousand men went out into the desert, whereas approximately twenty thousand women fled to remote areas to concentrate on their spirituality.[35] Books such as *Forgotten Desert Mothers* have begun to fill in gaps in our knowledge, introducing readers to women such as Amma Theodora and Amma Synkletica, desert mothers whose teaching skills and wisdom earned them the title "teacher" in the early centuries of the monastic movement in Egypt.[36] Gradually some of these hermits formed communities with one another, and agreed to live according to the rules devised by the founder or adopted from the popular Rule of St. Benedict. Early on, this gave some women the opportunity to serve as spiritual leaders to communities of women.

That so many people found this to be an attractive option is due to biblical as well as cultural influences. The celibate ideal was partly drawn from the example of Jesus, who was perfectly pure and single, and his mother, Mary, who was recast in the fourth century as perpetually virginal. The apostle Paul explicitly stated his wish that all could be single as he was, so that they would have no entanglements distracting them from this urgent work (1 Cor. 7). But celibacy was also largely rooted in cultural assumptions about the opposition between the spiritual realm, which was thought to be good, and the physical realm, which was deemed evil. Christian thinkers imported this negative view of the material world into their writing. Rejecting the idea of a good creation that God can and does speak through, they taught that the physical world and its delights detracted from the spiritual life. Many celibates, therefore, forswore not only sexual relations but also food that tasted good, comfortable clothing, beds, a full night's sleep, and everything else that might give the body pleasure.

In the writings of some male church leaders, the negative pronouncements about the body intensified when it came to the female body, a fact that is not surprising, perhaps, given that they were celibates struggling against sexual thoughts about women. (Unfortunately, happily married people were not the ones writing theology, or Christian thinking about sexuality and physicality might have been very different.) So, for instance, women were encouraged not to bathe very often because of the shamefulness of their bodies. And, because Eve was assumed to be sexually weak and therefore vulnerable to the temptation presented to her, all women were considered sexually weak as well as dangerous. Tertullian (ca. 160–220) expressed these sentiments:

> And do you not know that you are (each) an Eve? The sentence of God on this sex of yours lives in this age: the guilt must of necessity live too. *You* are the devil's gateway: *you* are the unsealer of that forbidden tree: *you* are the first deserter of the divine law: *you* are she who persuaded him whom the devil was not valiant enough to attack. *You* so easily destroyed God's image, man. On account of *your* desert—that is, death—even the Son of God had to die.[37]

Because of this, he believed that women should not adorn themselves with beautiful things, but should constantly be in mourning because of the guilt they had inherited from Eve. Clement of Alexandria (ca. 150–215) agreed, since he taught that "a woman should blush for very shame that she was of the same gender as Eve."[38] Later writers such as Jerome (ca. 340–420) and Ambrose (ca. 340–397) picked up on this idea and instructed women to weep and mourn because they were women.

Since sexuality became linked to the first sin and the ruin of the human race, virginity then came to symbolize salvation and the purity of the church. However, because all women were thought to be sexual by nature by virtue of this link to Eve, their celibacy was assigned a different meaning by male writers. A man, it was thought, elevated his nature through a denial of his sexuality, whereas a woman transcended hers. In fact, writers such as Jerome went so far as to call virginal women "female men of God," or those who have overcome their femaleness. In fact, at the turn of the third century, a burning question in North Africa was: are virgins still women?[39]

Male writers had quite a bit to say about how women should act, and why. They deemed daily fasting appropriate for women because food was thought to incite sexual passions, whereas drinking water and eating simple vegetables would cool these passions. Jerome believed that the ideal woman living in Christian community would be pale and thin from fasting or, even better, she would hide her face, because "Jesus is jealous. He does not choose that your face should be seen of others."[40] In addition, women's talking was considered inappropriate, not only because it was active rather than passive, but also because it was associated with openness and looseness. Silence was preferable, since it symbolized their being virginal and closed. This, at least, was what some of the prominent male writers thought. How much women in monastic communities believed this, or lived up to it, is another thing entirely.[41]

For the women themselves, celibacy may have been attractive for a number of reasons. First of all, it represented the highest spiritual calling, according to church teaching at that time, and to choose it demonstrated what they considered most important about their lives, that is, their spiritual health. The life of study and worship appealed to thousands of women, often to the distress of parents, particularly those of the nobility. Asceticism represented a rebellion against a woman's family and the social expectations laid upon her. Eastern church writer John Chrysostom (347–407), in his treatise *On Virginity*, compared the betrothal of young aristocratic women to slaves waiting to see who their future masters were going to be; the families made the decision while the daughter was shut inside. A life of celibacy also meant avoidance of the restrictions placed on women by marriage, restrictions due to the large number of pregnancies and the potentially fatal stress of childbirth, but more especially due to a lifestyle that required being a servant to their husbands. In fact, historian Joyce Salisbury has found that women in these early centuries expressed more sentiment against marriage itself and the strictures it places on women than on sexuality, which so disgusted the male writers. For instance, a Spanish noblewoman, Theodora, likely wrote the story of Helia in the early fifth century, in which Helia decided as a child to be celibate, wanting "not to be subject to the curse of Eve, but rather to participate in the blessings of Mary."[42] Marriage and the resulting lack of freedom were the curse, rather than sexuality itself; the blessings of Mary had to do with freedom to stay in the house of God.

Of course there were severe rules to be followed in monastic houses as well, and therefore some scholars contend that religious women were just as constrained through monastic vows of obedience as other women were by their marraige vows. However, the meaning of obedience is different when the rules are shared among many, and when they are understood as beneficial to spiritual formation. Further, in asceticism a woman could construct her life in contradistinction to the social norms of the dominant culture, or even her own family's expectations. Rather than measure her success by a politically or economically advantageous marriage, or because of the number of heirs she bore to a family line, in monastic life her value was measured by a totally different standard: faithfulness to God. Women monastics lived under a set of rules that might seem onerous to us but that allowed the women to determine for themselves a different shape for their lives. The monastic houses themselves often had quite a bit of leeway in determining the nature of the community; some of them, in fact, were answerable directly to the pope with no bishop overseeing them.[43] In any case, the ideals expressed by men regarding women's silence and enclosure were often subtly reconfigured by women, or disregarded altogether.

Perhaps it would be appropriate to close the chapter with a glimpse at a fourth-century woman named Melania. Her story was very popular, and thus presumably attractive to women and influential in helping them think about their lives. Melania was one of the many ascetics whose activities were described by Palladius, a monk who traveled around to monastic communities and wrote what he observed himself and the stories he heard. Palladius tells us that Melania encountered a woman named Alexandra, who had herself enclosed in a tomb with a hole for receiving food, a hole so small no one could see her. Why? asked Melania. "A man was distracted in mind because of me, and rather than scandalize a soul made in the image of God, I betook myself alive to a tomb, lest I seem to cause him suffering or reject him." Shocked, Melania asked her how she spent her time. The reply: "Spin, pray, rehearse patriarchs, prophets, apostles, martyrs." This answer would have pleased the patristic writers, but Melania simply walked away, not interested in hiding or spinning.[44]

A couple of other vignettes from Melania's life introduce her miracles. First she saved a woman from the surgeon's knife when he was about to cut out an undelivered stillborn baby. In this story she explicitly rejected the idea that reproduction is filthy and affirmed that no bodily part is vile since all were created by God. Her view stands in contrast to that of many male writers for whom reproduction was despised in the overall negative attitude toward sexuality and toward women's bodies, which were considered particularly odious. Besides, Melania noted, all "patriarchs, prophets, apostles and other saints" were born through the birth canal, which means it isn't intrinsically evil, as her male opponents argued. Her other two miracles addressed women gripped by demons that had closed their mouths. They couldn't talk or eat and were consequently in danger of starving. This, we might note, was precisely what the advice of the church fathers for women tended toward; it is the logical conclusion of their instruction to be silent and to fast as signs of being closed, pure, and virginal. Melania's miracle? To open their mouths again.[45]

Conclusions

Given the recent scholarship about women's official positions in the church, we can see what was invisible before: that women functioned in all sorts of officially recognized roles, from widow and martyr to deacon, presbyter, and bishop. Some women also carried on ministries, including serving the sacraments, that received approval on the local level but earned them severe censure from higher up in the church hierarchy. The clues continue to mount that our old assumptions about women's silence and passivity in the early church have to be revised.

Additionally, when we consider the hugely popular stories of women such as Thecla, Nino, Melania, and others, we find that women did not fully embrace the more negative assessments of female bodies given by male church writers; in fact, they called into question the men's overall devaluing of women by celebrating the strength, wit, and holiness of these women heroes.

8

ABBESSES, MYSTICS, AND REFORMATION WOMEN

Women in the Medieval Western Church

As in the earlier centuries, most women and men in Western society in the Middle Ages worked simply to push their lives forward. Since most did not live the privileged life of the nobility, they had to grow enough to eat, to pay the manor lord, and to keep their children alive. For peasants in that era (as for many in ours), everyone had to contribute to the family economy just to subsist.

However, some families were neither noble nor peasant but developed home industries that required the joint labor of men, women, and children. If her husband died, or went off to find glory in a crusade, a woman often perpetuated the family business, which meant that even in the medieval era some women were financially independent. In *Between Pit and Pedestal: Women in the Middle Ages*, Marty Williams and Anne Echols examine data such as tax records from various European cities and discover that women were involved in hundreds of professions, including both the typically feminine, such as thread and ribbon making, yarn spinning, silk spinning, candle making, laundry, street vending, and ale making and selling, and also surprising businesses such as money lending and running apothecaries. Women owned interests in trading ships, or owned the ships, or even owned shipping enterprises. Cologne had some female town assessors and women involved in customs and setting tolls for toll roads. Women worked in bookmaking, even outside convents, and in illustrating, selling, and repairing them as well. Starting with a Dominican convent at Nuremberg, women entered the carpet making trade. And women were lay doctors, barbers, surgeons, druggists, and, of course, midwives and nurses. Some of these women may very well have understood their work as their vocation, as service to God and humanity, though the records are slim. Space does not permit a comprehensive description of women's work in various professions, and the ensuing discussion will continue the focus on women in the church, but the information above should at least caution us against assuming that women were either monastics or wives tending the home fires.

In order to understand how women functioned in the church in the Middle Ages, the next sections will offer examples of women's various public roles in the medieval church. First of all there were the queens who converted their pagan husbands, introducing whole regions of early medieval Europe to the Christian faith. Other wealthy women founded and funded monasteries, and often led them as well. These abbesses, the spiritual and managerial heads of abbeys, were often immensely influential in their regions and in the lives of the men and women in their monastic houses. Other abbesses, as we shall see, were playwrights, musicians, theologians, artists, poets, and preachers. Finally we will examine the ideals and practices of the Beguine movement, in which women rejected rules of enclosure but vowed to commune with each other for spiritual development and service to the poor.

Christianizing Queens

Clotilde was a Christian princess married off by her father to Clovis, the pagan king of the Franks. She convinced him to allow their first son to be baptized, but when the baby died, he thought that demonstrated the superiority of goddess worship. Finally he himself was baptized along with three thousand of his men, after this new faith seemed to help him win a battle (echoes of Constantine). One historian observes: "Clotilde accomplished what none of the clergy, Arian or Catholic, could seemingly bring about."[1] Such influence apparently ran in families, since Clotilde's great-granddaughter, Bertha, was married to Ethelbert, the pagan king of Kent. At her request Pope Gregory the Great sent a retinue of missionaries headed by Augustine (known now as Augustine of Canterbury). On Christmas Day 597 Ethelbert and ten thousand Anglo-Saxons were baptized, thanks not only to Augustine of Canterbury and the rest of the delegation from Italy, but to Bertha, the Christian queen. Pope Gregory expressed his thanks to her in a letter extolling her as another "Helena," the Christian mother of Constantine.[2]

Wealthy women also promoted Christianity by founding and funding convents. Their wealth helped establish Christian presence and Christian practice in areas that were pagan or only nominally Christian. Families of the nobility were concerned about the amount of money directed to these religious houses, either to which noble princesses retired or which they simply supported. From the seventh century on, both in England and on the continent, charters for convents show the generosity of wealthy women, and most notably queens, who could bequeath huge parcels of land to found religious communities.[3] The royal nuns at Kent had enough money at their disposal to fund Boniface's mission work in Germany. "Abbess Eadburh of Thanet ruled a double monastery with extensive lands, a fleet in the isle's harbor, and a large, expensive scriptorium and library. Eadburh thought nothing of Boniface's request that she have Peter's epistles copied in gold for him,"[4] and this in addition to the books and vestments she had already sent.

In Anglo-Saxon England, women could inherit and bequeath land, livestock, household furnishings, clothing, jewels, books, and slaves among other things. They could swear legal oaths and receive compensation for crimes committed against them or people under their care (rights that were lost to them following the Norman conquest). Women of certain classes ran autonomous households and could dispose of their property independently of male relatives. While lower-class women were employed as wet nurses, corn grinders, weavers, serving maids, and seamstresses, women of more means engaged in a variety of occupations including baking, cheese making, and the production of lace and fine embroidery, even for religious purposes such as making the stole of St. Cuthbert.[5]

Abbesses

It is not surprising, then, that in the seventh and eighth centuries the church in Anglo-Saxon England offered significant opportunities for women to exercise leadership. It was during those years that the great double monasteries—a men's house and a women's house together under one head—were founded and led by women such as Hild (or Hilda) of Whitby. Hild (614–680) established several monasteries in East Anglia and was the abbess of the double house at Whitby from 657 until her death. This means she was the spiritual leader for the men and women monastics who had taken vows there. Under her care and supervision, Whitby became the focal point of religious life in that region; for instance, during that time the Synod of Whitby (664) was convened to settle the question of when to celebrate Easter, and she sanctioned the first religious verse in the Old English language. Not only that, but Bede, the eighth-century church historian, observed that under her guidance Whitby was "a nursery for bishops" since five bishops were nurtured and trained there.[6]

Among other prominent Anglo-Saxon women religious, another bears mention here: Leoba (Leobgyth, 700–779). She was a nun, highly respected for her learning and her holy life at a convent in Wimborne, until she was invited by her relative, Boniface, the most famous missionary to what is now Germany, to assist him by establishing women's monastic houses in that country. Despite her abbess's reluctance to let her go, she traveled to Germany, taking along some other nuns, and began her work as abbess in the convent she set up. Known throughout the region as an erudite person, she became a close personal friend and spiritual mentor to Queen Hiltigard, who put pressure on her to live at the court with her and Charlemagne in Aachen. Princes and bishops came to her for advice: "because of her wide knowledge of the Scriptures and her prudence in counsel they often discussed spiritual matters and ecclesiastical discipline with her."[7] Leoba declined a place at court in favor of continuing her ministry of teaching Scripture and theology in monastic houses in northern Germany and encouraging the monks and nuns to holy living.[8]

Boniface considered her a peer and admired her skill, according to her biographer, and he

> commended her to . . . the senior monks of the monastery who were present, admonishing them to care for her with reverence and respect and reaffirming his wish that after his death her bones should be placed next to his in the tomb, so that they who had served God during their lifetime with equal sincerity and zeal should await together the day of resurrection.[9]

However, when she died, the monks at Fulda declined to bury her with Boniface; they were afraid that her popularity would result in a stream of pilgrims, men and women, who would demand entrance to the monastery to honor her.

Like Leoba, other abbesses over double monasteries garnered the respect of men and women under their tutelage and spiritual care and functioned as spiritual leaders to men and women. In these establishments, the vows of new members, both male and female, would be made to the abbess just as they would be made to an abbott, and obedience was due the abbess as the superior. Apparently not all men were happy with this setup: there is a document that contains deliberations about how to handle a monk who refused to genuflect before his Mother Superior because of her sex, and what to do about a nun who then refused to kneel before this same monk/priest in the confessional.[10] But this case seems to be the exception that proved the rule. Thousands of monks lived in monastic houses and did not fuss about offering their highest respect and obedience to a woman, or receiving their spiritual guidance from her.

Furthermore, the abbesses functioned as quasi-bishops, holding authority not only over their monastic houses but over the surrounding regions, and exercising not just ecclesiastical and spiritual leadership but civil control as well. This happened because some monasteries, and even religious orders, were granted permission to come directly under papal protection, which meant they were free from any local bishops' interference. The women's Benedictine community at Brindisi, Italy, for instance, oversaw the thirty-six churches in the villages on monastery land, and the Clerkenwell community, an order of canonesses, controlled territory in eleven counties around London, and had authority over sixty-four parishes there until Henry VIII gave this jurisdiction to the bishop of London.[11] The abbesses of these communities were the spiritual and legal overseers of all the people in their monasteries' lands.

This phenomenon, of abbesses holding quasi-bishop status, occurred in monastic houses all over Europe, in what are now France, Germany, Italy, and Spain. Some of the abbesses were even called bishops on their tombstones; in addition to Theodora (see chap. 7), there is an inscription to *episcopa Terni* (Bishop Terni) mentioned in the Council of Tours, and in the cemetery of the Basilica St. Valentiniane an inscription says (*Hono*) *rabilis feminia episcopa* (Honorable Woman Bishop). As historian Joan Morris puts it, the church has forgotten, but the very stones cry out.[12]

For abbesses who headed convents, the ordination ceremony was identical to that of abbots, and the garments and jewelry worn were indicative of the abbesses' pastoral and episcopal office. Just like bishops and abbots, abbesses wore the alb, a long robe worn over secular garments; the stole, a band of silk draped over the shoulders; the crozier, the staff that resembles a shepherd's crook; the pectoral cross; the ring, sometimes even inherited from a bishop; gloves; and a miter, or liturgical headdress.[13] Tellingly, if you look up "crozier" or "miter" in a modern dictionary, you will likely read that these are items used by bishops and abbots and symbolize high liturgical office; this shows the lack of awareness that abbesses were invested with the same authority by the same symbols. Even the women in the communities were sometimes referred to with liturgical titles such as *sacerdotes*, which is the Latin term used to designate priests in some places in the Vulgate (the Latin version of the Bible translated by Jerome in 405 CE). The woman who headed a group of canonesses was sometimes ordained as *Sacerdos*

Maxima, and sometimes as an archdeacon. A medieval German historian describes a terrible storm in which the "priests of both sexes" were hit by lightning.[14]

The point of all this is to demonstrate that women have participated in the work of the church in surprisingly powerful and prominent ways, though the memory of their work has mostly been lost in the selective writing of history. In another telling example, we have the fact that Oxford University grew from its roots in a double monastic house founded by a noblewoman, Frideswide (680–727). According to the most reliable account of her life, she refused the man her parents chose for her and fled to a remote spot. When her suitor chased her down and found her, he was struck blind, as the story goes, and Frideswide had to restore his sight.[15] At that place, where Christ Church, Oxford, now stands, she founded her religious community of men and women, which under her care became a center of learning and intellectual innovation. Her feast day is still celebrated in Oxford (October 19) at her shrine, which was destroyed in 1528 in Henry VIII's dissolution of the monasteries, but renovated in the nineteenth century. In the words of a medieval English scholar, Frideswide was the one "whose leadership was the initial heartbeat of the ecclesial, academic and civic life in Oxford."[16] Ironically, women were not allowed to matriculate into Oxford University until the twentieth century.

Happily, in the past thirty years books, letters, poems, plays, and songs written by women religious in the Middle Ages have been uncovered at an astounding rate. Whereas scholars used to assume that we couldn't know much about women's lives and spirituality in that era because of a lack of texts, we now have firsthand accounts that allow fascinating glimpses into their worlds. Hildegard of Bingen (1098–1179) is a good example. Most people had never heard of her a few decades ago, but now her theological visions have been translated and retranslated from Latin into many modern languages; volumes of her letters and her poems have been released; her music has been recorded by modern musicians; her artwork with its rich symbolic sets of meaning is reproduced for book covers and posters; and her book of medicine has been made available to those who enjoy homeopathic remedies.

Why the Hildegard craze? For one thing, she was gifted in so many areas, as theologian, poet, composer, artist, doctor, and also preacher. For another, her life and activity belie the idea that only men contributed and can contribute to the church and to society. Born in 1098 to a noble family in central Germany, she entered a cell with a hermit woman, Jutta, when she was eight years old. Her parents considered her their tithe to God since she was the tenth child, but also gave her up to a religious life because she claimed to have visions from God even as a child. Other noble families left their daughters under Jutta's care, and soon there was a women's community attached to the men's Benedictine house at a place called Disibodenberg. When Jutta died, Hildegard became the abbess and moved the women down the Rhine River, where she set up an independent women's house. There she wrote a long theological book called *Scivias*, which was purportedly based on a vision she had, though some scholars suggest she framed it as a vision because otherwise no one would read a book of theology written by a woman. In any case, the bishop of Mainz thought it was beautiful and helpful, so he promoted it to the pope, who also found it inspiring and therefore gave his blessing for Hildegard to go on preaching tours in southern Germany and France. She wrote poetry and music for the sisters in her convent to use in worship, and she put together a book of medicine, since like many Benedictine leaders, she learned basic healing skills to minister to her sisters and to those who came to the convent seeking help. Her letters demonstrate that she was a politically astute person, as she instructed the pope to act better, carried on a correspondence with Eleanor of Aquitaine, and advised Eleanor's husband, King Henry I of England, to do his job better as well. Despite all this, she called herself "a feather on the breath of God."[17]

Though Hildegard was exceptionally talented, she was not unique in the scope of her influence. Almost two centuries earlier, Hroswitha of Gandersheim (ca. 932–1002) made her mark in poetry, drama, and writing of history. She was not an abbess but a canoness at the abbey at Gandersheim in Saxony. This abbey was a center of female learning in western Europe; it boasted an excellent school for girls of the nobility and a large library; it minted its own coins; the abbess had a seat on the imperial diet (court); and she had her own army for defending the holdings of the abbey. Hroswitha took advantage of all of this, reading widely in the classical authors and also in early Christian writers. But rather than simply reiterate their negative view of women, she playfully takes the stereotypes of women as lascivious wretches who tempt men, and recasts them as courageous heroes who defend the gospel and chastity against paganism and preying men. She was the first Christian dramatist and the first Saxon poet and historian; in all, she wrote six plays, eight legends, two epics, and a short poem, and defended her writing by linking her talent to the gift of God and her actual writing to the strength of God. As part of her defense, but also implicitly as a call to other women, she wrote: "I was eager that the talent given to me by heaven should not grow rusty from neglect."[18] In the end she also refers to herself as "the Strong Voice of Gandersheim."

Thousands of women whose names are not remembered participated in monastic life in the Middle Ages. More women than men founded religious orders and set up religious houses, so that from the seventh century until the Reformation there were twice as many nuns as monks. This is not surprising, given that convents were the only place where a woman could develop a life of study and prayer, and also spend her life in roles of spiritual usefulness. There they could be intercessors for the souls of their loved ones, the church, and the civil rulers, but also engage in copying Scripture manuscripts, educating the children of nobility, and offering succor to the sick and the poor. A study of French nuns in the eleventh to thirteenth centuries found that, despite the writings of the early church fathers calling on them to deny their female selves, these women saw themselves as whole religious people. In the society outside their cloisters, they were treated as "religious," meaning monastic, in the same way that men were, and this was their primary understanding of themselves.[19] They were busy with the same things as their male counterparts: prayer, holy living, education of the young, and service to the poor. They often felt at liberty to engage in theological reflection.

Beguines

In the thirteenth century, when urbanization was gaining momentum in northern Europe, a lay women's movement centered in the Low Countries began to create a different space for women to live out their lives. Refusing the strict rules of enclosure that were placed on female monastics by the Catholic hierarchy, the first Beguines simply intended to pray, study Scripture, discuss spiritual issues among themselves, and serve the poor in their cities. At the outset, most remained in their families, though gradually some chose to live in small groups to encourage each other in lives of worship and charity. By the end of the century, there were communities called Beguinages, which were small cities in and of themselves, replete with churches, hospitals, cemeteries, streets lined with convents, and also small houses where the older or wealthier Beguines could choose to live. The movement was never formally organized into a religious order, and the women involved never took vows of chastity or poverty, though many lived virginal lives and chose to earn money in order to give to the poor.

The Beguines functioned without official sanction, since they made the church hierarchy uneasy for a number of reasons. First, they resisted enclosure, refusing to stay hidden within convent walls, though the church imposed this (with varying degrees of success) on traditional religious women for centuries. Second, and related to this, the Beguines in cities all over Europe insisted on lives of meditation coupled with activity. They preferred to work in order to support themselves and, as mentioned, to alleviate others' suffering. That the individual women or their groups were self-supporting meant that poor women could be part of the movement, whereas only wealthy women with significant dowries had been welcomed into Benedictine houses throughout the Middle Ages. And third, their spirituality involved visions and a profound emotional component, as evidenced by the writings of some of the prominent women involved. In an age of swooning, courtly love poetry, they wrote of intense longing for God, using many images for the intimate relationship between the soul and God by capitalizing on bride imagery.

Hadewijch of Antwerp, for instance, employed the conventions of courtly love poetry in her writing, in which the faithful lover-knight longs for the lady, who proves to be fickle and demanding. Strikingly, however, she casts the soul as the constant knight and God as the *minne*, the fickle lady, because the sense of God's presence is sometimes there and sometimes not.[20] But, according to Hadewijch, it is the very absence of God and the desire that this darkness creates that draws the soul to union with God. She believed that when she loved those around her, but received only scorn in return, she could identify with God in Christ's humanity; in the suffering of human life we find Christ. Typical of the Beguine writers, hers is a mysticism based on daily interactions with others, not a withdrawal from the world.

Conclusion

Many other women could be mentioned here whose writing demonstrates their profound engagement with God, wise interaction with the powerful ecclesiastical and civil authorities, and respected spiritual leadership. Some of these women wrote in Latin, such as Hildegard, in order to enter the theological conversations of their day, but most chose to write in the vernacular, and their works are often among the first pieces of literature in their respective mother tongues.

Women in Reformation Europe

The Reformation changed the religious playing field for everyone, but it had particular implications for women. For most people (since most were married), the more positive assessment of marriage was a welcome development. The Catholic reformer Erasmus, for instance, asserted that wedlock, not monasticism, is the holiest kind of life, and in this assessment he is affirming something that male writers in the early church despised: sexuality in general and women's sexuality in particular. In his treatise *The Institution of Marriage*, Erasmus observes that marriage was instituted by God in paradise for human happiness, in contrast to other sacraments which were instituted on earth as remedies for human brokenness. "Jesus who presides at weddings, made us equal in so many ways. He redeemed us by the same death, he washed us in the same blood. . . . Forget about your birth, and hers; what about your rebirth? Can you consider her beneath you, when God accepts her as a daughter, and Christ as a sister?"[21] Luther agreed with Erasmus that marriage was superior to celibacy, but still did not embrace sexuality as a gift from God. In fact, he retained the old notion that sex always involved sin, demonstrated by the "bestial desire and lust" that it involved, but God overlooked the sin because of progeny. In his revulsion to sex he goes so far as to compare it to having a seizure.[22]

Another change grew from the Protestant reformers' different understanding of the authority of the church. Since the reformers touted the idea of the "priesthood of all believers," the role of the church and the clergy in salvation was diminished. Diane Willen, a scholar of early modern England, suggests that the Reformation effectively demoted the parish priest and elevated the male head of the household as the leader for spiritual development. Bringing religion into the home gave some women an increased role in the spiritual formation of their children. This, she suggests, spurred the Protestant reformers to be more concerned about women's proper place in the home and about women's definition of themselves as "goodwives" than earlier Christian writers had been.

However, this new emphasis on women's spiritual usefulness in the home, along with the Protestant practice of deemphasizing good works and dissolving religious orders, meant that places for women's spiritual work outside the home diminished. For instance, nuns had worked in St. Bart's hospital in London as part of their service to God, but after the Reformation nursing became a secular job in England. Willen observes: "The Reformation had brought the secularization of the hospitals and deprived single women of the option of holy orders. Rather than a spiritual avocation, their work had become menial employment."[23] Now the women who worked there toiled for incredibly low wages in horrible conditions.

In addition, all the Reformers attacked institutions that had exalted women or permitted their significant involvement: monasticism, feast days that honored female examples of Christian faithfulness, church processions in which women actively took part, and the veneration of Mary.[24] They effectively removed "the female element" in their expression of the faith, even visually; whereas at the front of churches worshipers previously may have seen Mary, and perhaps St. Margaret, St. Anne, and baby Jesus, now alongside the crucifix were only male Reformers or male evangelists.[25]

The Reformers generally married and proclaimed this a new freedom for monastic women, but were unable to see the loss of freedom that closing convents meant for thousands of women. Luther did push for universal education for all children, girls and boys, because like other Protestants he advocated lay reading of Scripture. Although this was good for the masses of girls, women no longer had a place for serious ongoing study. Men who left monasticism could still study or teach at universities (e.g., Martin Luther), and many became ministers in Protestant congregations. But no universities were open to women's study, let alone teaching, and, of course, women's spiritual leadership was rejected as well. Women who left monasticism generally lived like widows, if they were older, or they married and poured their lives into their families (e.g., Katarina Luther).

To live enclosed, or not live enclosed, that was the question, and significantly, a much higher percentage of women's communities than men's attempted to retain their way of life, even in Protestant areas. As an extreme example, when Duke Ernst of Brunswick introduced Protestant ideas in his territory, all the men's houses disbanded without pressure, and all the women's houses refused to listen to Protestant teachings. In the towns of Walsrode and Medingen the nuns locked the convent gates and fled to the choir in the chapel. Duke Ernst pleaded with them personally, but to no avail, so he had a hole smashed in the choir wall so that they would have to hear the Protestant sermon. In another town, Lune, the women sang through the Protestant sermon being imposed on them. In German territories many Catholic monastic houses persisted, either because the Lutheran nobles still wanted them, or because a ruler decided to allow them to dwindle on their own; in these cases, they would not be allowed to take in any novices. Some German princes allowed them to convert the entire house into a Protestant monastic establishment and retain their lifestyle. These examples demonstrate that it wasn't devotion to the pope, but the vitality of their own religious community and the lack of other meaningful options, that drove them to resist being disbanded. In England/Ireland the crown took the property, and monks and nuns went back to families or fled to the continent; in the Netherlands, all the houses were taken over as well.[26]

Sometimes nuns were forcibly removed, since they refused to leave their homes in their communities of women. The nuns in the Order of St. Clair, for instance, with their monastery surrounded, "soaked in the abundance of the wine of anguish, and sang compline in tears."[27] Family members were sent to beg them to come out; young men went to promise marriage to some of them; officials came to threaten the abbess with imprisonment if the sisters did not cooperate.

Yet there were also women who left monasteries and felt freed; probably this was especially true of women who had been put in a convent against their will in the first place. One noblewoman, Ursula of Munsterberg, published a tract in 1528 to correct her relatives' misinterpretation of her decision to leave the convent. She articulates a typical Protestant disdain for practices such as taking the vows, the worship of Mary, and being required to take the Lord's Supper even if not prepared. She compares life in the convent to a deadly swamp that pulls people down.[28]

According to the Reformers, then, women were free to leave convents, free to marry and use their teaching skills in their homes. But when women took the very Protestant notion of the "priesthood of all believers" too far, male leaders began to reassert restrictions on women. So, for instance, when Frau Voglin began preaching in the hospital church in Nuremberg in 1524, the city council took action against her. In 1521, several women were inspired by the preaching of Thomas Müntzer to begin preaching themselves, but by 1529 several of these women had been banished from the city. In fact, the city council was even against women getting together to discuss religious topics. In another German city, Memmingen, the city council decreed that maids could not speak of religion when they were drawing water at neighborhood wells. City councils tried to keep women from discussing the Bible, though none went as far as King Henry VIII of England, who, in 1543, forbade women to read the Bible. Women did engage in prophetic ministries, prophesying about the end of the world or, when war seemed imminent, about the fortunes of various leaders. One historian observes that they were taken as seriously as their male counterparts—which was not very much, except within small groups that accepted direct revelation.[29]

Both Luther and Calvin explicitly rejected the idea of women preaching. Luther observed that there might be exceptions—if no men were there to do it, for instance—but argued that women were less capable of preaching. Calvin allowed that there might be an occasion when a woman speaks, but the ordinances were for order and therefore Christians could not willingly abrogate this rule.[30]

Women did publish religious material, both Catholic women religious (nuns) and Protestant. These writers were for the most part noblewomen, though some middle-class women wrote hymns, religious poems, and polemical material. Argula von Grumbach was one such noblewoman; she complained in her "Letter to the University of Ingolstadt" about the violence against Catholics that Protestants were perpetrating. She linked herself to female biblical characters to justify her taking up the pen. Better to be punished by people, she said, than "to sin against God by keeping silent about the truth."[31] Her ideas were not addressed though she was called such lovely names as silly bag, female devil, heretical bitch, shameless whore, and wretched and pathetic daughter of Eve.[32]

Katherine Zell, married to the Swiss reformer Matthew Zell, like Katarina von Bora Luther, performed huge feats of hospitality as the Reformation produced refugees who needed lodging and new converts who desired to learn from the leaders. Zell, however, took up the pen on occasion, producing tracts that defended clergy marriage, her husband against libel, and, along the way, her right to take up the pen. Primarily her ministry focused on feeding and housing people and visiting people imprisoned for their faith. At her husband's funeral, she gave an address but had to justify it by comparing herself to Mary Magdalene, who did not aspire to be an apostle but who gave news of the resurrection to the disciples.[33]

The most public statement of faith, in the form of martyrdom, was made by women ranging from Anabaptists in Germany and the Low Countries to Catholics in England. Many of the Anabaptist women could articulate very fine points of theology supported by a broad and deep knowledge of Scripture. Their testimonies, like their sisters' in the early church, served to convert the skeptical and encourage the faithful as they made the ultimate sacrifice for their faith. And Catholic missionaries, such as Luisa de Carvajal in England, were imprisoned for spreading Catholicism. Specifically she was accused of being a priest in woman's clothing. Ironically, she had far more opportunities to promote her faith after being arrested. Other Catholic women suffered more than imprisonment. Margaret Clitherow, for instance, was crushed to death for harboring priests in her family home and for teaching children the Catholic Catechism.

Conclusions

During the Middle Ages thousands of (noble)women spent their lives in prayer and fasting, study and writing, worship and service, in the context of monastic communities. Some of the leaders of these communities exercised their considerable gifts in many areas of human life: music, literature, visual arts, politics, church renewal, theological reflection, and certainly spiritual direction. By the end of the era, lower-class women could join the Poor Claires or the Beguines and also pursue a religious vocation. Other laywomen simply participated in the life of the church through feast and fast days, through the celebration of mass and church festivals, and through pilgrimage and prayer.

With the arrival of the Reformation, the options for women's religious expression changed, and it is difficult to assess whether the Reformation improved the lot of women and in what areas, though it is easy to point to ways in which it limited their options for education and for leadership. The women who left the monasteries, unless they married a prominent Reformer, became invisible to history. Yet, if the primary religious focus for Protestants became the home, then for laywomen there may have been more intimate participation in the communal life of faith than for laywomen under Catholicism. The things of the faith, including the reading of Scripture, corporate prayer, and instruction of the young, were in their realm, rather than that of priests, monks, and nuns.

9

CHANGING THE WORLD

Women in Missions, Social Reform, and Church Work in American Evangelicalism

Two Windows of Opportunity for Women to Lead

In the mid seventeenth century, about a hundred years after Luther and Calvin died, a form of Protestantism arose that pushed the doctrine of the "priesthood of all believers" to its logical extreme. The Religious Society of Friends, known popularly as the Quakers, taught that God could and would speak to believers directly as they waited quietly for the inner light, so they rejected the structure (and the politics) of the Church of England and every other church; to them, traditional church was mere formalism. Of course, in a country where the monarch is the head of the church, to lambaste the church and its clergy publicly is tantamount to treason, and that, coupled with their pacifism and refusal to take oaths, made it fairly dangerous to be a Friend. However, George Fox, the first leader, found protection at Strathmore Hall, the estate of Margaret and Thomas Fell, after Margaret heard Fox preach in 1652 and was converted. (Thomas was a wealthy judge who was sympathetic to the Friends but never joined.) Margaret Fell worked tirelessly for the promotion of Quakerism: she hosted meetings at Strathmore Hall, offered long-term hospitality to Fox and other Quakers, pleaded before the king for the release of imprisoned Quakers, including Fox, and wrote sixteen books and countless tracts in support of Quaker beliefs. After Judge Fell died (1658), Margaret was subject to harassment and imprisonment for years at a time.

It wasn't just Friends' rejection of the institutional church that was offensive to critics, however, but the radical egalitarianism that character-ized them. From the beginning of the movement, the Friends explicitly affirmed the equality of all people in God's eyes and therefore invited all to speak in public assembly what God spoke in their inmost hearts. Women regularly testified to the inner light in local meetings, and many women traversed the countryside preaching; some even traveled to such far-flung places as the American colonies. Of the Quaker missionaries to Massachusetts Bay Colony in the seventeenth century, for instance, 40 percent were women, and this despite the fact that many faced imprison-ment in Boston for preaching their "peculiar doctrine" and some were hanged. Fell and a couple of her daughters went on preaching tours, closer to home in England, but encountered enough opposition because of their sex that she wrote a tract in 1666 with this heading:

Women's Speaking

Justified, Proved, and Allowed of by the Scriptures,
All such as speak by the Spirit and Power of the Lord Jesus.

And how Women were the first that Preached the Tidings of the Resurrec-tion of Jesus, and were sent by Christ's own Command, before he Ascended to the Father, John 20.17.

She argued from Genesis about the equality of men and women made in the image of God, from the Old and New Testament examples of women God empowered to prophesy, and from Jesus' treatment of women. With regard to the Pauline passages (1 Cor. 14 and 1 Tim. 2) she maintained that women who were tattlers or busybodies were forbidden by Paul to take authority, but that women who were part of the church were encouraged by Paul in other passages to pray, prophesy, and work hard on behalf of the gospel. She also argued from the prophecy in Genesis 3:15 that the seed of the woman would crush the head of the serpent, suggesting that since women are part of the woman's seed in Christ, then surely they will be active in crushing the work of the devil. Finally she suggested that since women as well as men are part of the bride of Christ, and in Revelation 22:17 the bride says "Come," then female Christians just as much as males should be calling people to Christ.[1]

Not quite fifty years after this tract came out, Susanna Wesley, a Church of England pastor's wife, came under fire for her spiritual leadership. While her husband, Samuel Wesley, was away for an extended time in London (around 1710), she began to hold Sunday evening prayers for her children and servants; this in itself was a lot of people, since she had nineteen children, ten of whom she raised to adulthood. Gradually these Sunday evening prayer services drew in the servants' families, the neighbors, and their friends, and soon the attendance had grown to more than two hundred people, even with some turned away at the door. The curate, the assistant minister, filling in for Samuel Wesley became jealous because his evening service drew only twenty to twenty-five people, so he wrote to Samuel that Mrs. Wesley was holding an "illegal conventicle." Samuel wrote a couple of times telling Susanna to desist, but this was her reply:

> If you do, after all, think fit to dissolve this assembly, do not tell me that you desire me to do it, for that will not satisfy my conscience: but send me your *positive command*, in such full and express terms as may absolve me from all guilt and punishment for neglecting this opportunity of doing good when you and I shall appear before the great and awful tribunal of our Lord Jesus Christ.[2]

With that challenge, Samuel acquiesced, recognizing what a serious thing it is to discourage someone from doing the work that perhaps God had laid before her.

Years later when her sons, John and Charles Wesley, clergymen in the Church of England, were engaged in revivalism work in England, they were criticized for allowing laypeople to preach. John responded with a tract called "Lay Preachers," in which he argued that the validity of their ministry could be seen by its fruits. When laywomen began to sense the call to preach, however, Wesley thought this a bit improper and requested that they stop. But Mary Fletcher responded by pointing out that their ministry could be justified using Wesley's own argument for lay preaching: "They shall be known by their fruits." During Wesley's lifetime some women in this new Methodist movement did gain reputations as powerful preachers, though soon after his death in 1791 the British Methodists withdrew their support of women leaders.

Nineteenth-Century Women in US Revivalism and Reform

In the United States, though, Methodism was just taking hold, and women tended to have more freedom to pray or speak in public worship. Some women traveled on horseback with their husbands who were pastors of many little gatherings of Christians in various places over a large area. (These itinerant preachers, called "circuit riders," faced grueling travel conditions in all sorts of weather, and various levels of hospitality, so usually wives did not go along.) One such circuit rider's wife, Fanny Newell, did accompany her husband, and she records in her journal how her husband would preach, and then after the sermon she would stand up and "exhort." This involved encouraging people to confess sins, or take the things of God seriously, though without preaching from a particular text. She observed that her exhorting would bring them to their knees, weeping.[3]

In the new African-American churches that broke from the main Methodist body (called, at that time, the Methodist Episcopal Church), women were grudgingly granted permission to preach. A prominent preacher and traveling evangelist, Jarena Lee, wrote about the struggles she faced until her church, the African Methodist Episcopal mother church in Philadelphia, finally approved of her preaching. She spent decades as a traveling evangelist, doing what she believed God had called her to do.[4]

The Free Will Baptists went one step further in their affirmation of women leaders: they approved women evangelists in the early decades of the nineteenth century. From New England to the western reaches of New York, women traveled and preached in churches, carrying letters of recommendation from home congregations. Some became rather well-known—Clarissa Danforth, for example—while others quietly went about their business. One such woman was Nancy Towle, who wrote in her autobiography about her conversion, her call into ministry followed by her reluctance to start preaching, her eventual obedience, and then her travels. She casually mentions doing preaching tours first with one sister, then another, and she describes the sweet fellowship of arriving in a city and finding other sisters carrying out the same work. And this was all before 1820.[5]

Hundreds of women preached as evangelists, started churches, and served as pastors in the United States in the eighteenth and nineteenth centuries, as Catherine Brekus shows in *Strangers and Pilgrims: Female Preaching in America, 1740–1845*. Further, they combined gospel preaching with fervent calls to improve the society throughout the nineteenth century.[6] Though he is often credited with being the first to promote women's vocal participation in public worship, the revivalist preacher Charles Finney (1792–1875) merely welcomed women's prayer and testimony; even that was a radical step for him, since his fellow Presbyterians found this shocking and unseemly. Women, they believed, should never have the floor in mixed assemblies, inside or outside of the church. (Apparently Finney did not defend Antoinette Brown, who in 1846 entered

Oberlin College, where Finney was a professor and later president; she was not awarded her degree until 1908 because she had done the theology track, which was supposed to be only for men.) In any case, women had been doing far more than simply giving testimony in Methodist churches and in some of the smaller Protestant denominations.

Women began to be involved in Christian service in other ways as well. Christian women began moral reform societies, which sought to rescue women from prostitution, get them converted, and train them in alternative vocations. These efforts partook of societal assumptions about women, in that they should work with women, but rejected the conventions of delicacy and propriety that would have made them silent. In addition to housing, feeding, and clothing the ex-prostitutes and their children, and offering them job training, some of these societies published lists of names of men seen entering brothels, shaming men and demanding an end to the double standard, which required sexual purity only from women. In the course of their work, the women saw how difficult it was for a woman to support herself, and they began to agitate for better-paid employment for women.

Thousands of women also organized, raised money, and went out stumping to end slavery and to make hard liquor unavailable in this country. These two movements—abolition and temperance—tapped empathy in women, since they demonstrated, among other things, women's vulnerability in society. Women (and men) initially fought hard liquor, not because they saw alcohol as intrinsically bad, but because alcoholism in men meant destitution for their families. In the early nineteenth century a woman generally could not hold property, so even if she inherited the house she was born in, it became her husband's as soon as they were married. If he became attached to strong drink, he could drink away the property, and the wife had no legal recourse. If she tried to keep the children fed and clothed by taking in laundry or working as a servant in a wealthy household, or later, by working in a factory, her husband could drink away her earnings as well. If hunger, homelessness, and humiliation weren't enough, many alcoholic husbands were violent as well (something that is still a large problem in our society), but it was extremely difficult for a woman to leave her husband. For one thing, her testimony was not valid in a court of law—like British women, American women were dead before the law—so she could not sue for divorce very easily. But more significantly, her children automatically would stay with her husband or the husband's family. Women had no legal rights to their own offspring in cases of divorce, or even when a husband died. So the temperance issue drew into public view the vulnerability of women, since increasingly the ideal of women's absolute economic dependence was being promoted in the society. Women fought against alcohol in order to protect women and children from male alcoholism that resulted in indolence, violence, and many ruined lives. Their rhetoric often included words of compassion for the men, sometimes casting them as victims of the demon alcohol itself or of saloon operators who abetted this demon in the community.

In the same way, women in the abolition movement had compassion for the men who were owned and abused, but they had particular empathy for the enslaved women. For one thing, slave women suffered differently from men in that they were completely vulnerable to rape, a situation depicted both in journals of slave women (Harriet Jacobs, for instance) and in novels that showed the heroic efforts of slave women to avoid the sexual violence of their masters. Not only did they have no legal protection, but apparently church bodies, afraid of losing the plantation owners' support, also refused to take up the cause of these abused women.

The other difference in slave women's experience was that they were the ones who generally raised their children, caring for them as best they could, despite long work hours and tremendous physical exertion. So when they went on the auction block or their children were sold "down the river," which meant down the Mississippi River into regions from which they would never return, the anguish was overwhelming. Reports by observers describe these horrendous scenes of women wailing and moaning over their children, even toddlers, who were ripped from their embrace. Countless narratives written or dictated by ex-slaves describe firsthand the despair of these events. This became one of the cornerstones of women's arguments against slavery: think of the mothers; think of the children.

In the early 1800s two sisters from South Carolina, Angelina and Sarah Grimké, started campaigning to abolish slavery; they understood the injustice of the entire system and had seen firsthand some of the unthinkable cruelty it allowed. As deeply Christian people, they believed that slavery was completely at odds with Scripture, since slavery denied that slaves were fully human or made in God's image, and it certainly did not promote love for one's neighbor. It became dangerous for them to stay in their home state, and in 1819 they moved to Boston, a hotbed of abolitionism, where they continued working to end slavery. However, when they attempted to hold an antislavery meeting, people surrounded the church where they were gathered, threw rocks through the windows, and tried to prevent them from leaving. The women linked arms and faced the hostile crowd on the streets of Boston. The opposition was not on account of their antislavery rhetoric or agitation; it was simply because they were women speaking to a mixed audience. Some of the pastors in Boston then collaborated on a letter asserting that women had no business speaking in public but should confine themselves to women's meetings. Sarah Grimké responded with several letters published in 1836 and now collected as a book called *Letters on the Equality of the Sexes*, demonstrating from Scripture that God created men and women equally in the image of God and for the service of God. In order to fight slavery, the Grimkés discovered they had to do the prior work of justifying their own activity; they had to argue for the right to have a voice in the discussion.

A similar thing happened to Elizabeth Cady Stanton and Lucretia Mott. Both women had been actively involved in fighting against slavery and had been elected to represent their regional societies at the World Anti-Slavery Conference in London in 1840. Stanton, who had traveled to London with her husband—in fact it was their honeymoon trip—and Lucretia Mott, a Quaker preacher, became friends, because after two days of deliberation about the issue, it was decided that women were to be sequestered in the balcony of the meeting house and not allowed to speak or to vote. Mott and Stanton realized, as the Grimkés had before them, that they would have to address the issue of women's place in society first, or they would have no effect in fighting against any other evil. It was no good trying to speak out against injustice for the enslaved, since they themselves had no voice. The seed of the women's rights movement had been planted.

Eight years later, during which time Stanton had several children and Mott traveled around preaching the gospel and fighting strong drink and slavery, they met again in Seneca Falls, New York. Stanton, who had been converted during a Finney revival, and four Quaker women, including Lucretia Mott, gathered to plan the first Women's Rights Convention, in July of 1848. Drawing on their deep conviction that God had created them as full human beings and that therefore their demands for just treatment were Christian indeed, they enumerated the ways in which women had been forced to be dependent and powerless in all areas of human life: no college except Oberlin open to them; no right to their own wages, property, or even children; no voice in most churches; no voice in the construction of laws that ruled them; no representation in the government over them, despite the requirement to pay taxes; men were made their masters at marriage, since women had to promise their husbands obedience, and men were legally permitted to "chastise" wives physically. They decried, among other things, that churches did not allow women to participate in decision making or in preaching, and did not even permit women to work on behalf of the social ills that their consciences prodded them to do. So, though they used the social contract and natural rights language of the Declaration of Independence, they drafted a Declaration of Sentiments largely fueled by their religious commitments.

When the day came, July 21, 1848, about 340 women and men gathered in the Wesleyan Methodist Chapel in Seneca Falls (now a national park), and Lucretia Mott's husband presided, since the women lacked the confidence to preside over men. At the end of the two-day conference, one hundred people signed the Declaration of Sentiments, including the pastor of the host church and a number of other men. Not surprisingly, though, other clergy were very upset and became the most vociferous opponents of the nascent movement. Antoinette Brown, who had been trained in biblical studies and theology at Oberlin College, involved herself in some of the early women's rights conventions and argued from the Greek with the irate clergy who were fearful of a woman who had "stept out of [her] place."[7] A few years later, in 1853, Brown was ordained in a Congregational Church in South Butler, New York, the first woman known to be ordained to pastoral ministry in the modern era. (In 1908 Oberlin finally granted her the degree she had earned.)

Phoebe Palmer was engaged at this time in revival work in New York City. Though never ordained, each week in her home Palmer held the Tuesday Meeting for the Promotion of Holiness, at which she preached on salvation and sanctification. The meetings started small, but grew until more than two hundred people attended each week, including Methodist bishops, college presidents (from a wide range of institutions such as University of Michigan, Northwestern University, Georgia University, Drew University, Syracuse University, Boston University, and American University), and other influential people. Palmer also traveled to England with her husband, Dr. Walter Palmer, during the Civil War, where she engaged in a preaching ministry in the style of a traveling evangelist. Her message was a "shorter way" to the experience of sanctification: you would lay yourself on the altar and trust that God would make you clean. Because this act of consecration to God demanded total surrender to God, everything else in life became secondary, something which flew in the face of societal expectations that women would sacrifice everything for their families. For some holiness women, their experience of sanctification was the ground of their feeling of empowerment for preaching ministry.[8]

Catherine Booth, who many call the cofounder of the Salvation Army (rather than simply the wife of the founder, since they worked side by side their entire adult lives), helped her then-friend William see women differently. In the 1850s he wrote to her: "But as to concede that [woman] is man's equal, or capable of becoming man's equal in intellectual attainments or prowess—I must say that is contradicted by experience in the world and [by] my honest conviction."[9] But Catherine did not accept that; she pointed out that if God used women as messengers in the Old Testament, who had the right to tell God that it wasn't acceptable now: "Who shall dare say unto the Lord, 'What doest Thou?' when He 'pours out His Spirit on His handmaidens.' . . . Who shall dare thrust woman out of the Church's operations, or presume to put my candle which God has lighted under a bushel?"[10] William was partly persuaded, but it wasn't until Catherine composed her famous tract "Female Teaching" that he became convinced. She published the tract in response to the vicious attacks against Phoebe Palmer for her ministry in England. Catherine began preaching with great success, and soon thereafter William suffered a prolonged illness, during which he was glad to have such a competent replacement—his wife. Gradually women in the Salvation Army began preaching to the crowds, more or less because there weren't enough men. But when it came to sharing responsibilities in the local stations, many men, themselves recently lifted out of the gutter, did not want women treated as their equals, and therefore declined to work in the Salvation Army. Others, however, did accept women, and since that first generation, women have planted local ministries and have run corps and stations all over the world, and the worldwide organization has had a woman as its head. (This is not to say that the Salvation Army is without problems in this area; it is still true that many corps are run by married couples in which the husband and wife bear the same rank, but he carries more authority.)

The temperance movement, begun in the early nineteenth century, gained momentum as the century progressed. In the years 1873–74, in more than nine hundred cities in the United States, Protestant women gathered at local churches and marched en masse to saloons, where they would stand or even kneel around the entrance, praying and singing. (Carrie Nation showed up with an axe to split open the kegs, but not many women took it that far.) This "Women's Crusade" gave birth to the Women's Christian Temperance Union (WCTU), which had as its main focus the eradication of liquor. However, its second president, Frances Willard, broadened the mission to include any type of reform sought by members. She dubbed it her "Do everything" policy, which encompassed activism regarding labor laws, prison reform, raising the age of consent (since in twenty states in the late nineteenth century it was ten!), free kindergarten, schooling for blacks in the South, healthy dress for women (particularly the end of corsets, bonnets, and high heels), vocational training for former prostitutes, relief for the poor, municipal sanitation in cities, day nurseries for children of working women, and women's right to vote, on the basis that it would mean protecting the home. In fact, she called it the "Home Protection Ballot," making the idea of women's suffrage seem reasonable to nice church women, since it fit their societally approved role as "guardians of the home." However, though Willard's appeal sounded very traditional, she had reinterpreted "home," subtly stretching its boundaries, and thus women's sphere of action, to include the whole world and every level of society. Willard took the traditional assumptions of the nineteenth century regarding women, particularly notions of women's moral and spiritual superiority, and used them to argue for women's political involvement in many areas of society.

Elizabeth Cady Stanton, on the other hand, in her work to improve women's lives, hoped to get women to reject gender essentialist assumptions about themselves. In the early years of the women's rights movement, Stanton was herself much closer to Willard's version of Christianity, since she had gone to the altar at a Finney revival meeting. By the end of the century, however, she distanced herself from conservative evangelicalism, as was demonstrated most clearly in her publication of *The Woman's Bible*. She had certainly agitated for political equality and the just treatment of women in public life, but in the last thirty years of her life she worked hard to address the ways in which women's gender identity and role expectations limited them. Stanton recognized that women's own ideas of themselves restricted their lives and that the Bible had been instrumental in the formation of these ideas; in all sorts of churches the Bible was used to teach women that they were God's afterthoughts, and that they were created for service to men and children. This prompted Stanton's publication of *The Woman's Bible* in 1895 and 1898, in which she and some biblical scholars commented on biblical passages dealing with women.[11] She didn't dismiss the Bible outright, but rejected its use as a tool to keep women "in their place."

Women in the Modern Missions Movement

In the meantime, thousands of Protestants relocated to places all over the world in order to convert people to Christianity, in what has been dubbed the modern missions movement. In 1812, when the first Protestant women departed for foreign places in service of the gospel, they were among the most educated women in the society. The focus of women's mission work was not only evangelism but also education and medicine, so much so that according to missions historian Dana Robert, women's "commitment to the social and charitable side of mission transformed the face of American missions."[12] She notes that even in the most proclamation-oriented evangelical missions organizations and denominations, women engaged in ministries of compassion. This may have been in part because of assumptions barring women from preaching directly—though, of course, women often assumed leadership roles on mission fields that would not have been allowed in their home churches—and it may have been related to the fact that the thousands of single women missionaries formed deep relationships with the people they chose to live among.

Women who initially went out as missionary wives or "assistant missionaries" had developed by the end of the century their own very successful missions organizations and a gender-based mission theory, "Woman's Work for Woman." Mission boards had relegated women to the care of women and children, but this meant facing the horrible plight of women, and working to make their lives better. Female missionaries labored to end practices such as infanticide, child marriages, footbinding, polygamy, and *suttee* in India, in which wives were burned alive on their husbands' funeral biers. They also tried to address illiteracy and lack of health care among women, and to ameliorate the harsh conditions for abandoned or divorced women. Accounts of their activities appeared in women's periodicals and were read avidly by thousands, who in turn gave money to further this "Woman's Work for Woman." Groups such the "Women's Mite Society," so named because of the commendation Jesus gave to the poor widow who gave her "two mites" as an offering (Luke 21:1–4), gathered tremendous amounts of money to support missionary women and their ministries.

However, women became increasingly dissatisfied at how the money they raised was being spent, and so the Woman's Union Missionary Society was formed in 1861. For one thing, they were displeased that the needs of foreign women were downplayed and money channeled to more traditional missionary activities, such as building churches and evangelizing men. For another thing, they felt as if they couldn't take care of the women they supported since single female missionaries were paid far less than single male missionaries. Furthermore, during the war women had engaged in nursing or running family businesses or farms, and afterward they had new skills and confidence with which to organize mission efforts. Not surprisingly, following the Civil War, separate women's missionary boards were created in a number of denominations. With full responsibility to run mission enterprises themselves, they sent their own missionaries, mostly single women, and set their own agendas. This meant that the humanitarian work that women sought to do among women was not only permitted but now even celebrated.

All this organizing, administering, and traveling to distant places in the world offered some women opportunities to develop skills as well as space to reflect on the plight of women as women. This had a complex result: they could either compare their relative ease with the harsh conditions under which women lived elsewhere and simply be thankful for how much better things were for them, or they could recognize, perhaps for the first time, that women were not treated fairly in their own culture either.

In any case, in the early twentieth century these women's missionary societies were subsumed into general missionary boards, usually against the wishes of the women involved. Since women had no voting power in their denominations or larger mission agencies, they were powerless to stop this change. In *Western Women in Eastern Lands*, Helen Barrett Montgomery asked pointedly, are the *men* ready for it? "Are they emancipated from the caste of sex so that they can work easily with women, unless they be head and women clearly subordinate?"[13] Her fear was well-founded since, as soon as the missions societies were integrated, suddenly women had no place in leadership, had no real control over mission agenda any longer, and couldn't even lead prayer in joint meetings.

In the meantime, however, women were functioning as evangelists and even pastors in many places in the United States. Among women in the Reformed tradition, for instance, the call to do city mission work was strongly felt. Janette Hassey's book *No Time for Silence* describes the courage and determination of some Moody Bible Institute women who in the early twentieth century evangelized in Chicago. The ministry of women, however, was much more widely practiced and accepted (though never fully) in the Holiness churches, such as the Wesleyan Methodists, the Nazarenes, the Salvation Army, the Church of God (Anderson), and some sectors of the Methodist family of churches. The Wesleyan Methodist Connection, for instance, was ordaining women as pastors as early as the 1850s in Rochester, New York, and a move to "disapprove the licensing and ordaining of women as ministers" in the 1864 General Conference failed, though regional bodies were given freedom to decide this issue for themselves.[14] Throughout the late nineteenth century and into the early twentieth century, many women functioned in that denomination not only as missionaries, but as evangelists, church planters, and pastors. Donald Dayton, in *Discovering an Evangelical Heritage*, suggests that in the 1920s in some of these Holiness denominations the percentage of pastors who were women was around 30 percent.[15]

In Pentecostalism, women also initially experienced some leeway for their leadership. The Azusa Street Revival, which began in 1906 and touched off the modern Pentecostal movement, had at its inception men and women, blacks and whites, involved in preaching and leading. The Assemblies of God, the largest Pentecostal denomination formed in this era, owes its existence in part to a pair of women who worked tirelessly in evangelism. At least two denominations were also formed by women: the Pillar of Fire Church begun by Alma White, which was not Pentecostal but explicitly feminist, and the Foursquare Gospel Church, founded by Aimee Semple McPherson.

By the middle of the twentieth century, things had changed in both the Holiness groups and the Pentecostal denominations. For one thing, there was general societal pressure for Rosie the Riveter and all her friends to leave the workplace so men returning from World War II could find jobs. The GI Bill also allowed many more men to get a college education, and even in the denominations in which women had been very active, men with degrees were preferred over women without them. In addition, Holiness groups have been influenced by all the organs of neoevangelicalism: the publication of *Christianity Today*; the rise of the large evangelical seminaries such as Fuller, Gordon-Conwell, and Trinity Evangelical; and Christian radio and TV. These Holiness groups also joined the National Association of Evangelicals (formed in 1942) and began to downplay some of their own distinctions in order to gain credibility with the denominations that predominated in the organization. The affirmation of women's leadership was one of those distinctions that was played down.

In the meantime, women in the oldline Protestant churches, often former missionaries, were pressing for expanded opportunities for leadership. In the congregationally organized churches, such as the Disciples of Christ and the Northern Baptists, for instance, ordination of women was theoretically possible long before it became widely practiced, since individual churches could decide whether or not to do it. The United Methodist Church was the first of the large Protestant denominations to ordain women as full clergy, in 1954. In African-American denominations, the African Methodist Episcopal Zion Church ordained women beginning in the 1890s, and the African Methodist Episcopal Church began in 1948. The largest Presbyterian body affirmed women's full ordination in 1956 and two out of the three of the Lutheran bodies in 1970. (The Lutheran Church Missouri Synod still denies women that role.) In 1976, at their General Convention, the Episcopalians voted to affirm women as priests and bishops, though on account of the rancorous response, a clause was added that bishops could refuse to ordain women in their dioceses.[16] The Southern Baptist Convention, which had allowed churches to decide the issue for themselves, had more than 1,130 ordained women when it ruled in 1991 that women could not be ministers.[17]

Conclusions

The sense among many evangelicals is that only "liberal" churches ordain women, and that women had never been in ministry until the feminist movement prodded these "liberal" women and "liberal" churches to move in that direction. They are unaware of the long and rich history of women's participation in leadership of the church: the deacons, the widows, and those called priests and bishops on their tombstones in the early centuries of the church. They don't know about the abbesses who acted as bishops, caring for the spiritual health of hundreds of men and women in their monasteries, as well as hundreds of other people residing in the parishes under their jurisdictions.

People who advocate "traditional" roles for women in the home and the church likely do not know about the long history of women's preaching and church planting and of the huge missions networks they ran a century before mainline churches began ordaining women. People still make statements like the one at the beginning of chapter 7 about how women have never exercised leadership before and therefore shouldn't now, but as we have seen, women have often had much more leadership, in various times and places, than critics are willing to acknowledge.

Those who assume that women's work is primarily in the home may be unwilling to acknowledge that women are called by God to all sorts of vocations, and will likely keep entering them at higher rates: politics, education (including elementary, secondary, and higher education posts), the church, parachurch organizations, medicine, literacy, the visual arts, music, literature, and so many other fields. It is worth celebrating that many women are thinking beyond just having a job; they are taking seriously God's calling for their lives. In other words, rather than simply meeting societal, church, and family expectations, they are thinking in terms of what they can do to participate in God's work in this world.

Part Four

I SAID
WHAT I MEANT,
AND I MEANT
WHAT I SAID

10

NOT COUNTING WOMEN AND CHILDREN

Linguistic Invisibility in the Church

As we drove home from church, one of the men in the back seat complained that the pastor should not have allowed his wife to speak from the pulpit. Offhandedly I asked this man if he might not see it as a growth experience, a chance for him to get outside his comfort zone. Maybe, I said, it was a case of "iron sharpens iron," a phrase from Proverbs 27:17. Without hesitation Fred, the driver, chimed in, "'Iron sharpens iron' does not apply to women." Why? "Because it says, 'Iron sharpens iron as one *man* sharpens another,'" he said. I pointed out that unless there is a concrete male person involved, the NIV (his preferred translation) uses "man" to designate people in general, as in "Man does not live on bread alone" (Deut. 8:3, NIV). How did he decide, then, when *man* included women and when it didn't? How would one know, for instance, whether the verse about God "who wants all men to be saved" (1 Tim. 2:4, NIV) applied to women? His response was simply this: common sense. His common sense told him that no woman could sharpen a man's intellect, but obviously women could be saved. In that moment, I learned something important about the language: that is, that the so-called generic use of the term "man" is, in fact, not generic. Fred had demonstrated that using the term left him the luxury to include or exclude women as he pleased. Furthermore, his freedom to invest the term with a certain meaning meant that he could use it to reinforce his stereotypes. Every time he heard the words "As iron sharpens iron, so one man sharpens another," he once again assigned it a male connotation, which reinforced his belief that men can and women cannot perform this function. I was left wondering how much of his Bible applied only to men.

Now for a positive example of the same phenomenon. I grew up memorizing verses from the King James Bible about having the power to become sons of God and singing songs such as "Rise Up, O Men of God." My friends and I had been addressed in congregational settings as "brothers" more times than I could remember; in fact, I would have had no cause to remember because I wasn't even noticing. It felt fine because that was all I knew. Years later, in the context of a "ladies'" Bible study, the leader called us "women of God" and something changed inside me; I felt a huge wave of relief. Perhaps for the first time I realized that God wasn't translating me into a male when God "looked" at me; perhaps God was fine with my being a female; maybe God intended that in my creation. I was surprised at my reaction, since I had not consciously thought that God wanted only "sons of God" or "men of God" or "brothers," but somehow that message slipped in with all the masculine language. This is to say, our words not only display our thoughts but also mold and form and reinforce our thoughts in subtle but powerful ways.

What both of these experiences illustrate is that regardless of intent, when we use masculine terms they do not function in generic ways. Because of the ambiguous nature of a word that sometimes is intended to designate male human beings and sometimes all human beings, the meanings bleed into each other. When one says "man" as in "the steps of the righteous man," the intention may be generic but maleness is not absent. The speaker may even flesh it out concretely as someone who is faithful to his wife, good to his children, and loves God. The "generic" has male overtones. In the 1970s, when academic organizations started suggesting that inclusive terms should replace what the American Psychological Association refers to as the "pseudo-generic masculine," it was not an arbitrary decision. What the scholars in these organizations recognized is that masculine words never did function very well as generics, because there was always the ambiguity of application. Further, the use of male language for all of the human race suggests rather forcefully that male experience is the norm for human beings and female experience is "other," pertaining only to women. One writer suggests that using "man" and "mankind" for the whole race is the same as using brand names instead of the generic, as in Kleenex rather than tissues, or Vaseline instead of petroleum jelly, and it has similar effects. All other brands of tissues or kinds of humans are linguistically invisible and therefore out of mind.[1]

But of course there were (and are) skeptics. For instance, in the 1980s, Christian scholar Vernard Eller asserted that "'man' words have functioned perfectly, communicating their various thoughts without a hitch to countless generations of both the learned and unlearned."[2] This position fails to acknowledge that the (pseudo-)generic "man" has functioned perfectly, but not in the ways intended: it has enshrined male experience as normative and rendered women and women's experience invisible, even when its users were not intentionally endeavoring to do so. Eller also fails to recognize the fundamental ambiguity of a term that sometimes is intended to refer to male human beings and sometimes to all human beings, or that the principle for deciding which meaning is at play is nothing other than an unconscious use of stereotypes allowed by the ambiguity—as Fred so clearly exhibited on that drive home from church.

In fact, this invisibility of women in the "generic" man is illustrated in the very history of the usage. It was argued in Britain that since women were "dead before the law" (a situation that also plagued American women until the first women's movement went about changing it in the 1800s), a woman could be linguistically designated by the man's name (Mrs. John Samson) and with the "generic" term "man." Simply, a woman did not exist as a legal entity, but moved in most cases from being represented by her father to being represented by her husband in any legal proceeding. Failing those options, a brother, an uncle, or some other male guardian could stand in. A woman could not vote (obviously!), hold property, or even have custody of her own children if her husband died or divorced her. John Kirby proposed the use of "man" to designate all people as a grammar rule in 1746, though it was already part of common usage much earlier, for instance, in Shakespeare's writing and the King James Bible; it was embedded officially in British law in 1850 by act of Parliament.

In other linguistic habits, the female is not completely subsumed under a male counterpart but is cast in a subordinate role to the male. The modern hymn writer Brian Wren, in his book *What Language Shall I Borrow?* gives a whirlwind tour of how male domination has been explicitly stated or depicted in metaphors by the leading thinkers in almost every field in Western history.[3] For instance, in philosophy men have been assumed to be rational while women are irrational, and of course, rationality is very highly valued.[4] Scientists, beginning with Francis Bacon, have often used the metaphor of "penetrating the inmost secrets of nature" or "unveiling the mysteries of nature," with nature always characterized as female. It is an image of the rational male (sexually) conquering the wild and preeminently physical female. In the economic and political arenas, particularly since industrialization, the fundamental human work of birth, of care for human beings, of attending to old age and dying is rendered invisible by the constant rhetoric of profit. We could add that ships, machines, cities, and other things that men have typically controlled have been referred to with female pronouns, though this is not considered grammatically correct any longer, precisely because of the dominating male and subservient female images that it implies.

Not only are males dominant in our linguistic conventions, but things female are consistently devalued. We can identify words that have come to carry demeaning attitudes, such as "hussy," which used to mean simply "housewife" and "gossip," but originally referred to the group of women who attended a childbirth. (Now it is generally used to denote a sexually promiscuous woman.) There are pairs of words that are grammatically parallel but value the people differently: as in bachelor and spinster, for instance, or tomboy and sissy. To call a girl a tomboy is often a compliment, a promotion, if you will, but to call a boy a sissy is highly offensive and constitutes a social demotion, since the female is perceived as less valuable than the male. The same dynamic is at play with names: parents can choose a name for their girl babies that is typically used for boys, but rarely the other way around. And if enough girls are named Taylor, for instance, boys won't be named that any longer.

Then there are the pairs that historically had somewhat parallel functions, before the female word changed. "Mistress," for instance, used to simply mean the female counterpart to "master," though obviously it now carries a different connotation. "Lord" and "lady" in a similar fashion were those who owned the manor, though now the male term is used almost exclusively in religious settings and the female term carries ornamental or sexual overtones when applied to women (as in "sit like a lady" or "foxy lady" or "lady of the evening," whereas "foxy lord" just doesn't have the same ring to it). "King" and "queen" have retained some parallelism, though there is a difference in power evoked with these terms, and there are also the sexual overtones for queen (as in "drag queen"). Even "madam" and "sir" are unequal, since madam can refer to a woman who runs a brothel, but sir doesn't have sexual connotations.[5] We might well ask why the female terms in these pairs have consistently become sexualized. Relegating women linguistically to only one part of their existence represents an incredible reduction of their personhood; their bodies and their roles are sexualized either because of male fear of or fascination with female sexuality. In either case, women are clearly under the male gaze, and this is reflected in how we use language.

People often use pairs that are not grammatically parallel in ways that imply the inferiority of women. For instance, why should men be referred to as "men" while their counterparts are called "girls," as in, "The man gets the girl he wanted in the end." To use a term that denies women full adulthood implies their perpetually dependent nature, and excuses men from having to take them seriously as peers. Though the next example is archaic, one still hears it: "man and wife," denoting the personhood of the man, whereas the woman is mentioned only by her role in his life. (Using "husband and wife" on the other hand implies that the significant thing about both people being discussed is that they are married to each other.) "Gentlemen, you can take your seats here on the main floor, and ladies, you'll find yours in the balcony." This seating arrangement still pertains in some church governing bodies where men are the sole actors in church governance; this linguistic habit is more prevalent but points to the same thing: an ornamental status for women. It accentuates differences that have no bearing on issues at hand and perpetuates the illusion that women should be passive while men run the world.

In everyday speech we often use different adjectives for the same attitude, depending on the gender of the person being described: strong men, aggressive women; decisive men, pushy women; firm men, hard-nosed women; forceful men, shrill women, to name only a few. Yet we might speak of compliant women, pushover men; quiet women, mousy men; sympathetic women, soft men. Human characteristics are appraised differently depending on who is acting them out. Language is used to articulate and reify different gender expectations and to express through implication and insinuation the lower status of women. Women are supposed to be compliant and quiet, but not strong, decisive, firm, or forceful in their speech.

In many ways, then, our language communicates the superiority of everything male and a disdain for the female. Why might this matter? Paul Smith, a Southern Baptist pastor for many years, made this observation: "Language is our means of classifying and ordering the world. Therefore, if the rules which underlie our language system are invalid, then we deceive ourselves daily."[6] Our language, in other words, not only shows our wrongheaded thinking, but also reaffirms our misperceptions. This, he argues, is not a healthy Christian place to be.

As Christians, we should be greatly concerned about such misuse of language for at least three reasons: our need for theological consistency, the demands of Christian love, and our ability to communicate the good news of the gospel in our society. First of all, Christian theology demands an accurate use of language about women and men—otherwise we might inadvertently communicate things at odds with our own stated

theological positions. To subtly imply the inferiority of women and superiority of men undermines people's ability to believe the core of the
faith: that all of us bear God's image equally, that all are equally sinful,
and that all may receive grace equally and participate in the redeemed
community together. If our language practices elevate maleness and masculinity (theologian Letty Russell estimated that before the usage began
to change, the average English speaker heard "man" used "generically"
ten million times over the course of life),[7] if our preaching focuses on
male characters in Scripture, if we hear more about the "weaker vessel"
than about being made in the image of God, and if we experience all the
other misuses of language mentioned above, it is probably impossible
to resist subtle (or not so subtle) messages about the relative worth of
women. If our linguistic practices go unexamined, it is likely we communicate something at odds with our own theology.

As we move from theology to lived Christianity, we find that Christian love demands a use of language about each other that is respectful and welcoming. Language that demeans individuals or groups of
people can hardly be called loving, and even ways of speaking that
render women invisible or of lesser significance do not reflect the way
that Jesus treated women. Further, it is a requirement of Christian
love that we acknowledge the pain inflicted on others by the way we
speak—even when it is pain we never intended to cause—and work
at expressing ourselves more lovingly and carefully. Sometimes my
students object, claiming that we shouldn't have to be "politically correct" just because some feminists make a fuss, but that is like saying
we should not "give in" to the civil rights movement and use respectful
terms for African-Americans.

Furthermore, as Paul and other New Testament writers demonstrated,
we should be self-reflective about how we present the good news of the
gospel. Outdated language conventions should not stand in the way of
people hearing something that could open them up to the love of God.
When Paul says, for instance, "I have become all things to all people,
that I might by all means save some" (1 Cor. 9:22), he is advocating a
particular mission strategy: act and speak like the locals so that the message gets through to the audience. Don't let people be turned off to the
message because of a faulty method. In this context it could be worded:
"Don't bring disrepute to the gospel by a use of language that points to
chauvinistic attitudes or insensitivity." In this regard, remember this
warning: "When secular values of masculine priority are brought into
the church, it is much more serious than the bias that is evident in the
workplace. Jesus' harsh words were never for the average sinner, but
rather for the religious leaders whose distortions of spiritual things were
truly dangerous because they used their authority to keep people from

God. Sexism, like all ungodly things, keeps people from God—especially on Sunday morning at 11 o'clock."[8]

Again, it is irrelevant if a pastor or worship leader thinks that people should not take exclusive language as an insult; the fact is that some people do, and as Christian communicators it is incumbent on them to avoid language that is potentially painful, or even just distracting, to anyone. Besides, making the switch generally offends no one since those not attuned won't notice, while it makes a tremendous positive impact on those who do notice. So, on the one hand, if a preacher uses the phrase "sons of God" all through a sermon to refer to Christian believers, some people will not notice, but some in the congregation will have to expend energy bracketing the insensitivity in order to hear anything else that is said. On the other hand, if this preacher were to use "children of God," everyone could simply hear the welcome of God being expressed.

Because of the importance of theology, love, and the responsible communication of God's word, many Christian speakers have begun to employ gender-neutral language in reference to people. In this they follow the translators of the NRSV (New Revised Standard Version) and TNIV (Today's New International Version), who have endeavored to render Scripture into English more faithfully by using inclusive terms. Like other translators, these scholars had to consider how best to carry the sense of the original document into a different language and cultural setting, a particularly difficult task when moving from an ancient language to a current one. There is constantly a tension between the form of the word or phrase and the way that word or phrase functions to convey meaning. Let's look at a couple of examples. First, if one version of the Bible uses the word "denarii" in Luke 7 and another says "one day's wages," we don't accuse the second version of "changing the Bible." It is not "changing the Bible" but translating it in such a way as to convey the meaning more carefully. We view the substitution as helping the modern reader understand Jesus' words. Or consider that in Psalm 23:5, a literal rendition from the Hebrew is: "You have made my head fat with oil."[9] If the translators stuck to the exact form of the Hebrew words, this is what it would say. However, that phrase is meaningless to modern English speakers, and so translators try to convey the sense of the original verse using other words:

New International Version: "You anoint my head with oil" (making it sound like the King James Version)

Today's English Version: "You welcomed me as an honored guest."

The question is, is it better to stick to the form of the words but leave people confused, or worse, with a mistaken idea, or to look for what linguists and translators refer to as a dynamic equivalent (the stated objective of the NIV translators) that helps people understand the sense of the phrase or verse?

Another example, one more pertinent to the discussion at hand, is in Acts 17, Paul's sermon on the Areopagus in Athens. In traditional English versions of the text, Paul starts out his speech, "Men of Athens" (v. 22), though at the end of the passage we learn that there were women there, including Damaris, who is mentioned by name (v. 34). Is it more correct to say "Men of Athens" but leave readers with the mistaken impression that Paul is addressing a crowd of men, or to say "Athenians," as the NRSV does, since clearly women were there, and Paul certainly knew this, since Damaris followed him and became a believer? Furthermore, we know that Paul was in favor of preaching to women, since the previous chapter tells us he sought them out down by the river in Philippi as they were praying (Acts 16).

A final reason for Christians to employ precise language with regard to our human brothers and sisters is that, if unchecked, assumptions about male superiority and female inferiority will come into play when we begin thinking about God. Now we are back to the theological consistency mentioned at the outset. Do our words and images about God reflect the same biases regarding gender that our language does regarding people? Elizabeth Johnson observes: "The way in which a faith community shapes language about God implicitly represents what it takes to be the highest good, the profoundest truth, the most appealing beauty."[10] Is our penchant for using masculine images for God something that God's nature demands, or is it what we consider the most appealing beauty, given our society's preference for the male and subordination of the female?

Conclusion

It seems obvious that Christians, of all people, would want to be careful about how they use language. After all, one of the central images in Scripture for the incarnation is the Word who came among us, and one of the central tasks of the church is to bear the Word into the world. Therefore, we should use our words well, carefully, lovingly, extending welcome in the name of Jesus. Our patterns of language usage should demonstrate our belief that all people bear the image of God and all can be renewed in the image of Christ.

11

THE DISCARDED IMAGES

Reasserting Biblical Language for God

In our culture God is often pictured as an old man with a long white beard, in everything from Gary Larson cartoons to TV movies, and comedians still refer to God as "the man upstairs" or "the big guy." Even in church circles people make assumptions about God's gender. A Christian friend told me he once heard the story of Jesus' baptism read by a woman. When she came to the words of God from heaven (and in his retelling he adopted a mock soprano voice), "This is my beloved Son, listen to his words," he just couldn't take them seriously. It struck me that he really thinks that Almighty God, over all the universe, sounds more like him than like me, just because he sings bass. At some level he, and all the drama directors who choose men with deep, resonant voices to be the voice of God in Christmas pageants, assume that God *is* male, or is more like men than women.

Is that really what the Bible says about God? Is God a big man in the sky? The answer, of course, is no, although it is difficult to have a dialogue about our language for God, given the excesses in some circles—for example, the rejection of all male images in favor of exclusively female ones. Many conservative Christians are nervous about anything feminine when it comes to God language, fearing that they will step onto a slippery

slope and fall into goddess worship. Others fear that using female images for God will sound like a capitulation to feminist agitation, or that
they will somehow be identified with feminists. Others simply consider
it dangerous because it's something feminists do, and everything they
do is rejected out of hand.

To argue that we should not use female metaphors for God because
feminists do it, however, is to ignore the ways in which prominent writers throughout the history of the church have embraced these images.
In many eras of church history, female images of God were apparently
not as bothersome as they seem to be now. In fact, many folks used maternal images for God, or specifically for Christ, unabashedly affirming
the spiritual benefit one could receive from them. For instance, in the
second century Clement of Alexandria observed that "the Word is everything to his little ones, both father and mother,"[1] and John Chrysostom
a couple of centuries later compared Christ's nurture to a woman who
nurtures her offspring with blood and milk. Another fourth-century
writer, Ambrose of Milan, speaks of "the Father's womb" and the nour-
ishing breasts of Christ. To this list we could add Bernard of Clairvaux
(d. 1153) and Anselm of Canterbury (d. 1109), who each used explicit
mother images to describe God. But the history of this usage has been
lost, so much so that conservative Christians think that modern feminists
"invented" this language for God.

This chapter, then, is simply a plea that we rediscover the full range of
images for God given to us in Scripture, and in particular that we interact
with the female ones, since they have been overlooked so often in modern evangelicalism. Though they may initially make us uncomfortable,
we affirm them because we know that our thinking about God should
be formed by Scripture, all of Scripture, including the female images
of God we find there. Recovering feminine images of God is important,
first of all, because the very fact that they are in Scripture means they
have something to teach us about God and that they contain invitations
to draw near to God in particular ways. Through them we can learn to
hear the welcome of God in feminine terms. Secondly, remembering that
God is pictured as female as well as male will keep us from imagining
that God *is* male; it will guard us from reducing God to someone quite a
bit more like us, that is, a gendered being. The female imagery, in other
words, reminds us that the male images of God are not absolute, but are
metaphors that point to various characteristics of a God who is beyond
biological sex and its associated gender. Finally, embracing the feminine
metaphors for God has significant implications for our anthropology,
or our theological understanding of what it means to be human: if only
a father's love, for instance, can teach or reflect God's love to children,
then a mother's love is inferior, not worthy of the metaphor. Clearly this

implies that men are intrinsically more capable of bearing God's image in the world, which in turn suggests that they are more like God than women are. On the other hand, using feminine images for God affirms that women can reflect God's image, love, and presence in the world. Perhaps that is one of the reasons these feminine depictions of God appear in Scripture.

Before we begin our survey of biblical metaphors for God, a few words about metaphors in general are in order.

Speaking of Metaphors

We talk of spending time, saving time, wasting time, using time wisely, and investing time in something as if it were money or some other measurable thing. We can hardly speak without using metaphors, either in our mundane speech or in our communication to and about God. As Sallie McFague, a contemporary theologian, observes, it used to be assumed that metaphors were employed as poetic embellishments and were not necessary, that the thing could have been said without a metaphor. Now scholars are more of the opinion that we resort to metaphors when we have no other way of talking about something. She comments: "Here, metaphor is a strategy of desperation, not decoration; it is an attempt to say something about the unfamiliar in terms of the familiar, an attempt to speak about what we do not know in terms of what we do know."[2] When we're speaking of God, we are attempting to speak of the infinite in terms of the finite.

Furthermore, metaphors are not used, in Scripture or in everyday parlance, simply to describe something, but to draw the hearers in to a certain experience. "The essence of metaphor is understanding and experiencing one kind of thing in terms of another."[3] To use a wider variety of biblical metaphors for God is not simply a matter of gaining a fuller understanding of the complexity of God, though obviously that is part of it. Rather, we do it in order to open ourselves up to a fuller and richer relationship with God. Modern hymn writer Brian Wren comments in this regard: "Naming God truthfully is especially important if language shapes and angles thinking and behavior, since untruthful God-language will then hinder our encounter with God and our knowledge of God."[4] To expand our use of metaphors for God is not, as some evangelicals characterize it, simply an attempt to be politically correct, nor is it just an attempt to be sensitive to women in the congregation (though this latter is critically important for a Christian community that is characterized by love).[5] The primary reason for carefully considering the language and the metaphors we use for God is this: our understanding of God, our worship of God, and our ongoing interaction with God depend on it. If God is the one to whom we are entrusting our very beings, then surely our concepts of God will influence many things about our lives. We engage in this for the good of our souls!

Another observation about the nature of metaphors is that it is in their nature to be incomplete. That is, all our metaphors fail in two ways: for one thing, metaphors are partial. In other words, no one metaphor can fully depict the subject because each refers only to a certain slice of that subject. This is true even if the subject is mundane: fog, for instance, may come on cat's feet (showing fog's gentle presence), but it might also be thicker than pea soup (identifying the frustrating, blinding nature of fog). The more complex the subject, the more it will demand a variety of metaphors to display its many and varied characteristics. When we consider love, for instance, something abstract and very powerful in human experience, we find thousands of attempts to use images to describe and understand it. In a similar way, Scripture writers give us many metaphors for God because of the immensity of the subject. No single metaphor for God or our relationship with God can bear the weight of that reality and that relationship. Rather, each image or word picture offers one piece in the mosaic of God's face, and taken together they give us a fuller conception of God and draw us into richer communion with God. Conversely, when we ignore the partial nature of metaphors and focus on only one metaphor for God, we are likely to forget that it is a metaphor. Then we begin to confuse the metaphor with the reality to which it was supposed to point.

Not only this, but metaphors also fail because they are imprecise in that there is never a metaphor in which all the aspects of the first element point to something in the second. With regard to God-language we could say that every metaphor says something true about God, but if pressed too far, says false and nonsensical things. Take, for instance, the words from Psalm 91: "You who live in the shelter of the most High . . . will say to the Lord, 'My refuge and my fortress.'" While we might recognize this as a powerful affirmation of God's constant care and protection when life seems stormy, at the same time we might admit it is a metaphor with severe limitations. After all, most aspects of shelters say nothing about God: the psalmist never meant us to think that God was actually akin to granite, or that God has a dank smell, or that God is chilly on the inside. Most characteristics of shelters have no usefulness in deepening our understanding of God, just as a great deal of what we know about light (particles, waves, color spectrum) may do nothing to draw us to God.

Another observation to make up front is that metaphors are rooted in human experience and appeal to human experience. It would be nonsensical to assert anything else, given that the whole point is that one understands and experiences the second element on the basis of familiarity with the first. "No metaphor can ever be comprehended or even adequately represented independently of its experiential basis,"[6] say the authors of a book about all the various metaphors that give us a coherent frame for understanding life. When it comes to metaphors for God, we can see that they reflect the personal experience of the writers of Scripture and appeal to the experience of the original hearers and readers. We never have psalms about being lost in a blizzard, for instance, or about being accosted by a skunk, since blizzards and skunks are not native to the Middle East. How else could people of ancient Israel understand God except in terms that were already part of their human experience? That God's covenant with Israel resembles a political treaty of the ancient Near East indicates that God interacted with them *in* their culture, not despite it, and *through* their human experience, not lifted out of it. Brian Wren comments: "Revelation is not disembodied, but incarnational: . . . it has to be in language drawn from the particularities of our physical makeup and our political, economic, and cultural experience."[7] God interacts with them in ways they can understand, rather than overwhelming them with an incomprehensible display of the inner workings of the Trinity, for instance. All language of God is, as Wren notes, in a sense incarnational; God condescends to the confines of the human—in this case, human language.

But this is not to say that God fits within human language. We have the (metaphorical) reminder in Isaiah 55:9 that God's ways are higher than our ways as heaven is higher than earth. So, though we affirm that metaphors are helpful because they are grounded in our experience, we also have to remember that our experience does not go far enough. Clearly this is true in the discussion of gender: in our experience, all personal beings have a sex, and so it is difficult to affirm God as a personal being, but not a gendered humanlike being. We cannot really imagine a God who transcends or encompasses both genders. McFague quotes a prayer that a friend prayed as a child: "Father-Mother God, loving me, guard me while I sleep, guide my little feet up to thee," which had the happy effect of reminding him of God's likeness to earthly parents, as well as God's uniqueness and difference from anyone else he knew.[8] God, in the end, is like us, but not like us.

That is why we need so many and such varied ways to speak about God. Let's turn our attention to some of the ways in which biblical writers employed metaphors to depict God.

Biblical Images of God

To set the context for the discussion, a few observations about God and gender in the Old Testament texts might be helpful. Given the milieu in which the Old Testament texts were written, it is significant that Israel's God was not pictured in a sexualized way. In the ancient Near East, long before the Greeks and Romans came along with their pantheons of gods and goddesses, the nations all around Israel had many male and female deities. Often the sacred texts of these groups depict particular goddesses as consorts or quasi-spouses of certain gods, sometimes eventuating in children and all sorts of drama. Scholars have written extensively on the ways in which the Old Testament depictions of God do and do not resemble the deities of the societies around the ancient Israelites,[9] but one profound difference is that, in contrast to the fertility gods and goddesses of Canaan and Babylon and Sumeria (and the highly sexual gods and goddesses of modern neo-paganism), the God of Scripture is never sexualized.

Significantly, the most personal name for God in the Old Testament, the name told to Moses at the burning bush, is not one that indicates maleness, or even what would have been considered male characteristics. Rather, when Moses asks, "Who should I tell them sent me?" the answer is: Yahweh, "I AM." The name has to do with the ever-present Being of God (some have understood the term as "I will be who I will be"), and the "I AM" points to the sufficiency, or the fullness of being, as well. The revelation of the name "I AM" is the foundation of Israel's relationship with God. This God, Yahweh, isn't having love quarrels with female deities, because the "I AM" is not so limited as to be male in gender, and certainly Yahweh did not need union with a female consort in order to be completed. Even the creation of humanity, both male and female in the image of God, points to the idea that God encompasses all human characteristics but transcends both sexes.

Yet, since humans generally come with a particular sex, many metaphors for God reflect gendered human experience, male and female. Others are nongendered, even nonliving. In fact, the range of images associated with God in Scripture is striking: everything from inanimate objects to plants and animals, from forces of nature to people in a variety of roles. Given this range, we don't ask which metaphor is most true (they all point to true aspects of God) but rather, how does God draw us into personal engagement through each of these metaphors? To think about God coming as water to a parched land probably evokes a different response in us than thinking of God as an immovable rock. Both images are meant to tap our experience and create points of contact through which God can communicate life into our lives.

The same is true of all the metaphors that compare God to a non-living entity: they are intended to draw us in through their evocative qualities. God is called a rock, a shelter, a shield, a burning fire, light, water, the sun, and even the wind, among other things. Though none of these metaphors can be taken on its own (they are definitely partial) and none can be pressed too far without saying untrue things of God, these metaphors are still enriching to our worship and to the development of the life of faith.

The biblical writers also use plants and animals at times to convey some aspect of God. Each metaphor, again, points to certain characteristics of God but doesn't capture God's whole essence. When God is compared to a cedar of Lebanon or a beautiful flower, we know that something besides photosynthesis is intended, and, Narnia notwithstanding, clearly God is not a literal lion, though there are instances of such a comparison. For example, God is said to be like a "lion to Ephraim" and a "young lion to Judah" that will maul the prey (Hosea 5:14) and a leopard lurking along the way (Hosea 13:7). God, according to this picture, is strong, fierce, and to be feared because of coming punishment, not tame, not on anyone's little leash. Hosea 13 continues: "I will fall upon them like a bear robbed of her cubs, and tear open the covering of their heart" (v. 8) because they had made idols, silver calves, that they were kissing, worshiping. Furthermore, in Deuteronomy 32:11–12, God is said to be like an eagle teaching her young to fly (see also Exod. 19:4; Job 39:27–30). None of these images gives us a full picture of God, but taken together they tell us something of God by way of things that we can observe in nature.

The same applies to the human images of God in Scripture; they are not comprehensive, as if we could fully understand God with one metaphor; neither are they completely fitting, as if all the points of comparison hold true. If you asked someone who grew up in the church to list the images of God that come to mind, probably God as king, master, or father would top the list. The feminine metaphors have been given so little airtime in American Christianity that students have told me there are no such references. (Calling God "mother" is heresy, according to some of them—which means they would have to excise many passages from their Bibles.) The church in the modern era has enjoyed the male metaphors for God and suppressed the female because "God can't be both at the same time!" However, like the metaphors from nature, the human images of God are varied, but not in opposition to each other. In other words, if God is pictured as a rock and an eagle, we don't reject one or the other because they are opposites—one living and one nonliving—though surely a nonliving and a living image would be nonsensical together if taken literally. If we can embrace that span (nonliving/living), surely a collection of metaphors that spans male/female can be embraced as varied, rather than as in opposition to each other. Besides, if we're going to be faithful to God and learn to be so from Scripture, we cannot overlook a group of images simply because they make us uncomfortable or don't fit our preferred picture of God.

Female Images of God in Scripture

Let's look, then, at a few of the female images of God in Scripture. First, there are some explicit uses of womb and birth imagery. At the end of the book of Job, God asks Job where he was during the creation (Job 38:8–9), "Or who shut in the sea with doors when it burst out from the womb?—when I made the clouds its garment, and thick darkness its swaddling band," and later (v. 29): "From whose womb did the ice come forth, and who has given birth to the hoar-frost of heaven?" Despite whatever potential there was for misunderstanding, the writers of Scripture did not shy away from explicit images of God birthing creation.

We also have examples of God birthing Israel: "You were unmindful of the Rock that bore you; you forgot the God who gave you birth" (Deut. 32:18). Isaiah 46:3–4 speaks of God having carried the remnant of Israel from the womb and borne with them since having birthed them. Obviously this does not mean that we are supposed to think that God has a womb any more than we are to think that God has a literal hand when the psalmist says God stretches out a hand to save Israel. These passages do suggest though that it is appropriate to think of God in a birthing role, and let the metaphor work in us affectively. Can we imagine the sorrow of a mother forgotten by her own young? Can we empathize with God, the mother forgotten by the people of Israel?

Further, we could note here the link between the Hebrew word for womb, *racham*, and the plural form *rachamin*, which is translated as "compassion," "love," and "mercy," in numerous passages throughout the Old Testament. The related verb is often translated "to show mercy," and the adjective *rachum*, rather than being translated as "womb-like" (though the form of the word could suggest this) is translated "merciful." The merciful love of God is like womb love, like the love of one who carries a baby in her womb. Many people would have powerful associations with this word, either from carrying a baby or from watching the great care that pregnant women (usually) take for their babies.[10]

In the New Testament, birth imagery is employed again, this time by Jesus in his conversation with Nicodemus. You must be born again, or born from above, Jesus says (John 3; see also James 1:18; 1 Pet. 1:3). Jesus uses so radical an image that Nicodemus is flummoxed; again, there isn't a sense that birth is an off-limits image just because it may cause confusion. How differently this metaphor speaks than if, for instance, Jesus had said that coming to him was like starting Hebrew school all over again, something Nicodemus would have readily understood. It is ironic that so many people who describe themselves as "born-again Christians" are opposed to the very idea of the image Jesus uses here to teach Nicodemus.

Then there are images of God as a woman in labor, when the people fail to live justly and obediently. Isaiah 42:14 reads: "For a long time I have held my peace, I have kept still and restrained myself; now I will cry out like a woman in labor, I will gasp and pant." This image of God is loaded with the pain and inevitability of labor, of God laboring to bring Judah to obedience. Jesus also speaks of his hour having arrived, alluding to a woman whose hour of labor has come.

There are other maternal images, such as God as nursing mother: "Can a woman forget her nursing-child, or show no compassion for the child of her womb? Even these may forget, yet I will not forget you" (Isa. 49:15). This image is picked up in 1 Peter 2:2–3: "Like newborn infants, long for the pure, spiritual milk, so that by it you may grow into salvation—if indeed you have tasted that the Lord is good." God is pictured by the psalmist as mother of a weaned child: "But I have calmed and quieted my soul, like a weaned child with its mother" (Ps. 131:2). In the last chapter of Isaiah, Jerusalem too is pictured nurturing the returned exiles as a mother nurses her children: an image of comfort and abundance (Isa. 66:12–13).

Like the word for womb, which is linked to a common word for the love of God, the Hebrew word for breast, *shad*, is linked to one of the names for God in the Old Testament: *El Shaddai*. Apparently some earlier scholars observing the link between *shad* (breast) and *El Shaddai* concluded that the word *shadu* had come to mean "mountain," which justified translating *El Shaddai* as "God Almighty." But more recently some have suggested that the ancient Hebrews, not afraid to assign female anthropomorphisms to God, intended *El Shaddai* to be a maternal image and thus should be translated "God with breasts." The basis for this argument is that this name appears in Genesis six times, always in the context of a fertility blessing. For instance, Genesis 28:3, "May *El Shaddai* bless you and make you fruitful and numerous," or "I am *El Shaddai*: be fruitful and multiply" (Gen. 35:11). The final use of this name for God appears in Genesis 49:25, which says, "by *Shaddai* who will bless you with blessings of heaven above, blessings of the deep that lies beneath, blessings of the breasts and of the womb," a mixture of fertility, womb love, and breast references.[11]

God is also like a comforting mother, Isaiah 66:12–13 tells us: "For thus says [Yahweh] . . . As a mother comforts her child, so I will comfort you." Jesus uses this imagery again in his lament over Jerusalem just before his death. As he stands outside the city looking back over it, he weeps and cries out (Luke 13:34): "Jerusalem, Jerusalem . . . How often have I desired to gather your children together as a hen gathers her brood under her wings, and you were not willing." Here is a tender, protecting, nurturing image of Jesus as mother—Jesus, who is our fullest picture of God.

Feminine imagery for God is not limited to birth and motherhood, however. In Psalm 123:2, God is pictured as the mistress of a household to whom the female servant looks up, and God is a midwife in Psalm 22:9: "Yet it was you who took me from the womb; you kept me safe on my mother's breast." In an image that may have had added resonance for women, God is the wise midwife who delivers people and gives them the assistance they need even when they are as helpless and ignorant as newborns. God is also depicted as the one who gives bread, something that was a woman's job in the cultures in which Scripture was written: God gave manna in Old Testament times; Jesus described himself as "the bread of life" given by God (John 6:31–35). Jesus uses other images of women's work in his parables to depict the activity of God: God is the woman looking for a lost coin (Luke 15:8–10); God is the woman working yeast into a lump of dough (Luke 13:20–21; Matt. 13:33). Johnson observes that it is "obvious that the *imago* is flexible and returns to its giver, so that women who are genuinely in God's image in turn become suitable metaphors for the divine."[12] Jesus compares God to a woman because women bear the image of God.

It is interesting that in a number of instances the writers put male and female images of God back to back, apparently not minding the clash. In fact, the clash may have been an intentional reminder that Yahweh supersedes all conceptions of gender. In the Job passage mentioned earlier, for instance, images are paired:

> Has the rain a father, or who has begotten the drops of dew?
> From whose womb did the ice come forth,
> and who has given birth to the hoar-frost of heaven?
>   (Job 38:28–29)

This is a wonderfully balanced set of poetic images of God who begets and God who births. Of course to beget and to birth are logically impossible, but should we really reject some of Scripture just to make it easy on ourselves? (Is it any more impossible than the claim in Hebrews that Jesus is both the high priest *and* the sacrifice?) The Isaiah 42 passage mentioned earlier illustrates this as well:

> The Lord goes forth like a soldier, like a warrior he stirs up his
>   fury;
> he cries out, he shouts aloud,
> he shows himself mighty against his foes.
> For a long time I have held my peace, I have kept still and re-
>   strained myself;

> now I will cry out like a woman in labor, I will gasp and pant.
> (vv. 13–14)

God is a mighty warrior shouting out and frightening the enemy, and yet God is the woman in labor crying out. Here, Yahweh is depicted with both masculine and feminine images; both men and women can relate their experience to the image, and thus be moved by the image. Again, in Psalm 123:2, we find such a pair: "As the eyes of servants look to the hand of their master, as the eyes of a maid to the hand of her mistress, so our eyes look to the LORD our God."

In the Gospels we see that Jesus did the same thing in his ministry. First of all, he directed his healing to men and women alike (Luke, particularly, alternates male and female healing stories), and these miracles function not only to bring physical wholeness to the people but as signs of the new creation. They are pictures of God at work in women's and men's lives. There is also a delightful balance of images in Jesus' parables: in Luke 13:18–21, God is the farmer who plants the mustard seed and God is the woman working yeast into the lump of dough. In Luke 15:1–10, God is the shepherd looking for lost sheep and God is the woman looking for a lost coin.

Finally, there is the interesting literary echo between Wisdom, in Proverbs 8, and the Logos (Word) in John 1. Personified as a woman, Wisdom is described as having been with God in creation, and, in fact, "created" or "conceived" before creation (v. 22). Wisdom claims that "whoever finds me finds life and obtains favor from the LORD" (v. 35). Some scholars have considered Sophia as a separate entity, which makes her rather like the pagan goddesses, consorts of male gods. Others have seen in Sophia a feminine aspect of God, which is helpful if we are affirming that God exhibits male and female personal characteristics, but is problematic if viewed in a ratio sort of way, as in, God is part female and part male. In any case, the description of Sophia in Proverbs 8 resembles statements made about the Word (Logos) in John 1, though the two are not identical. Whereas the woman Wisdom, or Sophia, is a personification of an abstract characteristic of God, the Logos is identified with God (John 1:1); and whereas Wisdom is created or conceived, the Word is already there at the beginning. Finally, Wisdom is involved in creation as an onlooker (Prov. 8:27–31), while the Logos brings things into being since the Logos is life, and gives life (John 1:3–4). Despite these differences, however, the literary resonance is strong and could serve to stress that the significance of Jesus is not in his maleness.

Indeed it is not his human characteristics that save us but that God condescended to become one of us. It is not ultimately his Jewishness, but his humanity that is important; if not, Gentiles would have no stake in his gospel. It is not his free status, but his humanity that counts; if not, slaves would be left out. It is not his maleness, but his humanity that is central to the incarnation; if not, men would have priority in salvation. As the early church affirmed, only that which has been assumed in the incarnation can be redeemed. In other words, Jesus became human in order to redeem humanity: women and men, Jews and Gentiles, slave and free. We are all equally redeemed through Jesus' death and resurrection because he shared in our humanity.

If we make Jesus' masculinity theologically significant, we have called into question his ability to extend salvation to everyone in the human race. His maleness is not the mechanism through which salvation comes, rather it is incidental. Yet it was probably not accidental, since a female teacher wandering around the countryside of first-century Galilee or Judea would not have had as much success (particularly among Jews looking for a messianic son of David). Neither would Jesus have made such a splash in his society if he had been a Greek rather than a Jew, or if he had been a slave and had no leisure to travel with his message. God obviously could anticipate these things and was wise enough to work in effective ways in that culture, but that does not mean we should pin theological meaning to pragmatic considerations. In John's Gospel, Jesus claims identification with the I AM in his various statements using that phrase, underscoring the gender-neutral nature of Jesus as savior.

One important implication is that Jesus' maleness does not need to be mirrored in those who represent him in this world. Elizabeth Johnson argues that it is neither Jesus' sex that is significant in salvation nor a person's sex that determines whether or not that person can bear the image of Jesus in the world: "The image of Christ does not lie in sexual similarity to the human man Jesus, but in coherence with the narrative shape of his compassionate, liberating life in the world, through the power of the Spirit."[13] In other words, we are not only made in the image of God, but we are remade in Christ's image; with God's help, we reflect Jesus as we follow after him and participate in advancing his work in this world. This is not on the basis of gender, but on the basis of our discipleship, which is consistent with descriptions of discipleship in the New Testament.

Why Feminine Images for God Are Important

First of all, Scripture contains feminine images for God that warrant our attention and appreciation if we are intent on learning all we can about God from the Bible. They play, in fact, an indispensable part of drawing us into relationship with the wonderful, complex God of the Bible. To picture God as a woman kneading bread or as a midwife using her wisdom to deliver a baby or as a mother holding a baby to the breast lets us engage with God in different ways than the king, lord, and father images do. How we learn about God has new possibilities when we think about images of God as mother. Many of us learned to think about what God must be like from looking at the ways our fathers interacted with us—or from looking at how they failed, and understanding God in contrast to their lack. If God is also like a mother to us, then we can and should consider what our mothers have demonstrated—or failed to demonstrate—about God's character. What new insights about the love and care of God might we learn from our mothers' interactions with us?[14]

In addition, the use of feminine images for God calls into question our conceptions of a male God, a god reduced to one gender, a god who is so limited and incomplete that he needs a female goddess to complete him (think of *The Da Vinci Code*). The constant use of masculine imagery and the resulting (nonscriptural) idea that God is male have very serious consequences. Among academic women and among women in the culture at large, interest has been growing in "women's spiritualities" or "women-friendly faiths," seen most notably in the rise of neo-paganism and Wicca. Often people attracted to these movements have experienced Christianity as intrinsically oppressive to women, because of both the historic practices of the church and a certain understanding of scriptural language about God. If the masculine metaphors for God are taken to mean that God *is* male, then men are more like God and have a greater stake in the faith; if God *is* male, men would also represent God more fully in the world, which justifies their domination over women. As Mary Daly so succinctly put it: "If God is male, then male is God."[15] It isn't female imagery for God that drives these women to goddess religion, but the very lack of female imagery in Christian circles that allows Christianity to function as a male-oriented religion.

This raises a serious question for all of us: have our distorted depictions of God and our implicit assumptions of God's maleness turned people away from experiencing the love and power of God in their lives? Do we need to repent of the practice of favoring certain biblical images of God at the expense of the gospel, of using one comfortable image of God—that is, God as father—even if it means obscuring the liberating nature of Jesus' message and the overflowing generosity of God?

In this regard, Catholic theologian Denise Carmody invites readers to listen to the reasons that goddess religion is so powerful and to consider the ways in which a distorted, male-centered Christianity has turned women away. Goddess religion affirms women's bodies, in contrast to the long tradition in Christian circles that has villainized female bodies as hypersexual and spurned them as intrinsically more linked to the rest of the created order (despite Adam's being the one created from the dust of the ground). Goddess religion celebrates women's power and their ability to exercise decision-making will over their lives, rather than requiring female submission to husbands, to male pastors, and by extension to all men. Finally, goddess religions celebrate female bonding and highlight women's participation in human history; this is in contrast to traditional Christian history, which largely renders women invisible, despite the fact that their labors have sustained the church for many centuries.[16] Carmody's list suggests that when nominally Christian people turn to neo-paganism we should listen to their reasons: some women are simply weary of being shut out of the inner sanctum; they are weary of male authority figures, both in writing and in the pulpit, telling them how to be (how to dress, how to be a good or happy wife, how to conceive of vocation, how to use or not use their gifts). They are weary of exclusively male imagery for the divine that subtly, but constantly, communicates that men are more like God, which makes women by nature inferior. They are fed up with the blatant sexism found in statements such as the one a pastor made to one of my students: "Silence is the gift that women give the church." To say such a thing not only denies women their place as disciples of Jesus who were to go and tell, but in the end robs them of their dignity as full human beings. Is it surprising that many women are leaving evangelicalism?[17]

To remedy the male-only God-language, some point to the words *Shekinah*, the glory of God that descends into the temple, and *Ruah*, the Spirit, both of which are female nouns in Hebrew.[18] In essence such words in Scripture assert that God has female or feminine components. But as Elizabeth Johnson and other theologians have pointed out, it is not enough to say that only a part of God is female or feminine, and it is especially troubling to say that the Spirit is somehow feminine while the other two members of the Trinity are masculine. Then we have a situation in which God is two-thirds male, and the two "masculine" members, the Father and the Son, send the "feminine" member out to do God's work in the world.[19] God cannot be divided up in this way, and besides, this model would further solidify a subordinate role for women as helpers assigned tasks by men.

It is also not helpful to suggest that God has "feminine characteristics" that we can enumerate in addition to the "masculine" ones, since how cultures assign characteristics to the respective genders appears to be largely arbitrary. Things like nurture or strength or wisdom are human characteristics and not capacities that either sex has a monopoly on. If we assert, for instance, that God is nurturing and gentle (i.e., feminine) and that God is also strong and bold (i.e., masculine) we have said nothing about God's gender qualities but have given religious sanction to our own definitions of women and men.[20] To assume that nurturing is intrinsically (biologically) linked to motherhood is something that our society has a stake in perpetuating—it certainly lets men off the hook on the parenting front—but is merely a sentimentalizing of motherhood.

Furthermore, to assert that the nurturing of God is feminine is to completely miss how the metaphor of "father" is used in the Old Testament. Surprisingly, there are not that many references to God as father in the Old Testament, and virtually every one of them refers to the care and compassion of the father who represents God.[21] In the first mention in the Old Testament of God being a father (2 Sam. 7:14; cf. 1 Chron. 17:13), God promises steadfast love to David and his descendants through a son whose throne will be established forever: "I will be a father to him, and he shall be a son to me." Most of the passages refer to God's care for the people as a group of helpless children; for instance, "Father of orphans and protector of widows is God in his holy habitation" (Ps. 68:5), or, "As a father has compassion for his children, so the LORD has compassion for those who fear him. For he knows how we were made; he remembers that we are dust" (Ps. 103:13–14). These passages emphasize the tender care of God as father, who notices the weakness of the children and treats them gently. It is not an image of control or dominating power in a family. In the Prophets, God is called "father" in the middle of the people's estrangement: "You, O LORD, are our father; our Redeemer from of old is your name" (Isa. 63:16). Or even more pointedly, in Jeremiah 3:19, in which God is the rejected father:

> I thought
>   how I would set you among my children,
> and give you a pleasant land,
>   the most beautiful heritage of all the nations.
> And I thought you would call me, My Father,
>   and would not turn from following me.

Directly following those verses is a plea for the people's return, and a prediction of their return in 31:9:

> With weeping they shall come,
>   and with consolations I will lead them back,
> I will let them walk by brooks of water
>   in a straight path in which they shall not stumble;
> for I have become a father to Israel,
>   and Ephraim is my firstborn.

When the Old Testament writers wanted to evoke the intimate care and compassion of God, they employed father or mother images, which suggest that these are similar rather than opposite images. Obviously the power of both these images is in the way in which they resonate with people's experience as parents themselves. "Parental love is the most powerful and intimate experience we have of giving love whose return is not calculated (though a return is appreciated); it is the gift of *life as such* to others. Parental love wills life and when it comes, exclaims, 'It is good that you exist!' Moreover, in addition to giving life, parental love nurtures what it has brought into existence, wanting growth and fulfillment for all."[22] This is how father and mother imagery is used in the Hebrew texts. In fact, when the Old Testament writers want to focus attention on the power, authority, or discipline of God, they employ different images, such as king, lord, and she-bear.

Metaphors not only draw us in but inform our thoughts and actions. This is to say that our concepts of God will determine how we understand our service to God in this world. Picturing God only as a sovereign king who makes humans the rulers over creation in his stead produces different feelings and actions than if we also imagine God as a mother who brings forth life—who gives us life, along with everyone and everything else. Again, if we think of God as an artist who creates everything and pronounces it good, then God's declaration is an aesthetic judgment and evokes a certain response in us. We might feel awe before God's creativity as well as a sense of duty to care for God's beautiful piece of work. However, as theologian Sallie McFague observes, if we see God as mother bringing this whole universe into existence, almost like giving birth, then the assessment is not an aesthetic one, but a parental one: the "very good" arises out of deep compassion. We are not saying that God *is* our mother, but that the mother metaphor brings home a deeply Christian understanding of how God relates to the world: with intimate, unfailing love. This parental love will work for betterment of created things; it will continually ask, are my offspring flourishing? It is a love that draws in the last and the least because that is what fathers and mothers do. In this model, we are called to be concerned about the well-being of all because we were all brought into being by the same parent; we are in this complex and glorious web of relationships together.[23]

Objections to Feminine Imagery

It is commonplace for moderate evangelical scholars to state that "God is not male" but then to reject the use of images that would help to make that message clear to Christians in the pews. It can hardly be surprising that people who go to church and never hear anything but masculine pronouns and masculine titles for God should think themselves completely orthodox for claiming that God *is* male, or that God *is* father. Metaphors are like a finger pointing to the moon: they help direct attention, but one shouldn't confuse the moon with one's own finger.[24] Many people, however, do just that and confuse their favorite metaphor for God with God's actual nature. They ignore the range of metaphors for God in Scripture and forget that our language and our metaphors are only partial—never adequate—containers for the fullness of God. Once this happens we end up worshiping something that is less than God, something reduced to fit our comfort zone. Brian Wren observes, "No image is adequate. To select one image and bow down to it is idolatrous. If we draw on a variety of God-images and let them balance, enrich, and clash with one another, we shall be following the instincts of biblical faith and the methods of many biblical voices. Allowing God-images to *clash* is important, because it reminds us that we are approaching that which is beyond all images."[25] It is just this clash, however, that many seek to avoid as they ignore feminine imagery for God.

One common objection to female imagery, even for those who do recognize the variety of images in Scripture, is that most metaphors for God in Scripture are male. Of course, the preponderance of male metaphors in evangelical preaching is misleading, since female images are so routinely overlooked, but still, in Scripture the balance is toward masculine images. People who judge this imbalance as grounds for sticking with male metaphors are claiming, explicitly or not, that some metaphors for God are definitive and others less so. However, the frequency of a metaphor cannot be the arbiter of its truthfulness, since all are given to teach us of God and engage us in worship. The Bible does not invite us to count up all the times God is referred to as rock as opposed to water to determine whether God is more rocklike or waterlike. Both images, rock and water, are supposed to deepen our interaction with God, no matter how many times they appear. If we take Scripture seriously, we are supposed to use them and learn from them, and in the same way we are supposed to embrace all the personal images of God. The fact that female metaphors are used of God at all shows that they have something to communicate to us. In fact, one could argue that if God never desired to be thought of in female terms then likely there would be no female images of God in Scripture.

Another objection people raise is that Jesus called God "Father" and so should we. However, Johnson notes that in the Gospels the use of the term grew: Mark (who likely wrote the first Gospel) uses it the least, and John (who likely wrote the last of the four Gospels) uses it the most, although even in John the I AM is the most important theological designation Jesus uses for God. In any case, the parables of Jesus give us many images of God, including landowner, baker, farmer, woman cleaning the house, shepherd, and father. "Taken as a whole, the Gospel tradition demonstrates variety and plurality in Jesus' speech about God rather than the exclusive centrality of speech about God as father. To select this one metaphor and grant it sole rights does not follow the pattern of Jesus' speech."[26]

In the New Testament, outside the Gospels there is a surprising dearth of the title "Father" in direct prayer or in reference to God. Even though Jesus, when he gave them the instructions on prayer, invited his followers to call God "Father," they did not take this as a rule that forbade them to call God other things. In the eleven prayers recorded in the New Testament outside the Gospels, the early Christians addressed God with other titles, but never as "Father." Every time in Acts, for instance, when direct prayers are recorded, the prayers use terms such as "Lord," "Sovereign Lord," and, in Stephen's prayer, "Lord Jesus" (see Acts 1:24; 4:24; 7:59–60; 10:13–14). Paul uses *marana tha* (Our Lord, come!) in 1 Corinthians 16:22. The remaining recorded prayers in the NT are all found in the book of Revelation. Here, too, no prayers are directed to the "Father"; instead we have names such as "Lord God Almighty" (twice), and once each for "Lord and God," "Holy One," "Lord God, the Almighty," and "Lord Jesus" (see Rev. 4:11; 11:16–17; 15:3; 16:5, 7; 22:20).[27]

In simply speaking of God, the New Testament writers also used the designation "Father" much less than other names; in fact, they used it only about one time in twenty when God is named outside the Gospels, according to Paul Smith. He found that the references to God in the NT outside the Gospels break down as follows: 1,055 times as God, 476 times as Lord, and only 78 times as Father.[28] This is not to invalidate the image of God as Father, since in a previous paragraph we rejected deciding a metaphor's worth based on frequency, but to decenter the image. It is to remind us that using "Father" exclusively, or even primarily, is not a biblical practice.

Besides that, when people claim that we have to call God "Father" because Jesus taught us to do so in the Lord's Prayer, they overlook the fact that we often pray without using all the rest of the words of that prayer. Jesus' closest followers did not interpret the Lord's Prayer as demanding we always address God as Father, and neither did they think that the other phrases of the prayer were the only words they should speak to God. Though "hallowed be thy name, thy kingdom come, thy will be done on earth as it is in heaven" are powerful requests worth saying to God, it is safe to say that most people who go to God in prayer do not stick solely to the words of the Lord's Prayer to make their requests or express their worship. Appropriately they cry out to God in the language of their own hearts. Why is it assumed that we must always begin our prayers with some form of "Our Father" but then we are free to use our own words in the body of the prayer?

Other objections to female imagery for God seem to gather around the idea that it is inherently dangerous to employ such metaphors, the feminine imagery for God in Scripture notwithstanding. For instance, some people are afraid that feminine imagery is sexual and therefore would be inappropriate for God. Donald Hook and Alvin Kimel assert that God is not male, but that masculine pronouns should be used because "The decided advantage of masculine pronouns is that they do have a long precedent for carrying nonsexual connotation. Female pronouns do not."[29] This is, of course, a very problematic assertion, because masculine pronouns are *not* neutral, which is why so many conservative Christians of all stripes consider God to be male. The pseudo-generic pronouns never could function completely as generics because masculine pronouns (and images) are, after all, well, masculine. Even in the eighteenth century some expressed uneasiness with masculine pronouns being used generically, but particularly since the 1970s, the terms "man" and "mankind" and the use of male pronouns to designate all people or any people, male or female, has given way to a more specific usage: man means a male and masculine pronouns are recognized to be referring to males. Since that is true for speaking about people, then there is nothing generic about applying a masculine pronoun to God.[30]

Furthermore, the male metaphors for God are just as gendered as the female metaphors; it is simply that their "sexual character is cloaked."[31] In other words, male images for God are not gender-neutral, they are male. "Today I have begotten you," for instance, is certainly a metaphor of male sexuality, but the maleness of the image is downplayed and overlooked. Given the fear of and fascination with female sexuality down through the history of the church, not to mention the current fixation on it, introducing female metaphors seems to some like sexualizing God, and linking God to the sexuality most feared: female sexuality. To reduce female God images to their sexual component is parallel to the sexualization of women we observed in the pairs of nouns discussed in the previous chapter. If things female are reduced to their sexual difference from things male, then the first attribute we think of when we think of the female is sexuality. But if we remember that all humans, women as well as men, are much more than just their sexuality, we might conclude that female metaphors would have a range of things to teach us, just as male metaphors do. Female images for God are not nonsexual (just as male images are not nonsexual) but neither are they simply sexual; they are richer and more complex than that. In the end, using female imagery points out the fact that neither masculine nor feminine language for God is gender-neutral, and it reminds us that God cannot be reduced to either male or female.

Another fear regarding female metaphors is that their use will lead to goddess worship. The argument here rests on an erroneous picture of the religions of the ancient Near East and how the Yahweh religion compared with them. Ever since interest in female spiritualities began growing thirty years ago, adherents of goddess religion have depicted ancient Canaanite religion as an idyllic, female-centered system that was overcome by the masculine deity of the Israelites. Christians have, for some reason, taken this at face value, even though the most explicit showdown between Yahweh and a pagan deity recorded in Scripture was between Elijah and the prophets of Ba'al, a decidedly male character (1 Kings 18). Furthermore, Tikva Frymer-Kensky, a scholar of ancient Near Eastern religions, has shown that a mythological golden age of goddess worship never existed in that area, because, first of all, the religions in the ancient Near East included numbers of gods, not just goddesses, and there was a male high god, *El*, over them all. This was not an era of female ascendancy in the divine or human realm, given that there was still a male in control, dominating the activities of the gods and goddesses subordinate to him. In addition, the goddesses were usually consigned primarily to fertility, which is simply a reflection of a society that valued women only for their child-bearing capabilities, whereas men could be praised for their artistic skill, their prowess in battle, or any number of other achievements. She argues that a religion with fertility goddesses is not liberating for women but consigns them to a single, albeit important, slice of human life.[32]

To sum up, the difference between Yahweh and Canaanite deities is not that Israel's God was male and Canaanite deities were female. Rather, the primary difference is that ancient Hebrew faith was monotheistic rather than featuring a pantheon of religious figures. The *Shema*, the verses out of Deuteronomy 6 that form a central affirmation of faith for Jews even today, emphasizes that God is one; monotheism instead of polytheism is the foundational difference. But the *Shema* says nothing of God's gender, and this is another huge contrast to the paired gods and goddesses in Canaanite religion. Yahweh is not sexualized, not a male god in need of a female consort in order to create the cosmos or rule over it.

We could ask those who are fearful of falling into goddess worship merely through embracing female metaphors for God, why are female images more dangerous than male images? Given the male and female divine beings that populated ancient Near Eastern religion (and paganism of every sort since then), why would embracing female images of God lead to paganism any more than using masculine images tempt us to consider worshiping Ba'al of ancient Canaanite religion, Oden who is called "All-Father" in the Scandinavian pantheon, or Shiva in Hinduism? Many religions worship male deities, and some even call their gods "king," "lord," or "father," but that doesn't make these same evangelicals fear to use those male metaphors for God. Rather, as mentioned earlier, the attraction of nominally Christian people to goddess religion might be in direct proportion to the extent to which God has been assumed to *be* male in Christian tradition.

The irony in all this is that rejecting female metaphors for God, and implicitly (or explicitly) promoting a male view of God, boils down to the same error as those who claim that God *is* female: in the end each position simply mirrors the other, one side claiming God is male, the other side claiming God is female, and both reducing God to something less than the depiction of God in Scripture.

Some evangelicals fear that using female metaphors for God, particularly birthing images, would mean an automatic blurring of the line between God and the creation.[33] This fear is unfounded, first, because there are verses in Scripture that describe God in just those ways (see "Female Images of God in Scripture" in this chapter). Second, it seems to be built on the dubious claim that women have a unique connection to the physical world, as if all human beings aren't made of the same chemicals and subject to the same forces of growth, aging, and death. The linking of women to earth and men to spirit or rational thought is certainly foreign to the texts of our faith, but as early Christian writers embraced aspects of Greek philosophy, such ideas entered Christian imagination. Scripture designates only the human relationship to the created order. Furthermore, if one were to take the fathering or mothering images literally, then the line between parent deity and offspring world would be blurred equally by either parent's participation. It must be a holdover from a premodern understanding of conception to claim that if God gave birth to the world, this would make the earth the same substance as God, but if God fathered the world that would not be the case. Today we know that the substance of an offspring is derived in part from the mother and in part from the father.

Some people fear using female images for God simply because they know that feminists do it. To declare something wrong, however, just because those we disagree with do it, has always drawn Christians into odd and even heretical positions. It is not a reliable way to make decisions. (Oliver Cromwell refused to take a drug that would have saved his life just because the Jesuits used it.) Especially when it comes to points of theology or worship practices, each thing must be judged on its own merit.

In addition, many evangelicals assume all feminists to be radical—by which they mean antimen, antifamily, and pro–female superiority—and therefore write them off entirely. But to cast a whole movement in terms of the extreme elements is never fair; it is a cheap way to discredit the movement's main message and to ignore the perspectives of the majority of people in the movement. (To do this with feminism is like writing off Christianity on the basis of the radicalism of Christian militia groups.) In actuality, Christian feminism is diverse: there are feminists of many theological stripes, including evangelicals, progressive Catholics, process theologians, liberation theologians, and so on. People who advocate biblical feminism should not be lumped in with those who have rejected large portions of the Bible, for instance. Further, we should be careful not to blame feminism for every perspective of a particular feminist with whom we disagree.[34] In other words, many scholars in the classic liberal tradition question the bodily resurrection of Jesus, and most of these scholars have been men. If a feminist scholar in that tradition rejects the resurrection, we should not attribute it to her feminism (as in, feminism will lead you to reject the resurrection) but recognize that she shares assumptions with others in the classic liberal tradition.

Another fear that some writers express about female imagery for God is that it seems to make God androgynous; that cannot be, they argue, if we are gendered and we are made in God's image. Or, to start at the other side of things, they assume that our sexuality is part of our spiritual identity and then turn to the *imago Dei* text and suppose that God too must contain these two genders in some spiritual sense. This is nonsensical, since gender arises from biological sex, and clearly God does not have a physical body with sexual characteristics. We could argue that God does encompass both masculine and feminine—in terms of roles and characteristics assumed for each gender in the cultures in which Scripture was written—but God is not simply a melding together of male and female spiritual essences. Conceiving of God as a blend of male and female in any sort of spiritual sense is not biblical at all but reflects the yin and yang, the male principle and the female principle, of Eastern thought. God's loving community is trinitarian and not pictured as sexual balance or completeness because of male and female aspects within God.

Finally, some theologians object to using female imagery for God because it doesn't fit their concepts of hierarchy in the universe. Vernard Eller, for instance, asserts that God "has addressed us only as his beloved, only as feminine correspondent to his own masculinity."[35] He argues, as do the others in this camp, that the subordinate position of humanity before God puts humanity in the female role vis à vis God, who is in the male role. Not only does this assume that God must in some sense *be* male, but, for the comparison to work, that male human beings are superior to female human beings. This gives transcendent justification for asserting the inferiority of women and requiring the submission of women to men. In other words, this gives religious significance and eternal permanence to male domination over women, since the male God is eternally superior to the female human race or female church. This also implies that God is like the gods of ancient paganism after all, one who needs a female consort.

Some may object here that the church *is* the bride of Christ since Scripture says so in various places in the New Testament; the model seems biblically warranted. However, this is simply another example of confusing a metaphor for reality. The bride/bridegroom imagery is not the only biblical way to think about our relationship with God: we are also adopted children, servants to a lord, subjects of a monarch, freed slaves serving a new master, disciples (or students/followers) of Jesus, friends of Jesus, parts of Jesus' body, stones in the temple God is building, members of a holy nation and a royal priesthood, and the blind, lame, unattractive outcasts who are brought in for a banquet. We have to hold all these metaphors in mind, even let them clash with each other (after all, we can't be both Christ's body and Christ's bride in any literal sense), in order to guard against confusing any one of them with *the way things are*. They each point to some aspect of the great mystery of God's communion with us.

Conclusions

The God of the universe is not containable in a building made with human hands, nor within the limits of human language, but we build buildings and we use language to create spaces to meet with God. To understand this immense and complex God, we allow all the metaphors given to us in Scripture to teach us and to draw us in.

UP AND OUT

At the end of their visit to Willy Wonka's chocolate factory, the little boy Charlie and his grandfather find themselves in a glass elevator with Willy Wonka, who exclaims gleefully: "I have been *longing* to press this button for years! . . . Up and out!" When Grandpa Joe realizes that Mr. Wonka intends to drive the elevator right through the roof of the factory, he is terrified.

> "But . . . but . . . but . . . it's made of glass!" shouted Grandpa Joe. "It'll break into a million pieces!"
>
> "I suppose it might," said Mr. Wonka, cheerful as ever, "but it's pretty thick glass, all the same."
>
> The elevator rushed on, going up and up and up, faster and faster and faster . . .
>
> Then suddenly, *CRASH!*—and the most tremendous noise of splintering wood and broken tiles came from directly above their heads, and Grandpa Joe shouted, "Help! It's the end! We're done for!" and Mr. Wonka said, "No, we're not! We're through! We're out!"[1]

Maybe we're a little like Grandpa Joe: maybe we are afraid the elevator will blast apart and we'll be adrift in androgyny if we admit that men and women are made equally in the image of God and that both bear God's likeness, or that what we hold in common as humans is far greater than any gender difference we can identify. Maybe we fear that the family will disintegrate if we suggest that the most loving and mutually respectful way to organize a marriage is in equal partnership rather than hierarchically, with a husband-boss. Maybe we are nervous that the church will shatter into a million pieces if we affirm that God used women as word-bearers in Scripture and as active ministers—including leadership—throughout the history of the church and continues to do it in our age as well. And maybe, if we recognize that God is not male, but, in fact, pictured in Scripture with a variety of masculine and feminine images, everything will feel so out of control that we'll start shouting, "Help! It's the end! We're done for!"

But the elevator did not break. It simply traveled up and out.

What is our "up and out"? Perhaps it is getting free of the culturally formed ideas of women, men, marriage, church, and God; perhaps it involves being freed to *be* the church in this world, characterized by supreme love for God and sacrificial love for the other.

What would "up and out" mean when it comes to biblical images of God? Perhaps we could embrace all the metaphors for God, to see what they teach us, and more, to allow them to draw us in. Perhaps we would come into a state of wonder again at this God who comes to us, tapping at the door of the mundane moments of our lives, speaking to us through metaphors we can understand, and yet who transcends them all.

And once we contemplate again God's immensity we could ask, what does it mean that we are made in the image of this wonderfully complex God? For one thing it means living less artificially, less constrained by societal expectations and even church expectations and more according to who we are. Men can in fact be nurturing and even emotionally expressive, just as God is portrayed in Scripture, and women can be strong and decisive, even aggressive as a she-bear, because all of these are human characteristics and ways in which we mirror God. If God made us unique individuals, we probably shouldn't be trying to wedge ourselves into narrow slots of femininity and masculinity, but rather we should be living out our personalities, our callings, our very selves, in thankfulness to the one who made us.

And so, "up and out" means a new basis for all of our relationships: we each bring that whole complex and mysterious thing called "myself" into interaction with others, curious to know others who are also formed in God's image, eager to share the life given us by God. Within the redeemed community it will mean trusting one another with our hopes and doubts, encouraging each other with prayer and empathy, loving one another in foot-washing humility. All of these things will pertain to the highest degree in Christian marriage, as the husband and wife work together to live out their callings and use their unique gifts and talents to bear God's presence in this world. To the best of their abilities, they will promote the human happiness and the spiritual wholeness of the other, as part of their sacrificial love. In the end, "up and out" will mean that we stop playing roles and learn to know and be known; we stop seeking privilege and learn to honor the other; we stop vying for power and learn to love deeply and honestly.

Linked to all of this, of course, is a renewed appreciation of all the stories of women in the Bible, including those of women who acted courageously and wisely, and who even proclaimed the Word of God. Perhaps we would notice that they are not only mothers, wives, daughters, and sisters, but also worship leaders, military and political leaders, and poets. Perhaps we could put away our embarrassment that God tapped women to be prophets and to serve as redeemer figures to their people. We might take seriously the discipleship of the women around Jesus, and see the way he welcomed their participation in his ministry, and commissioned them to "go and tell" at the end. Then we might have to admit that God does things that we may not even be comfortable with: women on the streets of Jerusalem on the day of Pentecost, women as evangelists, as apostles, as coworkers in the gospel. We may recognize that there isn't even any gender distinction regarding gifts, since there is not a men's list and a women's list (1 Cor. 12; Eph. 4), and the Holy Spirit distributes these gifts not according to our comfortable categories but for the good of all according to the divine will.

When we recognize all those things, then it's "up and out." Then we can relax in the delightful creativity of God, who works in such surprising ways. Then we can lift our voices up together in worship and join hands to serve God fully in our homes, our churches, and our world. May we all be faithful to this call!

NOTES

Introduction

1. Penelope Eckert and Sally McConnell-Ginet, *Language and Gender* (Cambridge: Cambridge University Press, 2003), 10.

2. A fine resource in this regard is Elaine Storkey, *Origins of Difference: The Gender Debate Revisited* (Grand Rapids: Baker Academic, 2001).

3. Norm Wakefield and Jody Brolsma, *Men Are from Israel, Women Are from Moab: Insights about the Sexes from the Book of Ruth* (Downers Grove, IL: InterVarsity, 2000); Rosalind Barnett and Caryl Rivers, *Same Difference: How Gender Myths are Hurting Our Relationships, Our Children, and Our Jobs* (New York: Basic Books, 2005).

4. Barbara Ehrenreich and Deirdre English, *For Her Own Good: Two Centuries of the Experts' Advice to Women* (New York: Anchor Books, 2005).

5. See the introduction to Lisa Graham McMinn's *Sexuality and Holy Longing: Embracing Intimacy in a Broken World* (New York: Jossey-Bass: 2004), 1–11.

6. Paul Smith, *Is It Okay to Call God "Mother"? Considering the Feminine Face of God* (Peabody, MA: Hendrickson, 1993), 10.

7. Catherine Clark Kroeger and Nancy Nason-Clark, *No Place for Abuse: Biblical and Practical Resources to Counteract Domestic Violence* (Downers Grove, IL: InterVarsity, 2001).

8. Sarah Heaner Lancaster, *Women and the Authority of Scripture: A Narrative Approach* (Harrisburg, PA: Trinity Press International, 2002), 15.

9. Linda Hogan, *From Women's Experience to Feminist Theology* (Sheffield: Sheffield Academic Press, 1995), 165.

Chapter 1 Made in God's Image

1. J. Richard Middleton, *The Liberating Image: The* Imago Dei *in Genesis 1* (Grand Rapids: Brazos, 2005). For a brief summary of these views of the *imago Dei*, see Stanley J. Grenz, *The Social God and the Relational Self: A Trinitarian Theology of the* Imago Dei (Louisville: Westminster John Knox, 2001), 192–203.

2. John Eldredge, *Wild at Heart: Discovering the Secrets of a Man's Soul*, new ed. (Nashville: Thomas Nelson, 2006).

3. Elizabeth Johnson, *She Who Is: The Mystery of God in Feminist Theological Discourse* (New York: Crossroad, 1993), 70.

4. Loren Cunningham and David Joel Hamilton, *Why Not Women? A Fresh Look at Scripture on Women in Missions, Ministry, and Leadership* (Seattle: YWAM Publishing, 2000).

5. Alvin Schmidt, *Veiled and Silenced: How Culture Shaped Sexist Theology* (Macon, GA: Mercer University Press, 1989).

6. Dorothy Sayers, *Are Women Human?* new ed. (Grand Rapids: Eerdmans, 2005).

7. *The Mishnah*, trans. Herbert Danby (Oxford: Oxford University Press, 1974), 138.

8. Ibid., 141.

9. Judith R. Baskin, *Midrashic Women: Formations of the Feminine in Rabbinic Literature* (Hanover, NH: Brandeis University Press, 2002), 53–54.

10. See Tertullian, "Adorning Women," in Barbara MacHaffie, ed., *Readings in Her Story: Women in Christian Tradition* (Minneapolis: Fortress, 1992), 27–33; also Jerome, "Christian Asceticism," in MacHaffie, *Readings*, 33–40; "Calvin on the Creation of Woman," in MacHaffie, *Readings*, 72–74.

11. Victor Hamilton, quoted in Grenz, *Social God*, 270.

12. Mary Evans, *Woman in the Bible: An Overview of All the Crucial Passages on Women's Roles* (Downers Grove, IL: InterVarsity, 1983), 16. See Exod. 18:4; Deut. 33:7, 26, 29; Ps. 33:20; 115:9–11; 124:8.

13. Jean M. Higgins, "*Anastaium Sinaita* and the Superiority of Woman," *Journal of Biblical Literature* 97, no. 2 (1978): 255, as quoted in Grenz, *Social God*, 275.

14. John Stackhouse Jr., *Finally Feminist: A Pragmatic Christian Understanding of Gender* (Grand Rapids: Baker Academic, 2005), 66–67.

15. Stanley Grenz, *Sexual Ethics: An Evangelical Perspective* (Louisville: Westminster John Knox, 1990), 42.

16. Alice Bellis, *Helpmates, Harlots, and Heroes: Women's Stories in the Hebrew Bible* (Louisville: Westminster John Knox, 1994), 48.

17. See esp. Catherine Brekus, "Suffer Not a Woman to Teach," chap. 7 in *Strangers and Pilgrims: Female Preaching in America, 1740–1845* (Chapel Hill: University of North Carolina Press, 1998).

18. B. T. Roberts, *Ordaining Women—Biblical and Historical Insights* (Rochester: Earnest Christian Publishing House, 1891; reprint by Light and Life Press, 1992), 34.

19. Karl Barth, *Church Dogmatics* 3.4, "The Doctrine of Creation," as quoted in Elizabeth Clark and Herbert Richardson, *Women and Religion: A Feminist Sourcebook of Christian Thought* (San Francisco: HarperSanFrancisco, 1977), 254, 255–56.

20. John Piper and Wayne Grudem, eds., *Recovering Biblical Manhood and Womanhood: A Response to Evangelical Feminism* (Wheaton, IL: Crossway Books, 1991).

21. Cited in Grenz, *Sexual Ethics*, 42.

22. See, e.g., "Luther on Female Preaching," in MacHaffie, *Readings*, 75–76; "Calvin on the Silence of Women," in MacHaffie, *Readings*, 76–79.

23. Rebecca Merrill Groothuis, *Good News for Women: A Biblical Picture of Gender Equality* (Grand Rapids: Baker Books, 1997), 141.

24. Johnson, *She Who Is*, 64.

25. Ibid.

Chapter 2 Women Characters in Scripture

1. Alice Bellis, *Helpmates, Harlots, and Heroes: Women's Stories in the Hebrew Bible* (Louisville: Westminster John Knox, 1994), 74.

2. Bellis discusses Phyllis Trible's view in *Helpmates, Harlots, and Heroes*, 102–6.

3. According to the New Oxford Annotated Bible textual note linked to Isa. 8:3.

4. Craig Keener, *The IVP Bible Background Commentary: New Testament* (Downers Grove, IL: InterVarsity, 1993), 218. He observes that women did not sit at rabbis' feet, though he notes one second-century exception in which a learned rabbi's daughter married another learned rabbi. She tried to be part of the rabbinic discussions, though most rabbis ignored her contributions.

5. Richard Bauckham, *Gospel Women: Studies of the Named Women in the Gospels* (Grand Rapids: Eerdmans, 2002), 110–13.

6. Ibid.

7. *Diakonos* used by Paul with reference to himself in 1 Cor. 3:5; 2 Cor. 3:6; to Timothy in 1 Thess. 3:2; 1 Tim. 2:7; to Tychicus in Col. 4:7; to Apollos in 1 Cor. 3:5; to Epaphras in Col. 1:7; to Christ in Rom. 15:8; Gal. 2:17.

8. Catherine Clark Kroeger and Mary J. Evans, eds., *The IVP Women's Bible Commentary* (Downers Grove, IL: InterVarsity, 2002), 644.

9. Ute E. Eisen, *Women Officeholders in Early Christianity: Epigraphical and Literary Studies*, trans. Linda Maloney (Collegeville, MN: Liturgical Press, 2000), 47.

10. Erwin Nestle's text-critical edition of the Greek NT in 1927 changed it; so Eisen, *Women Officeholders*, 47; Eisen also cites Bernadette Brooten (ibid.).

11. See 1 Cor. 15:10; Gal. 4:11; Phil. 2:16; Col. 1:29; 1 Tim. 4:10.

12. Used for this section: Gordon Fee, *The First Epistle to the Corinthians*, New International Commentary on the New Testament (Grand Rapids: Eerdmans, 1987); Marion Soards, *1 Corinthians*, New International Biblical Commentary (Peabody, MA: Hendrickson, 1999); C. K. Barrett, *The First Epistle to the Corinthians*, Harper's New Testament Commentaries (New York: Harper and Row, 1968).

13. Fee, *First Epistle to the Corinthians*, 699–708; C. K. Barrett, *First Epistle to the Corinthians*, 330–33.

14. Used in this section: Richard Clark Kroeger and Catherine Clark Kroeger, *I Suffer Not a Woman: Rethinking 1 Timothy 2:11–15 in Light of Ancient Evidence* (Grand Rapids: Baker Academic, 1998); Gilbert Bilezikian, *Beyond Sex Roles: What the Bible Says about a Woman's Place in Church and Family* (Grand Rapids: Baker Academic, 1985); Gordon Fee, *1 and 2 Timothy, Titus*, Good News Commentary (New York: Harper and Row, 1984).

15. The problem is that the inconsistency is seen more in practice than in writing. For instance, John MacArthur argues against women speaking in church and also warns against displays of wealth, but one would have to see the women in his church to know whether they ignore the specific guidelines set out in the text (gold, pearls, braided hair), though we could be certain that women are not in the pulpit.

16. F. F. Bruce, *Galatians*, New International Greek Testament Commentary (Grand Rapids: Eerdmans, 1982), 190.

Chapter 3 Supermodels for Jesus?

1. Michelle Graham, *Wanting to Be Her: Body Image Secrets Victoria Won't Tell You* (Downers Grove, IL: InterVarsity, 2005), 51.

2. See Jean Kilbourne, *Deadly Persuasion: Why Women and Girls Must Fight the Addictive Power of Advertising* (New York: Free Press, 1999).

3. Kim Chernin, *The Obsession: Reflections on the Tyranny of Slenderness* (New York: Harper, 1981), 110.

4. Naomi Wolf, *Beauty Myth: How Images of Beauty Are Used against Women* (New York: William and Morrow, 1991), 187.

5. Susan Brownmiller, *Femininity* (New York: Ballantine Books, 1985).

6. See, e.g., the Web site for the Canadian Association for the Advancement of Women in Sport and Physical Fitness (www.caaws.ca), which has links to many articles about women athletes, women's sports, and some of the challenges unique to women in sports.

For an academic analysis of the *Sports Illustrated* swimsuit edition, see Laurel Davis, *The Swimsuit Issue and Sport: Hegemonic Masculinity in* Sports Illustrated (Albany: SUNY Press, 1997).

7. See Naomi Wolf's discussion in the chap. titled "Work," in *Beauty Myth*.

8. "Highlights of Women's Earnings in 2006," US Department of Labor, US Bureau of Labor Statistics, Report 1000, September 2007, p.1. See www.bls.gov/cps/cpswom2006.pdf.

9. As quoted in Terry Poulton, *No Fat Chicks: How Big Business Profits by Making Women Hate Their Bodies—and How to Fight Back* (New York: Birch Lane, 1997), 39.

10. Wolf, *Beauty Myth*, 187.

11. See Robert Mankoff, ed., *The Complete Cartoons of the* New Yorker (New York: Black Dog and Leventhal, 2006).

12. Lisa Abend and Geoff Pingree, "Models Get the Skinny on Weight," *Time*, September 16, 2006. This article can be found on-line at www.time.com/time/world/article/0,8599,1535663,00.html.

13. Jean Kilbourne, *Killing Us Softly 3*, distributed by Media Education Foundation (Northampton, MA: 2000).

14. See Kerry Knowlton, "The Beast Within: An Exploration into Eating Disorders among College Women," www.sahe.colostate.edu/Journal_articles/Journal%202000_2001 .vol%2010/The%20Beast%20Within.pdf. See also Healthy Place.com, a community for those with eating disorders (www.healthyplace.com/Communities/Eating_Disorders/women_3.asp).

15. Mark Johnson, "NY Lawmaker Wants Model's Weight Guide," *Boston Globe*, January 31, 2007, www.boston.com/news/nation/articles/2007/01/31/ny_lawmaker_wants_models_weight_guide/. This article was also run by Fox News on January 31, 2007.

16. Bob Herbert, "Why Aren't We Shocked?" *New York Times*, October 16, 2006, www .nytimes.com/2006/10/18/opinion/118herbert.html.

17. Joan Jacobs Brumberg, "Are We Facing an Epidemic of Self-Injury?" *Chronicle of Higher Education*, December 8, 2006, B6–B8; Gregory Eells, "Mobilizing the Campuses against Self-Mutilation," *Chronicle of Higher Education*, December 8, 2006, B8–B9.

18. An exaggerated example of this is a book on dating from the late 1960s, Helen Andelin's *The Fascinating Girl* (Santa Barbara: Pacific Press, 1969), in which young women are instructed on how to "win" the man and how to make him feel superior and in control so that he will play his role. The ironic subtext is that the woman is in control throughout, despite appearing passive.

19. Biblical use of the word "flesh," from A. R. G. Deasley, "Flesh," in *Baker Theological Dictionary of the Bible*, ed. Walter Elwell (Grand Rapids: Baker Books, 1996), 259–60.

Chapter 4 The Good, the Bad, and the Downright Strange

1. Rodney Clapp, *Families at the Crossroads: Beyond Traditional and Modern Options* (Downers Grove, IL: InterVarsity, 1993), 13.

2. See chap. 1 for a fuller discussion of Adam and Eve's shared essence, function, and substance.

3. Elizabeth Johnson, *She Who Is: The Mystery of God in Feminist Theological Discourse* (New York: Crossroad, 1993), 68.

4. Stephen Post, *More Lasting Unions: Christianity, the Family, and Society* (Grand Rapids: Eerdmans, 2000), 58.

5. Ben Witherington III, *The Paul Quest: The Renewed Search for the Jew of Tarsus* (Downers Grove, IL: InterVarsity, 1998), 266–68.

6. John Stackhouse Jr., *Finally Feminist: A Pragmatic Christian Understanding of Gender* (Grand Rapids: Baker Academic, 2005), 72.

7. Quote from Luther's *The Estate of Marriage*, in Elizabeth Clark and Herbert Richardson, *Women and Religion: A Feminist Sourcebook of Christian Thought* (San Francisco: HarperSanFrancisco, 1977), 142.

Chapter 5 Mistaking the Industrial Revolution for the Garden of Eden

1. Stephanie Coontz, *Marriage, a History: From Obedience to Intimacy or How Love Conquered Marriage* (New York: Viking, 2005), chap. 1.

2. Ibid., 37.

3. Even in the later nineteenth century, two-thirds of families lived on farms, according to Jack Balswick and Judith Balswick, *The Family: A Christian Perspective on the Contemporary Home*, 2nd ed. (Grand Rapids: Baker Academic, 1999), 88.

4. Rosemary Radford Ruether, *Christianity and the Making of the Modern Family* (Boston: Beacon, 2000), 65.

5. Barbara Ehrenreich and Deirdre English, *For Her Own Good: Two Centuries of the Experts' Advice to Women* (New York: Anchor Books, 2005), esp. chap. 1.

6. Ruether, *Christianity*, 83.

7. Lewis Smedes, *Sex for Christians: The Limits and Liberties of Sexual Living*, rev. ed. (Grand Rapids: Eerdmans, 1994), 70.

8. This study conducted by Gallagher and a research team included three levels of interviews: 130 personal interviews with churchgoing Protestants from 12 regions of the US; a national phone survey of 2087 "religiously committed" Protestants and 504 nonchurchgoing non-Protestants as a comparison group; and 173 interviews with self-identified evangelicals. They also read evangelical periodicals, bibliographies, and books and participated in evangelical services in various regions of the country.

9. Sally Gallagher, *Evangelical Identity and Gendered Family Life* (New Brunswick, NJ: Rutgers University Press, 2003), 155–56.

10. James Dobson, *Complete Marriage and Family Home Reference Guide* (Wheaton: Tyndale, 2000), 305–6.

11. Gallagher, *Evangelical Identity*, 157.

12. Ibid., 166.

13. Ibid., 157–62.

14. Ibid., 170.

15. Ibid.

16. Mary Pride, *The Way Back Home: Beyond Feminism, Back to Reality* (Westchester, IL: Crossway Books, 1985).

17. John Piper and Wayne Grudem, eds., *Recovering Biblical Manhood and Womanhood: A Response to Evangelical Feminism* (Wheaton, IL: Crossway Books, 1991), 415. For a fuller example, see chap. 26, "Charity, Clarity and Hope: The Controversy and the Cause of Christ."

18. Gallagher, *Evangelical Identity*, 164.

19. Rebecca Merrill Groothuis, *Good News for Women: A Biblical Picture of Gender Equality* (Grand Rapids: Baker Books, 1997), 54–55.

20. Smedes, *Sex for Christians*, 24.

Chapter 6 Two Heads Are Better Than One

1. See esp. Table 4: "Traditional, Biblical, and Modern Marriages," in Jack Balswick and Judith Balswick, *The Family: A Christian Perspective on the Contemporary Home*, 2nd ed. (Grand Rapids: Baker Academic, 1999), 85.

2. Carl Jung, *The Psychology of the Unconscious* (New York: Dodd, Mead and Co., 1916), at www.brainyquote.com/quotes/authors/c/carl_jung.html.

3. Balswick and Balswick, *Family*, 79.

4. Lewis Smedes, *Sex for Christians: The Limits and Liberties of Sexual Living*, rev. ed. (Grand Rapids: Eerdmans, 1994), 156.

5. Francine Deutsch, *Halving It All: How Equally Shared Parenting Works* (Cambridge, MA: Harvard University Press, 1999).

6. M. Scott Peck, *The Road Less Traveled: A New Psychology of Love, Traditional Values and Spiritual Growth*, 25th anniversary ed. (New York: Touchstone, 2003); see the chapter titled, "Dependency."

7. Deutsch, *Halving It All*, 64.

8. Kathleen Gerson, "What Do Women and Men Want?" *American Prospect*, Special Report, March 2007, 8–11.

9. See, for instance, Kathleen Kendall-Tackett, *The Hidden Feelings of Motherhood: Coping with Stress, Depression, and Burn-out* (Oakland, CA: New Harbinger Publications, 2001), 19, where she cites research showing that women are twice as likely as men to be depressed at some point in their lives and that mothers of young children are particularly vulnerable.

10. Joan Williams, "The Opt-Out Revolution Revisited," *American Prospect*, Special Report, March 2007, 12–15.

11. Scott Coltrane, "What about Fathers?" *American Prospect*, Special Report, March 2007, 20–22.

12. See Deutsch, "Fighting over Practice and Principle," chap. 4 of *Halving It All*, 61–84.

13. Janet Gornick, "Atlantic Passages," *American Prospect*, Special Report, March 2007, 19–20.

14. See Faulkner Fox, "The Joint Project," chap. 4 in *Dispatches from a Not-So-Perfect Life: Or, How I Learned to Love the House, the Man, the Child* (New York: Three Rivers, 2004).

15. Deutsch, "Why Couples Don't Practice What They Preach," chap. 8 of *Halving It All*, 152–68.

16. See Betty Holcomb, "In the Care of Strangers: Day Care's Enduring Stigma," chap. 8 in *Not Guilty! The Good News about Working Mothers* (New York: Scribner, 1998).

17. See, for instance, Amy Caiazza, April Shaw, and Misha Werschkul, "Women's Economic Status in the States: Wide Disparities by Race, Ethnicity, and Region," Institute for Women's Policy Research, Washington, DC, www.iwpr.org/pdf/R260.pdf.

18. Deutsch, *Halving It All*, 228–29.

19. Ibid., 230.

20. Ibid., 225.

21. Ibid., 229.

22. Ibid.

Chapter 7 Seeing the Invisible

1. Jean LaPorte, *Studies in Women and Religion*, vol. 1, *The Role of Women in Early Christianity* (New York: Edwin Mellen, 1982), 1.

2. Joan Morris, *The Lady Was a Bishop: The Hidden History of Women with Clerical Ordination and the Jurisdiction of Bishops* (New York: MacMillan, 1973), 4–5. See also Karen Jo Torjesen, *When Women Were Priests: Women's Leadership in the Early Church and the Scandal of Their Subordination in the Rise of Christianity* (San Francisco: HarperSanFrancisco, 1993), 10.

3. Ute E. Eisen, *Women Officeholders in Early Christianity: Epigraphical and Literary Studies*, trans. Linda Maloney (Collegeville, MN: Liturgical Press, 2000); Kevin Madigan

and Carolyn Osiek, eds., *Ordained Women in the Early Church: A Documentary History* (Baltimore: Johns Hopkins University Press, 2005).

4. Eisen, *Women Officeholders*, 5.

5. Ibid., 16, 21.

6. Eisen rejects the idea that there was an egalitarian era (the first two centuries CE) and then increasing accommodation to patriarchy; the data suggest it was more complex than that.

7. Clement of Rome, *Letter to the Corinthians* 55, as quoted in Patricia Wilson-Kastner's introduction to *A Lost Tradition: Women Writers of the Early Church* (Lanham, MD: University Press of America, 1981), ix.

8. See Anne Jensen, *God's Self-Confident Daughters: Early Christianity and the Liberation of Women*, trans. O. C. Dean Jr. (Louisville: Westminster John Knox, 1996).

9. Eisen, *Women Officeholders*, 203.

10. See the extant fragments of *The Gospel of Mary* in Amy Oden, ed., *In Her Words: Women's Writings in the History of Christian Thought* (Nashville: Abingdon, 1994), 17–20.

11. Oden, *In Her Words*, 21.

12. Quoted in Eisen, *Women Officeholders*, 52–53.

13. Eisen, *Women Officeholders*, 69, 71, 73.

14. Ibid., 95.

15. Ibid., 99.

16. Morris, *Lady Was a Bishop*, 13–14.

17. Eisen, *Women Officeholders*, 94.

18. Ibid., 98, 90.

19. See Madigan and Osiek, *Ordained Women*, 210: appendix C lists the names and locations of inscriptions of female presbyters.

20. Ibid., 167.

21. Eisen, *Women Officeholders*, 129.

22. Ibid., 134, quoting from Haye van der Meer, *Priestertum der Frau? Eine theologiegeschichtliche Untersuchung* (Freiburg: Herder, 1969), 118.

23. Eisen, *Women Officeholders*, 14; see also the chapter "Women Deacons in the East: Canons and Comments" in Madigan and Osiek, *Ordained Women*, 106–32, which contains quotes from the *Didascalia Apostolorum* and the *Apostolic Constitutions* along with discussion.

24. Madigan and Osiek, *Ordained Women*, 8.

25. Ibid., 124–26.

26. Ibid., 4. See also their appendix F, which focuses on deacons' relationships.

27. Ibid., 67.

28. Letter 10.96, as quoted in Wilson-Kastner, *Lost Tradition*, ix.

29. See *The Martyrs of Lyons*, in Oden, *In Her Words*, 38–41. These quotes are from pp. 40 and 41.

30. Elizabeth Johnson, *She Who Is: The Mystery of God in Feminist Theological Discourse* (New York: Crossroad, 1993).

31. See Elizabeth Alvilda Petroff, *Medieval Women's Visionary Literature* (Oxford: Oxford University Press, 1986); Oden, *In Her Words*. Both contain excerpts of this narrative with informative introductions.

32. Bonnie Bowman Thurston, *The Widows: A Women's Ministry in the Early Church* (Minneapolis: Fortress, 1989), 7.

33. Ibid., 25.

34. Eisen, *Women Officeholders*, 152. *Testamentum Domini*, a fifth-century document, attests to the broadening function of the widows, at least in the East.

35. Morris, *Lady Was a Bishop*, 12.

36. Eisen, *Women Officeholders*, 92.

37. Tertullian, "On the Apparel of Women," excerpted in Barbara MacHaffie, ed., *Readings in Her Story: Women in Christian Tradition* (Minneapolis: Fortress, 1992), 27.

38. Richard Clark Kroeger and Catherine Clark Kroeger, *I Suffer Not a Woman: Rethinking 1 Timothy 2:11–15 in Light of Ancient Evidence* (Grand Rapids: Baker Academic, 1998), 21.

39. Joyce Salisbury, *Church Fathers, Independent Virgins* (London: Verso, 1991), 27.

40. Ibid., 35, and Jerome, "To Eustochium," quoted in Salisbury, *Church Fathers*, 32.

41. Salisbury shows many instances in which monastic women flouted the behavioral expectations of male writers, because at heart they simply did not believe themselves to be as loathsome as these men suggested.

42. Salisbury, *Church Fathers*, 75.

43. Penelope Johnson, *Equal in Monastic Profession: Religious Women in Medieval France* (Chicago: University of Chicago Press, 1991).

44. Salisbury, *Church Fathers*, 111–12.

45. Ibid., 113.

Chapter 8 Abbesses, Mystics, and Reformation Women

1. Mary Malone, *Women and Christianity*, vol. 1, *The First Thousand Years* (Maryknoll, NY: Orbis Books, 2000), 178.

2. Ibid., 179.

3. Lisa Bitel, *Women in Early Medieval Europe, 400–1100* (Cambridge: Cambridge University Press, 2002), 123.

4. Ibid., 124.

5. Carole Hough, "Women," in *The Blackwell Encyclopedia of Anglo-Saxon England*, ed. Michael Lapidge, John Blair, Simon Keynes, and Donald Scragg (Oxford: Blackwell, 1999), 485–87.

6. Michael Lapidge, "Hild," in Lapidge et al., *Blackwell Encyclopedia of Anglo-Saxon England*, 239.

7. See "The Life of Saint Leoba," in Elizabeth Alvilda Petroff, *Medieval Women's Visionary Literature* (Oxford: Oxford University Press, 1986), 113.

8. Some scholars have even suggested that the level of learning among nuns in Anglo-Saxon England might have been higher than among the monks, given the examples of people such as Leoba, Eadburh, or Bugga (Hough, "Women," 486).

9. "Life of Saint Leoba," in Petroff, *Medieval Women's Visionary Literature*, 112.

10. Morris argues that the practice was acceptable until the Renaissance, when the revival of classical authors brought their misogyny back into the church; at the Council of Trent, women's orders came under local bishops (Joan Morris, *The Lady Was a Bishop: The Hidden History of Women with Clerical Ordination and the Jurisdiction of Bishops* [New York: MacMillan, 1973]). Bitel suggests that according to archaeological and textual evidence, there were between sixty and seventy double houses in England and Ireland in the eighth and ninth centuries (*Women in Early Medieval Europe*, 147).

11. Morris, *Lady Was a Bishop*, 22, 30.

12. Ibid., 4.

13. Ibid., 130–31.

14. See, e.g., Josh. 6:4; Neh. 12:1. See Morris for a full discussion of *sacerdotes* (*Lady Was a Bishop*, 130–39).

15. John Blair, *Saint Frideswide, Patron of Oxford: The Earliest Texts* (Oxford: The Perpetua Press, 2004), 11.

16. From the *Life of Frideswide*, by William of Malmesbury, quoted in Malone, *Women and Christianity*, 1:204.

17. http://justus.anglican.org/resources/bio/247.html.

18. Quoted in Malone, *Women and Christianity*, 1:239.

19. Penelope Johnson, *Equal in Monastic Profession: Religious Women in Medieval France* (Chicago: University of Chicago Press, 1991), 229.

20. Saskia Murk-Jansen, *Brides in the Desert: The Spirituality of the Beguines* (Maryknoll, NY: Orbis Books, 1998), 70.

21. Erasmus, *The Institution of Marriage*, trans. Michael Heath, in *Erasmus on Women*, ed. Erika Rummel (Toronto: University of Toronto Press, 1996), 117–18.

22. Martin Luther, *Lectures on Genesis* (St. Louis: Concordia, 1958), 118–19.

23. Diane Willen, "Women and Religion in Early Modern England," in *Women in Reformation and Counter-Reformation Europe: Private and Public Worlds*, ed. Sherrin Marshall (Bloomington: Indiana University Press, 1989), 158.

24. Merry Wiesner, "Nuns, Wives, and Mothers: Women and the Reformation in Germany," in Marshall, *Women in Reformation and Counter-Reformation Europe*, 14.

25. Grethe Jacobsen, "Nordic Women and the Reformation," in Marshall, *Women in Reformation and Counter-Reformation Europe*.

26. Merry Wiesner-Hanks, "Introduction," in *Convents Confront the Reformation: Catholic and Protestant Nuns in Germany*, trans. Joan Skocir (Milwaukee: Marquette University Press, 1996).

27. Amy Oden, ed., *In Her Words: Women's Writings in the History of Christian Thought* (Nashville: Abingdon, 1994), 80.

28. Wiesner-Hanks, *Convents Confront the Reformation*, 41–63.

29. Wiesner, "Nuns, Wives, and Mothers," 15.

30. Martin Luther, "The Misuse of the Mass," in Barbara MacHaffie, ed., *Readings in Her Story: Women in Christian Tradition* (Minneapolis: Fortress, 1992), 75–76; John Calvin, *Institutes of the Christian Religion*, in MacHaffie, *Readings*, 76–79.

31. Lisa DiCaprio and Merry Wiesner, *Lives and Voices: Sources in European Women's History* (Boston: Houghton Mifflin Co., 2001), 214.

32. Ibid., 213.

33. For more on Zell, see Roland Herbert Bainton, "Katherine Zell," in *Women of the Reformation in Germany and Italy* (Minneapolis: Augsburg, 1971), 55–76.

Chapter 9 Changing the World

1. Full text available online at http://ccat.sas.upenn.edu.

2. John Whitehead, *The Life of Rev. John Wesley*, vol. 1 (Philadelphia: W. S. Stockton, 1845), quoted in Frank Baker, "Susanna Wesley: Puritan, Parent, Pastor, Protagonist, Pattern," in *Women in New Worlds*, vol. 2, ed. Rosemary Skinner Keller et al. (Nashville: Abingdon, 1982), 125.

3. Fanny Newell, *Diary* (Boston: Charles H. Peirce, 1848).

4. William Andrews, ed., *Sisters of the Spirit: Three Black Women's Autobiographies of the Nineteenth Century* (Bloomington: Indiana University Press, 1986), 25–48.

5. Nancy Towle, *Vicissitudes Illustrated, in the Experience of Nancy Towle, in Europe and America* (Portsmouth, NH: John Caldwell, 1833).

6. Catherine Brekus, *Strangers and Pilgrims: Female Preaching in America, 1740–1845* (Chapel Hill: University of North Carolina Press, 1998); Nancy Hardesty, *Women Called to Witness: Evangelical Feminism in the 19th Century* (Knoxville: University of Tennessee Press, 1999).

7. This quote is from the Puritan pastor Hugh Peters in his accusation against Anne Hutchinson. The full sentence is: "You have stept out of your place, you have rather bine a Husband than a Wife and a preacher than a Hearer; and a Magistrate than a Subject." The full text can be found in "A Report of the Trial of Mrs. Anne Hutchinson before the

Church in Boston," in *The Antinomian Controversy: 1636–1638: A Documentary History*, ed. David D. Hall (Middleton, CT: Wesleyan University Press, 1968), 382–83.

8. Susie C. Stanley, *Holy Boldness: Women Preachers' Autobiographies and the Sanctified Self* (Knoxville: University of Tennessee Press, 2002), 72.

9. From an 1855 letter from William to Catherine, quoted in Bramwell Booth, *Echoes and Memories* (New York: George H. Doran Company, ca. 1925), 163.

10. Ibid., 165.

11. Elizabeth Cady Stanton, *The Woman's Bible* (reprinted, Boston: Northeastern University Press, 1993).

12. Dana L. Robert, *American Women in Mission: A Social History of Their Thought and Practice* (Macon, GA: Mercer University Press, 1997), xviii.

13. Quoted in Susan Hill Lindley, *"You Have Stept Out of Your Place": A History of Women and Religion in America* (Louisville: Westminster John Knox, 1996), 300.

14. Ira Ford McLeister and Roy Stephen Nicholson, *Conscience and Commitment: The History of the Wesleyan Methodist Church of America* (Marion, IN: The Wesley Press, 1976), 60.

15. Janette Hassey, *No Time for Silence: Evangelical Women in Public Ministry around the Turn of the Century* (Grand Rapids: Academie Books, 1986); Donald Dayton, *Discovering an Evangelical Heritage* (Peabody, MA: Hendrickson, 1988).

16. Lindley, *"You Have Stept Out of Your Place,"* 309–17.

17. Barbara Brown Zikmund, Adair Lummis, and Patricia Chang, *Clergy Women: An Uphill Calling* (Louisville: Westminster John Knox, 1998), 155.

Chapter 10 Not Counting Women and Children

1. Janice Moulton, "The Myth of the Neutral 'Man,'" in *Sexist Language: A Modern Philosophical Analysis*, ed. Mary Vetterling-Braggin (Lanham, MD: Littlefield, Adams, 1981), 113.

2. Vernard Eller, *The Language of Canaan and the Grammar of Feminism* (Grand Rapids: Eerdmans, 1982), 20.

3. See Brian Wren, *What Language Shall I Borrow?* (New York: Crossroad, 1990), chap. 2.

4. Of course, when eros is the focus, being emotional is highly valued and the gender roles get reassigned a bit. See Christine Bartersby, *Gender and Genius* (London: Women's Press, 1999).

5. Paul Smith, *Is It Okay to Call God "Mother"? Considering the Feminine Face of God* (Peabody, MA: Hendrickson, 1993).

6. Ibid., 36.

7. Letty Russell, *Household of Freedom: Authority in Feminist Theology* (Philadelphia: Westminster, 1987), 45.

8. Smith, *Is It Okay*, 8.

9. Ibid., 20.

10. Elizabeth Johnson, *She Who Is: The Mystery of God in Feminist Theological Discourse* (New York: Crossroad, 1993), 4.

Chapter 11 The Discarded Images

1. In this regard, see the second chapter of Virginia Mollenkott's *The Divine Feminine: The Biblical Imagery of God as Female* (New York: Crossroad, 1993). This quote is from p. 8; the rest of the quotes in the paragraph are from pp. 9–10. Paul Smith quotes some of these writers; see *Is It Okay to Call God "Mother"? Considering the Feminine Face of God* (Peabody, MA: Hendrickson, 1993), 137–38.

2. Sallie McFague, *Models of God: Theology for an Ecological, Nuclear Age* (Philadelphia: Fortress, 1987), 33.

3. George Lakoff and Mark Johnson, *Metaphors We Live By* (Chicago: University of Chicago Press, 1980), 5.

4. Brian Wren, *What Language Shall I Borrow?* (New York: Crossroad, 1990), 61.

5. In the book *This Is My Name Forever: The Trinity and Gender Language for God* (Downers Grove, IL: InterVarsity, 2001), the editor, Alvin Kimel, outlines the concerns of those interested in "changing" language for God, focusing on two questions: whether masculine language for God fosters or justifies abuse against women, and whether masculine language alienates women from worship (see p. 7). However, he has overlooked the fact that many Christians who advocate using female images of God (even in public worship) do so not simply out of ethical concerns (how will this affect women and men who have no good male role models?) but out of biblical and theological concerns.

6. Lakoff and Johnson, *Metaphors We Live By*, 19.

7. Wren, *What Language*, 101.

8. McFague, *Models of God*, 97.

9. See, e.g., Tikva Frymer-Kensky, *In the Wake of the Goddesses: Women, Culture, and the Biblical Transformation of Pagan Myth* (New York: Fawcett Columbine, 1992); J. Richard Middleton, *The Liberating Image: The* Imago Dei *in Genesis 1* (Grand Rapids: Brazos, 2005).

10. See Smith, *Is It Okay*, 56–58.

11. Ibid., 65n17.

12. Elizabeth Johnson, *She Who Is: The Mystery of God in Feminist Theological Discourse* (New York: Crossroad, 1993), 75.

13. Ibid., 73.

14. See Roberta Bondi's expanded treatment of this idea in *Memories of God: Theological Reflections on a Life* (Nashville: Abingdon, 1995).

15. Mary Daly, *Beyond God the Father: Toward a Philosophy of Women's Liberation* (Boston: Beacon, 1973), 19.

16. Denise Carmody, *Feminism and Christianity: A Two-Way Reflection* (Nashville: Abingdon, 1982), 26–28.

17. Barna observes that women are leaving the church, though he attributes that to the undue spiritual burden they carry. See the article, "Women Are the Backbone of the Christian Congregations in America," at www.barna.org/FlexPage.aspx?Page=BarnaUpdate&BarnaUpdateID=47.

18. In fact, in the medieval Kabbalist tradition, *Shekinah* is one of the ten "parts" (the *Sefirot*) of God knowable to the soul. See Peter Schaefer, *Mirror of His Beauty: Feminine Images of God from the Bible to the Early Kabbalah* (Princeton, NJ: Princeton University Press, 2002), 10.

19. Johnson, *She Who Is*, 54.

20. McFague, *Models of God*, 99.

21. Assertion based on an NRSV Concordance search.

22. McFague, *Models of God*, 103.

23. For a full treatment of this idea, see McFague, *Models of God*.

24. Wren, *What Language*, 109.

25. Ibid., 132.

26. Johnson, *She Who Is*, 81.

27. Smith, *Is It Okay*, 82–83.

28. Ibid., 84.

29. Kimel, *This Is My Name Forever*, 16.

30. Gail Ramshaw, "The Gender of God," in *Feminist Theology: A Reader*, ed. Ann Loades (London: SPCK, 1990), 176–77.

31. McFague, *Models of God*, 98.

32. See Tikva Frymer-Kensky, "'Godwomen': Goddesses, Women, and Gender," chap. 3 in *In the Wake of the Goddesses*.

33. E.g., Elizabeth Achtemeier, in a *Christianity Today* article in 1993, argued, rather counterintuitively, that the main challenge to Old Testament faith was Canaanite Baalism because it taught identification of deity and world—but Ba'al was male.

34. And the theological differences should not be attributed automatically to a person's feminism. For instance, when Elizabeth Achtemeier, in a *Christianity Today* article, criticizes Rosemary Ruether because Ruether envisions a matrix of being that survives even when the individual does not, she fails to acknowledge that Ruether is writing in classical process thought categories. If a man had written this, he would be called a process theologian; but when a woman writes it, she is a feminist? There is a confusion of categories, so that whatever the critic doesn't agree with is attributed to the person's feminism.

35. Vernard Eller, *The Language of Canaan and the Grammar of Feminism* (Grand Rapids: Eerdmans, 1982), 46.

Conclusions

1. Roald Dahl, *Charlie and the Chocolate Factory* (New York: Puffin Books, 1964), 152.

Scripture Index

Old Testament

Genesis

1   14, 31, 32, 37, 38, 90, 91, 99, 100, 114
1:26   28, 31
1:27   28, 33
1:28   31
2   14, 33–38, 37, 90, 99, 100, 101, 114
2:18   34, 35
3   31, 38, 40, 41, 42
3:6   38
3:15   182
3:16   39, 102
18   43
25:5   44
28:3   213
29–30   100
31   99
34   47
35:11   213
36   46
39:6–7   87
49:25   213

Exodus

4   50
15   52, 53
18:4   234n12
19:4   211
20:17   100

Leviticus

15:19–33   58

Numbers

12   44, 53

Deuteronomy

6   224
8:3   197
24:1   101
32:11–12   211
32:18   212
33:7   234n12
33:26   234n12
33:29   234n12

Joshua

2   50
6:4   240n14

Judges

4   52, 53
5   52
5:24   52
11   48
19   39, 46, 100
19:24   47

1 Samuel

1 45
2 37
9:2 54, 87
16:7 87
16:12 55, 87
19 51
25:32–33 51

1 Kings

11:3 100
18 224

2 Kings

22 53
22:12 54
22:15 54
22:20 54

1 Chronicles

17:13 219

2 Chronicles

34 53

Nehemiah

6:14 54
12:1 240n14

Esther

4:16–17 52

Job

38:8–9 212
38:28–29 214
38:29 212
39:27–30 211

Psalms

22:9 214
23:5 203
33:20 234n12
68:5 219
103:13–14 219
115:9–11 234n12

123:2 214, 215
124:8 234n12
131:2 213
139:13–14 92

Proverbs

8:22 215
8:27–31 215
8:35 215
27:17 197

Isaiah

8 54
8:3 54, 234n3
42:13–14 214–15
42:14 213
46:3–4 212
49:15 213
55:9 209
63:16 219
66:12–13 213

Jeremiah

3:19 219
31:9 219

Daniel

1:3–4 87

Hosea

1–3 100
5:14 211
13 211
13:7 211
13:8 211

Micah

6:4 52

New Testament

Matthew

13:33 214
20:20–21 138

Mark

3   59, 106
3:32   59
3:33–35   59
5   58
7:9–13   48
10   28, 50
10:2–12   101

Luke

1:42–43   156
2   37
7   59, 60, 203
7:36–50   57, 103
7:39   57
8   60, 72
8:1–3   60, 102, 104
8:2   60
8:3   60
10   59
11:27   59
13   58
13:18–21   103, 215
13:20–21   214
13:34   213
14   58
15:1–10   103, 215
15:8–10   214
18   22
18:1–8   103
21:1–4   191

John

1   91
1:1   215
1:3–4   215
3   57, 103, 212
4   57, 61, 103
4:27   57
6:31–35   214
8   103
11   103
12   60
13   105

Acts

1:24   222
2   112
2:17–18   62
4:24   222
5   101
7:59–60   222
10:13–14   222
12   62
16   62, 204
17   204
17:22   204
17:34   204
18   63, 101
19   67
21:8–9   156

Romans

3   91
5   31, 68
6   91
8   91
12   113
15:8   235n7
16   62, 64, 66, 69, 138, 159, 160
16:1   62
16:3–4   63
16:6   64
16:7   63, 155
16:12   64
16:13   64

1 Corinthians

1   91
3:5   235n7
6:12–20   93
7   50, 68, 72, 111, 162
9:22   202
11   64, 69
11:3–16   153
11:12   68
12   71, 231
12:4–11   111
14   66, 182
14:23–24   66
14:26   66
14:28   65
14:30   65
14:31   66
14:33–35   65
14:34–35   64, 66
15:10   235n11
16:22   222

2 Corinthians

3:6   235n7

Galatians

2   91
2:11–14   66
2:17   235n7
3:26–29   70
3:28   69
4:11   235n11

Ephesians

1   37
4   71, 231
4:11–12   111
5   108, 110
5:15–20   108
5:21   108
5:22–24   108
5:25   110
5:25–33   108
5:28–29   110

Philippians

2   106, 107
2:4–6   147
2:16   235n11
4   62

Colossians

1   42
1:7   235n7
1:29   235n11
3   108, 110
3:12–17   107
3:18   107
4   62
4:7   235n7

1 Thessalonians

3:2   235n7
5:12   63

1 Timothy

1:19   66
2   67, 69, 182

2:2   67
2:4   197
2:7   235n7
2:8   69
2:8–15   64
2:9   69
2:11–12   69
2:11–15   66, 67
2:13–14   68
2:14   69
3:4   138
3:4–5   63
3:12   139
4:10   235n11
5   67
5:14   138
5:17   63

Philemon

2   62

Hebrews

4:14–5:10   113

James

1:18   212

1 Peter

1:3   212
2   110
2:2–3   213
3   110

1 John

3   106, 109

Revelation

4:11   222
11:16–17   222
15:3   222
16:5   222
16:7   222
22:17   182
22:20   222

Subject Index

abbesses, 169–74
Abigail, 51
abolition, 185–87
Acts of Paul and Thecla, 156
adam, 28–29
Adam, and Eve, 30–33, 38–40, 68, 99
African Methodist Episcopal Church, 184
Ammia of Philadelphia, 157
androgyny, 126–27, 226
Anna, 56, 156, 162
apostles, 156
Argula von Grumbach, 178–79
asceticism. *See* monastics
Athaliah, 49
Azuza Street Revival, 192

babies, women and, 141–42
Barth, Karl, 36–37
Bathsheba, 48
Beguines, 174–75
Bertha, 168–69
Blandina, 161
body, 92–93, 163
body image
    church and, 87–88
    consumerism, 79–80
    dieting and, 75–76
    eating disorders, 83–84
    media and, 74, 76, 78–80
    narcissism and, 80–81
    Scripture and, 87–88
    self-hatred and, 82–83
Booth, Catherine, 188–89
Brown, Antoinette, 188

calling, 194
Calvin, John, 178
Canaanite religion, 224
Carmody, Denise, 217–18
celibacy, 111, 160, 162, 164
childbirth, and salvation, 68–69
childcare, 144–45
children, 119, 121
Christ. *See* Jesus Christ
church
    bride of Christ, 227
    culture and, 123
    family, 110–11
    home, 62
    institutionalization and women, 154
    response to body image, 86–88
    women in medieval, western, 167–75
    women in early, 152–55
class, middle, 121
Clitherow, Margaret, 179
Clotilde, 168
Colossians 3:12–17, 107
communication, 134
compassion, 104, 219–20
convents, 169, 174, 177–78
creation
    delight in, 91–92
    Genesis 2, 33–42
    God and, 225
    marriage and, 99
    role of humans, 31
    stories, 27, 36
curse, 39–40
cutting, 86

Daly, Mary, 20
Danforth, Clarissa, 184
dating, 236n18
David, King, 48
daycare. *See* childcare
deacon, 62–63, 159–60
Deborah, 52–53
Declaration of Sentiments, 188
Delilah, 49
depression, 140, 238n9
Didascalia Apostolorum, 159
Dinah, 47
disciples, 60–61, 72, 138
discipleship
    compassion and, 104–6
    gender roles and, 58–71
    image of God and, 216
divorce, 101
Dobson, James, 124–25
domestic labor, division of, 132–36
domestic violence, 84–85, 89
dress, 88–89
dualism, 29–30

eating disorders, 83–84
economies, 119–21, 167–68
Elizabeth, 56, 156
Eller, Vernard, 199, 226–27
El Shaddai, 213
Ephesians 5, 108
equality, 70–71, 182. *See also* marriage:
    mutual
Erasmus, 175–76
Esther, 52
Eustochium, 157
Eve
    Adam names, 36
    converses with God, 43
    fall and, 38–42
    relation to Adam, 34–36
    sexuality and, 163
    See also Adam, and Eve
exercise, 92–93

fall, 38–42
family
    agrarian economy, 119
    Bible and, 98–101
    church as, 110–11
    industrialism, 121–22
    Jesus', 59, 106

    sacrifice for, 147
    sanctuary, 120–21
father, 219
fatherhood, 142, 146
Felicitas, 161
Fell, Margaret, 181–82
femininity, 90, 120
feminism
    Christianity and, 14–16, 225–26
    movement, 14
    theology and, 125, 244n34
Finney, Charles, 184
flesh, 91–92
Fletcher, Mary, 183
Forgotten Desert Mothers, 162
Free Will Baptists, 184
Frideswide, 172
friendship, 38
Frymer-Kensky, Tikva, 224

Galatians 3:26–29, 70
Gallagher, Sally, 123–26, 129, 237n8
gender, 16–18, 120
gender roles
    discipleship over, 58–71
    culture and, 13–14
    media and, 82
    sexuality and, 124, 127
    sexism and, 128
    spirituality and, 122
    traditional, 123–24
    variance of, 127
Genesis 2–3
    Christian tradition and, 36–38
    equality of humans in, 33–34
    fall and, 38–42
God
    compassionate, 37, 212, 219–20
    creation and, 225
    biblical images, 29, 205–6, 209–13,
        211–27
    gender and, 29, 209–10, 217–18
    one, 224
goddess religion, 217–18, 224–25
Gomer, 49
Gospel of Mary, 155–56
Grimké, Sarah and Angelina, 15, 186–87

Hadewijch of Antwerp, 175
Hagar, 43–44, 47
Hannah, 45

Helia, 164
"helper," 34–35
heresy, at Ephesus, 66–69
Hild (or Hilda), 169–70
Hildagard of Bingen, 172–73
Holiness Church, 192–93
home. *See* family
Hroswitha of Gandersheim, 173
Huldah, 53–54
humanity, fullness of, 136
husbands and wives, 109–10. *See also* marriage
Hutchinson, Anne, 241n7

"I am," 210, 216
image of God
    human equality in, 27–31, 72, 99, 204, 207, 230
    interpretations of, 28, 30
incarnation, 92
industrial revolution, 119, 120–21
Institute of Marriage, 175–76
intimacy, 131, 146
Isaiah, wife of, 54

Jael, 52
Jephthah, daughter of, 48
Jesus Christ
    family of, 59, 106
    humanity of, 30, 215–16
    humility of, 72, 107
    image of, 216
    love of, 109
    maternal images of, 206, 213–14
    reconciliation and, 42, 53, 102
    reference to God, 30, 221–22
    relation to women, 56–59, 102–4, 215
Jezebel, 49
Joanna, 60
Job, wife of, 49
Jochobed, 50
Judges 19, 46–47
Junia, 63–64, 155
justice, domestic labor, 134–36

Kilbourne, Jean, 83
Kuria, 158

language, inclusive/exclusive, 197–204
Lee, Jarena, 184
Leoba, 170

Letters on the Equality of the Sexes, 187
listening, 11–13
Logos, 215
Lot, daughters of, 45–46
love
    demands of, 104–7
    sacrificial, 110, 113, 220
    freedom to fully, 133–34
Luisa de Carvajal, 179
Luther, Martin, 176, 178

Macrina, 157–58
"male gaze," 74–79
Marcella, 157
marriage
    in the Bible, 97–115
    biblical basis for Christian, 98–104
    friendship model, 130
    money, 135
    mutual, 101–2, 104, 108, 110, 114, 131–34
    Reformation assessment, 175, 177
    sacrifice, 106–7, 109–10, 131
    "traditional," 117–29
    See also domestic labor
martyrs, 160–61
Mary and Martha, 59–60
Mary Magdalene, 60, 155–56
Mary, mother of Jesus, 55–56, 59, 61
Mary, mother of John Mark, 62
Mary of Bethany, 60
masculinity, 76–77, 79, 90, 120
McFague, Sallie, 207, 209, 220
McPherson, Aimee Semple, 192
Melania, 157, 165
metaphors, 207–9, 220–21, 227. *See also* God: biblical images
Methodism, 183–84, 192
Michal, 48, 51
Miriam, 50–53
missions movement, 190–93
monastics, 162–66. *See also* convents
monotheism, 224
Montgomery, Helen Barrett, 192
motherhood, 137–42
Mott, Lucretia, 187
Myrta, 157

National Association of Evangelicals, 193
Nation, Carrie, 189
neo-paganism, 217–18

Newell, Fanny, 184
Nino, 156
Noadiah, 54

objectification, of women, 75–76
ordination, 171, 193
Oxford University, 172

Palmer, Phoebe, 188
parables, women in, 103–4
parenting
   career and, 140–41, 143–44
   depression and, 140
   shared, 132, 136–47
Paul, 62, 64–65, 68–69
Paula, 157
Pentecostalism, 192–93
Perpetua, 161
Philip, daughters of, 156
Phoebe, 62–63, 159
polygamy, 100–101, 118
pornography, 85
Praxedis, 152
prayer, public, 67
preachers, 178, 188
presbyters, 158–59
Pride, Mary, 126
priesthood, of all believers, 113, 181
Priscilla, 63
prophesying, 65
prophets, 53–54, 156
prostitutes, 185
Prudentiana, 152

Quakers, 181
queens, 168–69

Rachel, 45
Rahab, 50
Rebekah, 44–45
Reformation, 175–79
Ruth, 50–51, 138

salary inequality, 80, 144
Salvation Army, 188–89
Samson, mother of, 44
Sarah, 43–46
Scivias, 173
Scripture
   affirming justice, 19
   Christian life and, 13

culture and, 12–13, 70
feminists and, 19–21
interpreting, 22
on motherhood, 137–39
service, Christian, 72
sex, and gender, 16
sexuality, 163–65, 175–76, 200, 223. *See also* celibacy; gender roles: sexuality and; virginity
sin, 40–41, 91, 102, 163
slavery, 15, 186. *See also* abolition
Sophia (Proverbs), 215
Sophia, deacon, 160
spiritual gifts, 71, 111–14, 136
sports, women in, 77–78
Stanton, Elizabeth Cady, 187, 190
submission, 67, 81–82, 108
suffrage, 189–90
Susanna, 60
Synkletica, Amma, 162

Tamar, 46, 48–49
temperance, 185–86, 189
Terni, Bishop, 171
Thecla, 156
Theodora, Amma, 162
Theodora, Bishop, 152, 155
Theodora (of Macedonia), 158
Theodora of Rome, 158
Theodora (Spanish noblewoman), 164
theologians, 157–58
theology, language and, 202–4
Theonoe, 157
1 Timothy 2:11–15, 66–70
Towle, Nancy, 184
Trinity, 37

Ursula of Munsterberg, 178

violence, against women, 84–85, 89
virginity, 163, 166
vows, 48

wages. *See* salary inequality
wealth, displays of, 235n15
Wesley, Susanna, 183
Whitby, 169
White, Alma, 192
Wicca, 217
widows, 161–62
Willard, Frances, 189–90

Willen, Diane, 176
Wisdom, 215
witnesses, 61
woman of Samaria at the well, 57, 61
woman who washes Jesus' feet, 57–58
Woman's Bible, 190
womb, 212
women
  at Jesus' tomb, 61
  healed by Jesus, 58, 60
  objectification of, 75–76
  violence against, 84–85, 89

Women's Christian Temperance Union, 189
Women's Rights Convention, 15, 187
Women's Union Missionary Society, 191
worship, synagogue, 65
Wren, Brian, 199, 207, 221

Zell, Katherine, 179
Zipporah, 50